Migration Law in Albania

Migration Law in Albania

Erjona Bana (Canaj)

This book was originally published as a monograph in the International Encyclopaedia of Laws/Migration Law.

Founding Editor: Roger Blanpain
General Editor: Frank Hendrickx
Volume Editor: Helen Oosterom-Staples

Wolters Kluwer

Published by:
Kluwer Law International B.V.
PO Box 316
2400 AH Alphen aan den Rijn
The Netherlands
E-mail: international-sales@wolterskluwer.com
Website: lrus.wolterskluwer.com

Sold and distributed in North, Central and South America by:
Wolters Kluwer Legal & Regulatory U.S.
7201 McKinney Circle
Frederick, MD 21704
United States of America
Email: customer.service@wolterskluwer.com

Sold and distributed in all other countries by:
Air Business Subscriptions
Rockwood House
Haywards Heath
West Sussex
RH16 3DH
United Kingdom
Email: international-customerservice@wolterskluwer.com

DISCLAIMER: The material in this volume is in the nature of general comment only. It is not offered as advice on any particular matter and should not be taken as such. The editor and the contributing authors expressly disclaim all liability to any person with regard to anything done or omitted to be done, and with respect to the consequences of anything done or omitted to be done wholly or partly in reliance upon the whole or any part of the contents of this volume. No reader should act or refrain from acting on the basis of any matter contained in this volume without first obtaining professional advice regarding the particular facts and circumstances at issue. Any and all opinions expressed herein are those of the particular author and are not necessarily those of the editor or publisher of this volume.

Printed on acid-free paper

ISBN 978-94-035-0804-7

e-Book: ISBN 978-94-035-0805-4
web-PDF: ISBN 978-94-035-0810-8

Printed in the United Kingdom.

For my lovely family
Sokol, Arnis and Enea

The Author

Erjona Bana (Canaj) is Associate Professor at the Faculty of Law, European University of Tirana (Albania), where she researches and lectures on European Union law, human rights and asylum and migration law. She was born in 21 January 1981 in Elbasan (Albania). Actually she is the Head of the Public Law Department (Faculty of Law) at the European University of Tirana. She received her Doctor of Law degree from the University 'Sapienza' of Rome (Italy) in 2010. Her doctoral thesis focused on the family reunification of migrants and refugee in international and European Union law. She is the author of several books, academic articles and research reports in her fields of expertise in Albania, Italy and Kosovo. She used to be the Coordinator of the Faculty of Law Programme at the Doctoral School of the European University of Tirana and the Head of the Department of Private Law of the Faculty of Law, European University of Tirana. She works as a researcher at UET Centre of the European University of Tirana on migration and asylum law. She is a member of the editorial and advisory boards of several scientific national and international reviews and a principal Member of the Jean Monnet Cathedra at the European University of Tirana.

The Author

Table of Contents

List of Abbreviations

AIDA	Albanian Investment Development Agency
ALL	Albanian Currency
BCP	Border Crossing Point
CARDS	Community Assistance for Reconstruction, Development and Stabilisation
CoE	Council of Europe
CPT	The European Committee for the Prevention of Torture and Inhuman and Degrading Treatment or Punishment
DAR	Directory for Asylum and Refugees
DBM	Department for Border and Migration
DCM	Decree of the Council of Ministers
DG	Relex Directorate-General for External Relations in European Commission
DG JHA	Directorate-General for Justice and Home Affairs in European Commission
DNA	Deoxyribonucleic Acid
DR	Directory for Refugees
EC	European Communities
ECHR	European Convention on Human Rights
EEA	European Economic Area
EEC	European Economic Community
EU	European Union
EURODAC	European Dactyloscopy
GDP	Gross Domestic Product
INSTAT	Albanian Institute of Statistics
IOM	International Organization for Migration
LPD	Local Police District
MEFA	Ministry for Europe and Foreign Affaires
MoC	Ministry of Culture
MoH	Ministry of Health

List of Abbreviations

MoI	Ministry of Interior
MoJ	Ministry of Justice
MPO	Ministry of Public Order
MoSWY	Ministry of Social Welfare and Youth
NGO	Non-Governmental Organization
NSDI	National Strategy for Development and Integration
OSCE	The Organization for Security and Co-operation in Europe
PAMECA	Police Assistance Mission of the EU to Albania
RA	Readmission Agreement
SAA	Stabilisation Association Agreement
SAP	Stabilisation and Association Process
TCNs	Third Country Nationals
TIMS	Total Information Management System
UN	United Nations
USA	United States of America
UNHCR	United Nations High Commissioner for Refugees

Preface

Migration has played a determining role in humanity's history and development and it continues to influence every field of life. Most political parties must account for migration in their platforms, whether they act in developed or developing countries. The modern world has lowered the obstacles encountered when moving across borders and the increased crossing of these 'lines' has made the practical impact of rules regarding immigration vital to acknowledge.

This volume seeks to provide a structured overview of immigration and asylum rules in Albania. An isolated Communist state following the Second World War, Albania did not follow its other Central and Eastern European States when they initiated liberal reforms in the 1960s, preferring a model of the absolute rule of social property and a centralized and planned economy. Only in December 1990, after the start of a student movement, did political pluralism and an open market economy enter the country, marking the start of social and economic reforms on Albania's unsteady path towards joining the European Union (EU). Opened to the world for more than two decades, incredibly reformed and now a candidate country to join the EU, Albania still faces many challenges in its politics, economy and society, both old and new. The EU's founding values include the rule of law and respect for human rights. Albania has not had to start from scratch to realise these values and some progress has been made. Constitutional amendments adopted in July 2017 marked the beginning of a comprehensive justice reform process. A cross-cutting justice strategy for 2017–2020 and an action plan were adopted in November 2016. As regards enforcement of human rights, additional efforts are needed in relation to gender equality, the protection of children and other vulnerable groups.

This volume aims to provide a sufficient and adequate framework of the rules that apply to immigration. The volume also highlights some of the challenges in the application, interpretation and development of immigration and asylum rules. Emigration is not included in the particular study of normative guidance. The objective is to trace the main institutional and legal procedures applicable to foreign citizens who seek to reside legally in Albanian, either by immigrating or by seeking asylum. We believe that this book is particularly relevant for those who wish to understand the way in which Albania processes immigration and asylum matters in the context of the current legislative regime. Since immigration and asylum law is a particularly dynamic field of law, the applicable legislation changes constantly and may change again before the publication of this book. The reader is thus advised that this volume includes all changes legislation up to 30 September 2018.

General Introduction

§1. Immigration History and Statistical Information

1. The Republic of Albania lies in southeast Europe. It borders Montenegro in the north, Kosovo in the northeast, the Former Yugoslav Republic of Macedonia (FYRM) in the east, Greece in the south and the Adriatic and Ionian Seas in the west. In spite of recent changes, the population of Albania (2,800,138 inhabitants per *CENSUS 2011*),[1] is ethnically homogeneous: ethnic Albanians represent between 95 to 98% of the population while other ethnic groups such as Greeks, Aromanians, Macedonians, Montenegrins and Roma constitute the small remainder.[2] Most Albanian residents practice Islam, though small groups of Christians – mainly Catholic in the north and Eastern Orthodox in the south – exist. Although precise figures are in dispute, most estimates state that approximately 70% of the population is Muslim, 20% Eastern Orthodox and 10% Roman Catholic. Religion was banned in 1967, making Albania the world's first officially atheist State. A legacy of secularism from the banning of religion during the Communist regime – freedom of religion was, for the most part, re-established with the regime's fall – and a history of religious tolerance from dating back to before 1944 prevents most enmity along confessional lines.

2. Albania declared its independence from the Ottoman Empire in 1912, but suffered from frequent regime changes and periodic occupation over the next thirty-two years, especially during the two world wars. After the departure of occupiers and the rise of the Communist Party in 1944, Enver Hoxha established a totalitarian regime that isolated the country for more than four decades. This national agoraphobia left the country poor and underdeveloped until it finally emerged from isolation in 1991, when the first pluralistic Parliament declared the Parliamentary Republic of Albania. Albania has since eagerly sought integration into the international and European systems. It has entered into a Stabilization and Association Agreement (SAA) with the European Union (EU), signing it on 12 June 2006 and entering into force on 1 April 2009. Albania joined NATO in April 2009 and obtained visa liberalization for its citizens within the Schengen area that same year.

1. On 1 Jan. 2018, the resident population of Albania is estimated to be 2,870,324 inhabitants. *See* http://www.instat.gov.al/al/temat/treguesit-demografik%C3%AB-dhe-social%C3%AB/popullsia/publikimet/2018/popullsia-e-shqip%C3%ABris%C3%AB-1-janar-2018/, (accessed 13 Apr. 2018).
2. Statistical Yearbook, 10 (INSTAT 2017); A. Bërxholi, *Veçoritë e vizualizimit të dinamikës së popullsisë*, 156 (Atlasi gjeografik i popullsisë së Shqipërisë, Akademia e Shkencave, Qendra per Studime Gjeografike, No. 15, 2005).

The country has made significant progress towards its accession to the EU, measured primarily in terms of meeting the EU's political criteria and establishing stable institutions that guarantee democracy, rule of law, compliance with human rights, the protection of minorities, regional cooperation and good relations with enlargement countries and the EU's Member States. It gained candidate status to accede to the EU in June 2014. Albania's application for membership of the EU was an important landmark for a former Communist country that, less than twenty years ago, was the poorest, most isolated most repressive and most inscrutable country in Europe.[3]Progress has been made on many fronts, though there is still a lot of work to be done prior to its EU accession.

3. Migration has been an essential part of Albania's history and still is to the present day, though it has changed both in size and nature since the fall of Communism. Albania currently has the highest rate of emigration, relative to its population, in Central and Eastern Europe. Since 1990, it has experienced mass internal and external migration. Between 1989 and 2001, approximately 710,000 people, or 20% of the population, lived outside the country. Of these, 600,000 are thought to have emigrated and a further 110,000 to be children born in migration.[4] However, this is a conservative figure and the actual number of Albanian migrants abroad is probably higher. Most Albanian migrants abroad have settled in Greece and Italy, due to their geographical proximity, cultural affinity and knowledge of the language. Approximately 600,000 Albanians live in Greece while another 250,000 live in Italy and still more live in other European countries and other parts of the world.[5] However, due to the number of irregular emigrants, accurate figures are scarce.

4. Albania has a long history of emigration and a very short one of immigration. Emigration before the establishment of the modern State was a significant feature of the region starting in the eleventh century at the latest, peaking in the centuries after the death of the national hero Scanderbeg (1468–1744). Emigration after the creation of the independent Albanian modern State can be divided into three distinct periods based on motive and scale: (1) an early outflow before 1944, (2) a smaller, but more harrowing outflow during the Communist era, and (3) a significant outflow following the 1990 fall of Communism. Before 1944, Albanians followed the pre-independence emigration paths of their co-nationals towards Argentina, Australia, France, Greece and the USA, either for political or, more commonly, for economic reasons.[6] The second phase of Albanian emigration is during

3. R. Panagiotou, *Albania and the EU: From isolation to integration*, 357–374 (Journal of Balkan and Near Eastern Studies, Volume 13/3, 2011).
4. INSTAT, *Migration in Albania, Population and Housing Census 2001*, 13 (Instituti i Statistikës, Tirana, 2004).
5. R. King & J. Vullnetari, *Migration and Development in Albania*, 7 (United Kingdom, 2003); K. Barjaba & R. King, *Introducing and Theorising Albanian Migration*, 1–28 (R. King, N. Mai & R. Schwandner & S. Sievers, eds., Brighton Sussex Academic Press 2005).
6. *See* J. Vullnetari, *Albanian Migration and Development: State of Art Review*, 373 (IMISCOE Working Paper No. 18, September, 2007); L. Ikonomi, *Diasporas and their Role in the Formation of the Public Policy and Economy of the Home countries: The Case of Albania,* 93 (IOM Policy Paper, 13

the Communist period (1944–1990). The Albanian people lived in complete autarchy for more than three decades under Enver Hoxha's totalitarian regime. People were denied the right to move internally or abroad.[7] Emigration was primarily political especially to the European countries. Emigration had come to a virtual halt, as it was officially prohibited and emigrants and family members left behind were ostracized or severely punished. Those leaving the country did so in small numbers and were mainly asylum seekers who left due to fear of persecution.[8] The 1990s radically changed this pattern. In the first years after the fall of Communism, emigration was seen as a short-term solution to dire poverty in Albania, but the sputtering 'transition' to a functioning capitalist economy and reliable democracy in Albania led many Albanians to consider emigration as a more permanent solution.[9] After decades of brutal totalitarian dictatorship, absolute lack of freedom, human rights violations and poverty, Albanians took the opportunity to leave.[10] Within a decade between 600,000[11] and 800,000[12] Albanians went abroad. Greece, Italy and other European countries were the main destinations. Albania quickly became the country with the highest migration outflow in Europe, when measured in terms of the ratio of migrants to overall population. Presently, approximately 25% of the total population and over 35% of the labour force has emigrated. Albania's migration flow has, since the early 1990s, been five times higher than the average migration flow in developing countries.[13] Albanian emigration continues until today, mainly

---

Mar. 2005); C. Nikas & R. King, *Economic Growth through Remittances: Lessons from the Greek Experience of the 1960s Applicable to the Albanian Case,* 235 (Journal of Southern Europe and the Balkans, Volume 7, No. 2, 2005).

7. M. Lerch, *Does Indirect Exposure to International Migration Influence Marriage and Fertility in Albania?* 114 (Springer Science + Business Media Dordrecht Research Paper, 2015).
8. Around 20.000 emigrants are thought to have left Albania during the period 1945–1990. *See Competing for Remittances*, 9, published by IOM Tirana, 2005; N. Mai & S. Schwander-Sievers, *Albanian Migration and New Transnationalism,* 939–948 (*Journal of Ethnic and Migration Studies*, Vol. 29, 2003).
9. In Greece, Italy, UK, Sweden, Switzerland, Germany, Canada and in the USA. *See* for more, N. Ragaru & A. Dymi, *Study on 'The Albanian-American Community in the United States: A Diaspora Coming to Visibility*', 41 (Albanian American Community, 2004).
10. A. Leka, *Albanian Migration during the post-Communist Transition and the European Integration in Global Era. An Intercultural Reflection,* 207 (*Academicus*, No. 8, 2009).
11. R. King, *Across the Sea and Over the Mountains: Documenting Albanian Migration*, 283 (*Scottish Geographical Journal,* No. 119, 2003); R. King & Vullnetari J., *Development Research Centre on Migration, Globalisation and Poverty,* 6 (Brighton, United Kingdom, Working Paper C5, 2003); J. Vullnetari *International Migration, Integration and Social Cohesion*, 59 (IMISCOE, Amsterdam, Working Paper No. 18, 2007).
12. *See* K. Barjaba, *Migration and Ethnicity in Albania: Synergies and Interdependencies*, 231 (Easton Institute for International Studies, Vol. xi, ISSUE 1, Summer – Fall, 2004); R. King & Vullnetari J., *Development Research Centre on Migration, Globalisation and Poverty,* 6 (Brighton, United Kingdom, Working Paper C5, 2003).
13. After the fall of the Communist regime, international migration unfolded in four main episodes: (1) The 'Embassy Migrants', Summer 1990. During June–July 1990 around 5,000 Albanians sought refuge in the embassies of Western European States in Tirana. Eventually they were allowed to leave for the West. Italy was the main recipient. The Albanian authorities liberalised the issuing of passports and the small-scale exodus continued. Altogether, from the 'embassy invasion' until early 1991, some 20,000 Albanians left the country. (2) The Main Mass Exodus, March and August 1991 The chaos in the run up to Albania's first democratic elections (won by the Communists) led to the first 'boat-people' exodus to southern Italy in March 1991; 25,000 migrants were accepted by and

for economic and social reasons, though policies within the EU may be slowing it down.[14] EU Member State policies that affect Albanian migration seek to stop, control and reduce migration flows, as opposed to liberalizing channels of legal migration. In sending countries such as Albania, labour migration is considered an economic and social phenomenon. In receiving countries thesis also considered a risk to public safety. Due to these increasingly strict policies, the flow of regular immigrants from Albania to Italy and Greece is declining.

5. Since the introduction of reforms, the Albanian migration picture has evolved. Albania has opened itself up much more to migrants, though the relative number of immigrants remains low. This opening has included changes in the legislative framework governing immigration and a closer resemblance between Albanian legislation and international conventions governing individual rights and State obligations in the field of migration. Albania has especially changed its legislation to improve its alignment with the standards of the EU necessary for its eventual accession. Albania has transposed all EU directives relating to immigration and asylum into its national legal system and participates in the negotiations on new migration and asylum measures at the regional level.[15]

6. Immigration to Albania has been scarce, and the country has attracted neither foreign workers nor other immigrants in significant numbers. Albanian society has

settled in Italy. A second boat exodus took place in August 1991, but most of the 20,000 arrivals were repatriated. The Italian authorities argued that whereas the 'first wave' could be treated as refugees fleeing a tense political situation, the 'second wave' arrived after democratic elections and, therefore, could not be given refugee status. Meanwhile, a larger-scale but unquantified exodus took place to Greece; and clandestine migration continued to Italy. Altogether during the period 1991–1993 an estimated 300,000 Albanians, one in ten of the population, left the country, the vast majority to Greece and Italy. (3) The Pyramid Crisis, Spring 1997. In the early months of 1997, the collapse of a pyramid scheme for the investment of private savings (including many emigrants' remittances) led to a period of political and economic turmoil verging on civil war in some parts of the country. This chaos produced another boat exodus to Italy in early spring 1997. Initially 10,600 Albanians were accepted by Italy, but further sea-borne migrations were repulsed, sometimes in tragic circumstances, notably on 29 Mar. 1997, when, as a result of a collision between an Italian coastguard vessel and a boatful of Albanian migrants, eighty-seven people, many of them women and children, lost their lives. As before, larger but unregistered crossings of the Greek border took place. Albanian communities already established by onward migration in other EU Member States, such as France, Germany and Belgium, were augmented by new arrivals and the evolving diasporic network spread to the UK. (4) Kosovo Crisis, In 1999 Albania was host to 500,000 ethnic-Albanian Kosovar refugees entering through northern Albania; some have used Albania as a transit route to seek asylum in other countries, including the UK. The Kosovar refugee crisis destabilised the already fragile economic and demographic situation, especially in northern Albania, and many northern Albanians mixed with the Kosovan outward migration to other European asylum destinations. *See* R. King & J. Vullnetari, *Migration and Development in Albania*, 7 (United Kingdom, 2003).

14. A. Leka, *Albanian Migration during the post-Communist Transition and the European Integration in Global Era. An Intercultural Reflection*, 220 (*Academicus*, No. 8, 2009); R. King, *Albanians in Italy and Greece: A Study in Migration Dynamics and Social Exclusion'*, 1 (Sussex Centre for Migration Research, University of Sussex Department of Politics, University of Dundee, 2003); *The World Fact Book. Europe: Albania*, 13 (Washington, DC, Central Intelligence Agency, 2009) available at https://www.cia.gov/library/publications/the-world-factbook/geos/al.html (accessed 18 Jan. 2017).
15. *See* E. Canaj & S. Bana, *E drejta e Bashkimit Europian*, 245 (Tirana, Onufri, 2014).

thus remained mostly homogeneous throughout the last century. Even though the situation has changed in recent years, with increasing immigration from the EU and also third countries, Albania has still only a small foreign population, though its exact size cannot be estimated with precision due to limited documentation and source material. The marginalized role of immigration is notable in immigration legislation, as this field of law only became sensitive to the requirements posed by democratic legislative procedures and by Albania's international obligations, especially in the field of human rights, during the 1990s. Nowadays Albania has to create incentives to attract foreigners who meet the legal requirements and criteria, in order to become an attractive place for tourists.

7. Albania was a major recipient of migration during the 1999 Kosovo crisis, eventually receiving up to 450,000 refugees and to a much lesser extent during the Macedonia conflict in 2001. According to official statistics provided by the Ministry of Labour and Social Affairs, approximately 6,000 foreigners entered Albania as migrant workers in the period 1996–2003. According to the latest data of Albanian Institute of Statistics (INSTAT) on *Arrivals of Foreign Citizens according to the Purpose of Travel* at the end of 2017 Albania hosted a community of in total 12,519 foreigners. They are mainly employed in the construction, trade, service and education sectors. Around 75% of them come from Turkey, China, Egypt, other Arab and Islamic countries, and EU Member States. The latter are mostly specialists working for Western companies that operate in Albania. The majority of foreign immigrants are employed in Tirana, the capital of the country, and a few other big cities.

8. The composition of immigration has changed in recent years, especially with the return of irregular migrants previously residing in the EU Member States to their countries of transit or origin, which include Albania. In 2005 Albania signed a Readmission Agreement (RA) with the EU whereby the country committed to take back its citizens residing irregularly in the EU and to accept nationals of other countries who had passed through Albania prior to entering the EU.[16]The entry into force of the European Community/Albania RA on the 1 May 2006 represents a historic step, not only in the formulation of a common European Communities (EC) readmission policy but also in the development of the EC's cooperation with the Western Balkans. Return and readmission are issues of growing relevance and concern for EU Member States as well as for third and accession countries, like Albania.[17]The Commission of the EU made the signing of the RA a prerequisite for the signing a Stabilization and Association Agreement (SAA) with Albania. RAs have emerged as one of the main instruments for achieving the EU objective to involve countries of origin and transit in the fight against irregular immigration and Albania has been a key player for the EU to realise this objective since as early as 1999. Albania is considered a country of origin and transit for Kurds, Indians, Pakistanis and Chinese on

16. The RA was negotiated in three rounds in May, September, and November 2003. It was ratified by the European Parliament in early September 2005 and by the Albanian Parliament in January 2006 and entered into force on 1 May 2006.
17. *See Return Migration and Reintregation in Albania*, 17 (IOM Tirana, 2013).

their way to Italy as well as for citizens of land-locked neighbours Kosovo and Macedonia and Albania itself.[18] According to the Albanian Ministry of the Interior (MoI), 66,009 Albanian citizens residing irregularly on EU territory were returned in 2013.[19] Even where the conditions governing returns are not complied with by the EU Member States, the Department for Border and Migration (DBM) of the MoI has processed all the requests for readmission of Albanian citizens since the entry into force of the RA.[20] The examination of the legal obligations assumed by Albania through the RA and the implementation of these commitments demonstrate that a substantial policy change has taken place since 2000.[21] Albania has not only adopted the necessary legislation, but has also established the institutional mechanisms and taken the operational measures necessary to comply with the EU's demands in the area of the latter readmission policy. The degree of compliance with EU demands is very high in the period that has followed the EU's decision to make

18. In practice, according to the Albanian border officials, Albanian citizens were returned to Albania by the competent authorities of the EU Member States without prior contact with Albanian authorities. This occurred especially by Italy and Greece. Returns from these countries took place at the border, and all procedures were carried out at the respective border points directly and without the involvement of the central structures. In most cases, the Albanian authorities were only informed of the return once the individual had arrived on the territory of Albania and had been registered by its Border Police. There have been several reported cases where border authorities did not receive prior notification of the returnee's arrival. Thus, official procedures of notification, as outlined in bilateral RAs, were not observed by the EU Member States.

19. *See Return Migration and Reintregation in Albania*, 19 (IOM Tirana, 2013).

20. The main actors involved in the negotiation of bilateral RAs on behalf of the Albanian government were the Ministry of Foreign Affairs (MFA), the Ministry of Public Order (MOP, currently being restructured and renamed the Ministry of Interior, MoI) and the Ministry of Labour and Social Affairs (MOLSA, renamed Ministry of Labour, Social Affairs and Equal Opportunities, MOLSAEO). MFA took the lead in the negotiations and signature, while MOPO provided technical advice and supervised their implementation. MOLSA organized social support for returnees, especially for vulnerable target groups such as victims of trafficking. In general, MFA is responsible for coordinating bilateral negotiations between Albania and other countries at the political level. It also signs and keeps records of RAs, as it does for all international agreements signed by Albania. The consular section in the Directorate of Treaties and International Agreements distributes information and informs operating structures about commitments assumed by Albania under various international agreements, including RAs. *See* C. Mackenzie, *Return and Readmission. The case of Albania*, 17–18 (IOM Tirana, 2006) available at https://www.albania.iom.int/publications/research/12%20Return%20and%20Readmission%20%20(last%20version).pdf (accessed 15 May 2018).

21. *See*, for example, the Readmission Agreement between the Government of the Republic of Albania and the Swiss Federal Council for the readmission of persons at the border and the passage of transit, signed on 29 Feb. 2000, that entered into force on 2 Jan. 2003; the Readmission Agreement between the Government of the Republic of Albania and the Government of the Kingdom of Belgium on the readmission of persons in an irregular situation, signed on 17 Apr. 2001, that entered into force on 1 Nov. 2004; the Readmission Agreement between the Council of Ministers of the Republic of Albania and the Government of the United Kingdom of Great Britain and Northern Ireland on readmission of persons, signed on 14 Oct. 2003, that entered into force on 16 Aug. 2005; the Readmission Agreement on the readmission of illegal residents between the Government of the Republic of Albania and the Government of the Republic of Bulgaria, signed on 11 Jun. 2002, that entered into force on 2 Jan. 2003; the Readmission Agreement on the readmission of illegal residents between the Government of the Republic of Albania and the Government of the Republic of Bulgaria, signed on 11 Jun. 2002, that entered into force on 2 Jan. 2003; the Readmission Agreement between the Government of the Republic of Albania and the Government of the Federal Republic of Germany on the readmission of persons, signed on 18 Nov. 2002, that entered into force on 1 Mar. 2003.

accession conditional on Albania's compliance in the area of migration policy. According to the European Commission the RA with the EU has been implemented in a satisfactory manner. However, Albania still needs to finalise the negotiations on its RA with Russia and the implementation protocols with Greece and Spain. Albania also needs to conclude RAs with a number of countries of origin of irregular migration including Morocco, Afghanistan, Iraq and Iran. Further efforts are needed to ensure that the policy framework on emigration for employment purposes is coherent and implementation is not weakened by contradictory legal provisions.[22]

9. The handling of transitory migrants in Albania has been less elegant. Until 2006, there were no legal provisions on irregular migrants in Albania. Following the 'pre-screening procedure' introduced in 2001, when irregular migrants were identified on Albanian territory or at the border, they were referred to an inter-agency team, made up of representatives from the United Nations High Commissioner for Refugees (UNHCR), the Organization for Security and Cooperation in Europe (OSCE), the International Organization for Migration (IOM), and the MoI's Directorate for Asylum and Refugees, which were expected to provide an early indication as to whether an individual apprehended by the authorities might be a refugee, economic migrant, or victim of human trafficking. This process was regulated and standardized through an Instruction of the Minister of Interior, on 12 June 2008, entitled '*On the Procedure to be Implemented by the State Police for Selection of Irregular Foreigners at the Border*' No. 1085; and Law No. 9959 of 17 July 2008, entitled 'On Foreigners.' In the event of irregular stay in the territory by a citizen of a foreign country an expulsion order is issued, requiring the irregular foreigner's voluntary departure. In the event of failure to leave voluntarily within the time period determined in the expulsion order, an expulsion order using coercion is issued. The individual subject of an expulsion measure by coercion is detained in a closed centre until the expulsion order is enforced; this period can last up to six months, and on justified grounds it can be extended for six more months. The number of removals of irregular migrants from Albania to their country of origin is clearly increasing, though still at a very low level in absolute figures: from nine in 2006 to thirty-six in 2007. In 2008, ninety-three irregular foreigners were removed from Albania. Albania faces serious obstacles in carrying out effective and sustainable removals to countries of origin, not the least among them being a lack of RAs between Albania and the countries of origin. Actually, Albania has one reception centre for irregular migrants in Karrec with a total capacity of 150 beds. The centre is equipped to accommodate men, women and families in three different departments. There is no facility for unaccompanied minors. The centre's poor maintenance has led to it deteriorating and immediate renovation is required. In 2015, 294 people were detained in Karrec, compared to 363 people who were detained in the

22. *See Albanian Progress Report*, 70 (European Commission, 2016), available online at https://ec.europa.eu/neighbourhood-enlargement/sites/near/files/pdf/key_documents/2016/20161109_report_albania.pdf (accessed 12 Apr. 2018).

first half of 2016.[23]However, Albania needs to increase its capacity to host irregular migrants, in particular near its border with Greece.[24]

§2. Overview of National Legal Instruments

I. Historical Overview

10. Albania, perhaps more than any other nation, offers a unique perspective on the entire international migration process, as, in the last three decades, it has gone from forbidding migration to having migration become an integral demographic and social process with more than half of the households reporting family members with a migration experience.[25] It has recently also began the transition from a migrant-sending country to a migrant-receiving one. Albania's new role has put migration- and development-related policies in a flux, as political and ideological tensions arise from development and security concerns, on the one hand, and Albania's vital role as a simultaneously migrant-sending and migrant-receiving nation on the other. Albania initially pursued a 'zero-immigration' policy orientation, which continued into the 1990s. In the 2000s, economic growth, political stability and perceived social safety led to increased immigration to Albania. This immigration consisted of the children and foreign spouses of Albanian emigrants who were considered foreigners due to citizenship laws and their birth abroad. Subsequently, in the second half of the first decade of the twenty-first century, the immigrant communities of, in particular, Tirana saw a growing number of Albanian emigrants returning to the country. At this point, the State had not reacted proactively to this migration flow. The new millennium also saw new migration to Albania, mostly from the EU, but, increasingly, from the USA and Turkey as well. Increasingly aware of these new migration patterns and the associated public concern, the Albanian State started to discuss the development and implementation of a migration policy, though this was not the sole motivation for this development. The EU accession process has also driven Albania to improve its legislative and policy framework for migration. The immigration laws that have come into effect due to this recently found interest must thus be understood in the context of dual imperatives: the need to respond to the

23. *See Albanian Progress Report*, 69 (European Commission, 2016), available online at https://ec.europa.eu/neighbourhood-enlargement/sites/near/files/pdf/key_documents/2016/20161109_report_albania.pdf (accessed 12 Apr. 2018).

24. In 2015, 2009 irregular migrants were intercepted, mainly entering the country from Greece. The vast majority of these interceptions occurred during the first half of 2015 (1,971). The second half of the year marked a sudden drop after the former Yugoslav Republic of Macedonia introduced legislative changes providing refugees/migrants with freedom of movement during seventy-two hours. *See Albanian Progress Report*, 70 (European Commission, 2016), available online at https://ec.europa.eu/neighbourhood-enlargement/sites/near/files/pdf/key_documents/2016/20161109_report_albania.pdf (accessed 12 Apr. 2018).

25. *See* C. Carletto & B. Davis, M. Stampini & A. Zezza *A Country on the Move: International Migration in Post-Communist Albania*, 767 (International Migration Review, 2006).

new realities of migratory fluxes and the need to implement EU legislation. However, while Albania has developed several initiatives with regards to emigration in the last twenty years, it has yet to build an effective and comprehensive *migration policy*.

11. The first legislative act to be considered in this sense is the Constitution of Albania adopted by referendum on 22 November 1998. The Albanian Constitution includes strong guarantees for the respect of human rights and fundamental freedoms, not only for Albanians, but also for foreigners and stateless persons.[26]When regulating the rights of immigrants, the Albanian legislator must respect the principles of non-discrimination and equality before the law.[27] An immigrant can be deported only under conditions specified in law and the process must be transparent and respectful of the immigrant's rights in the Albanian Constitution. Collective expulsion of foreigners is expressly prohibited.[28] Article 40 of the Albanian Constitution also provides that foreigners may find refuge in Albania according to law.

12. Since the return to democracy in 1991, different executives have developed migration laws in 1995, 2003, and 2013. The 1995 Migration Act, later modified by the 2003 Labour Migration Act, first regulated migration to Albania. The Act legally defines the government's responsibilities with regard to migration and emigrants: information, assistance, facilitating their integration into the receiving country's labour market, social and human services systems, and promoting the return of a migrant's social, human and financial capital. The aim was to manage migration flows in order to improve 'governability' and control over migrants. It also introduced the idea of immigrant incorporation, respecting the immigrant's culture of origin and not forcing immigrants to assimilate into Albanian society. Policies to discourage irregular immigration include informing and assisting potential immigrants with regard to legal migration opportunities, as well as encouraging decentralized cooperation between the local authorities of inter-border areas. Albanian authorities also engage in facilitating the entry, instalment into the labour market, legal regulation and social integration of Albanian emigrants in receiving countries. They have made persistent efforts to negotiate with receiving-country governments and ensure compliance with international conventions on labour and migration. In terms of taking advantage of the Albanian diaspora, the government promotes the voluntary return of successful emigrants and tries to harness their financial, human and social capital to boost the country's development.

13. In this context, the Albanian government adopted the *National Strategy on Migration and National Action Plan on Migration* in 2005 to elucidate priorities for

26. *See* Art. 16 of the Constitution of the Republic of Albania.
27. *See* Art. 17 of the Constitution. Art. 18 of the Constitution reads: '1. All are equal before the law. 2. No one may be unjustly discriminated against for reasons such as gender, race, religion, ethnicity, language, political, religious or philosophical beliefs, economic condition, education, social status or ancestry. 3. No one may be discriminated against for reasons mentioned in para. 2 if reasonable and objective legal grounds do not exist'.
28. *See* Art. 39 of the Constitution of the Republic of Albania.

immigration.[29] The Albanian Government developed this strategy with funding from the EU Commission's Community Assistance for Reconstruction, Development and Stabilisation (CARDS) Programme 2001 as well as support from the IOM technical and co-funding support programmes. This comprehensive migration policy for Albania set a number of priorities: combating irregular migration, encouraging the return and reintegration of migrants, promoting the link between migration and national development, protecting the rights of Albanian emigrants in destination countries, and improving the Albanian legislative and institutional framework for immigration. However, the effective implementation of these requirements was limited, mainly due to a lack of financial and human resources.

14. As regards institutional changes, the Department for Border and Migration (DBM) was established in October 2004 as part of the Ministry of Interior (MoI). It handles all matters related to the crossing of borders and migration, including readmission. Prior to this date, these competences were divided among several MoI departments, and none had overall responsibility for irregular migrants. In 2007 a Migration and Readmission Department was established within the DBM. This department has a special unit for readmission issues and coordinates with foreign migration services and border police units on the readmission of Albanian and foreign citizens. Prior to this date, a single specialist in the Unit for the Treatment of Foreigners and Migration dealt with return and readmission issues. The actual readmission of irregular migrants into Albanian territory is the responsibility of the Border Police. The Council of Ministers Decision No. 194, dated 5 April 2006 provided for the establishment of the National Institute of Diaspora (NID) attached to the Ministry of Foreign Affairs (MoFA) that handled Diaspora issues. This Institute has been charged, among others, with the task of implementing the existing strategies set out in the National Strategy on Migration.

II. Current Applicable Legislation

15. The Albanian law on immigration assumed its current form on the adoption of Law No. 108/2013 'On Foreigners' on 28 March 2013 as part of its effort to align Albanian law with EU law. This Law is fully compatible with: Regulation(EC) No. 810/2009 of the European Parliament and of the Council of 13 July 2009 establishing a Community Code on Visas (Visa Code)';[30] Directive 2009/52/EC of the European Parliament and of the Council of 18 June 2009 providing for minimum

29. V.K.M. Nr. 760, 19 Nëntor 2004 e Këshillit të Ministrave të Republikës së Shqipërisë available online at https://www.parlament.al/wp-content/uploads/2015/11/legjislacioni_shqiptar_2001_2009.pdf; V.K.M. Nr. 296, 06 Qershor 2005 e Këshillit te Ministrave të Republikës së Shqipërisë. available online at https://www.parlament.al/wp-content/uploads/2015/11/legjislacioni_shqiptar_2001_2009.pdf; *Strategjia Kombëtare për Migracionin dhe Plani i Veprimit për Migracionin: rruga drejt mena xhimit të Migracionit*, 1 (Tiranë, July 2005), available at http://shtetiweb.org/wp-content/uploads/2014/05/strategjia_kombetare_e_migracionit_alb.pdf (accessed 15 May 2018). *See* L. Ikonomi, *E dre jta migratore*, 105 (Tirana, 2014).

30. OJ EC 2009, L 243/1.

standards on sanctions and measures against employers of illegally staying third-country nationals';[31] Council Directive 2009/50/EC of 25 May 2009 on the conditions of entry and residence of third-country nationals for the purposes of highly qualified employment;[32] Directive 2008/115/EC of the European Parliament and of the Council of 16 December 2008 on common standards and procedures in Member States for returning illegally staying third-country nationals;[33] Council Directive 2005/71/EC of 12 October 2005 on a specific procedure for admitting third-country nationals for the purpose of scientific research';[34] Council Directive 2004/82/EC of 29 April 2004 on the obligation of carriers to communicate passenger data;[35] Council Directive 2004/81/EC of 29 April 2004 on the residence permit issued to third-country nationals who are victims of trafficking in human beings or who have been the subject of an action to facilitate illegal immigration, who cooperate with the competent authorities'; Council Directive 2004/114/EC of 13 December 2004 on the conditions of admission of third-country nationals for the purposes of studies, pupil exchange, unremunerated training or voluntary service Council Directive 2003/109/EC of 25 November 2003 concerning the status of third-country nationals who are long-term residents;[36] Council Directive 2003/86/EC of 22 September 2003 on the right to family reunification';[37] Council Framework Decision 2002/946/JHA of 28 November 2002 on the strengthening of the penal framework to prevent the facilitation of unauthorised entry, transit and residence';[38] Council Directive 2000/78/EC of 27 November 2000 establishing a general framework for equal treatment in employment and occupation;[39] Directive 96/71/EC of the European Parliament and of the Council of 16 December 1996 concerning the posting of workers in the framework of the provision of services.[40]

On 14 July 2016, the Albanian Parliament approved the Law No. 74/2016, which amends Law No. 108/2013 'On Foreigners' ('Law No. 74/2016').[41] Law No. 108/2013, as amended, regulates the regime for entry, stay, employment and the departure of aliens. The law stipulates the functions and competences of the State's authorities and other entities, be they public or private, Albanian or foreign, carrying out activities in the Republic of Albania which are related to non-nationals who seek to enter, those who enter, stay in and depart from the Republic of Albania. International agreements concluded with the government of other countries, ratified by law, may provide special and more favourable provisions for the citizens of these countries, which apply with reciprocity.

31. OJ EC 2009, L 168/24.
32. OJ EC 2009, L 155/17.
33. OJ EC 2008, L 348/98.
34. OJ EC 2005, L 289/15.
35. OJ EC 2004, L 261/24.
36. OJ EC 2004, L 16/44.
37. OJ EC 2003, L 251/12.
38. OJ EC 2002, L 328/(1).
39. OJ EC 2000, L 303/16.
40. OJ EC 1997, L 18/1.
41. These amendments were published in Official Gazette No. 146 and entered into force on 20 Aug. 2016.

16. Migration management actually is handled in a special section of the National Strategy for Development and Integration 2025 (NSDI). NSDI observes that despite the progress in the effective management of migration in Albania, after the implementation of the first National Strategy on Migration (2005–2010) and the Strategy on Reintegration of Albanian Returnees (2010–2015), several challenges need to be addressed: (i) prevention of irregular migration from the country, abuse with the visafree regime in the EU Schengen area; (ii) sustainable return of Albanians through provisions of support for reintegration; (iii) impact of migration development must be strengthened, *inter alia,* through promotion of human and financial investment of Albanians who are abroad; (iv) strengthening of structures of migration management and immigration policy and their implementation based on solid facts and in line with international standards including the securing of human rights of all the emigrants.[42]

17. With regard to asylum, the first Law adopted in the Republic of Albania was Law No. 8432/1998, dated 14 December 1998. This law was modified by Law No. 10060, dated 26 January 2009, that established the conditions and procedures for granting asylum or subsidiary protection and the statutes for asylum seekers, refugees and subsidiary protection, in accordance with EU law.[43]Actually Republic of Albania, in order to further harmonise its legislation with the EU Directive has adopted the law no. 121/2014 'On asylum in the Republic of Albania' which provides for the conditions and procedures for granting and cancelling refugee status, supplementary protection and temporary protection in the Republic of Albania, rights and obligations of asylum seekers, refugees and persons under temporary and supplementary protection, right to family reunification and also definition of conditions for integration of refugees and persons under supplementary protection in the Republic of Albania in compliance with the provisions of this law, the international conventions to which Albania is a party – most notably the 1951 Geneva Convention Related to the Status of Refugees and the 1967 New York Protocol – or

42. NSDI vision consists of the creation of an effective system of migration governance in Albania, through the attainment of the following strategic objectives: (1) Promotion of safe and regular routes of migration in Albania to prevent irregular migration, so as to streamline 70% of migration from Albania through regular bilateral agreements; (2) increasing the impact of emigration development by creating favourable legal and institutional mechanisms; (3) increasing sustainability of return migration by supporting reintegration of returned emigrants; (4) implementation, at an advanced level, of migration policies to ensure equal treatment of thirdcountry nationals and their integration in Albania in line with the international standards; and (5) consolidation of migration policies, the legal framework, the management and coordination structures, to ensure a better response to migration challenges. *See Albania – Migration Profile* 11 (IOM, Min. e Brendshme, 2016), http://www.mb.gov.al/files/documents_files/Profili_i_Migracionit_2016 (Eng).pdf (accessed 20 Feb. 2018); *See* L. Ikonomi, *E drejta migratore*, 106 (Tirana, 2014).

43. Council Directives No. 2004/83/EC, dated 29 Apr. 2004, and No. 2005/85/EC, dated 1 Dec. 2005, repealed by Directive 2013/32/EU of the European Parliament and of the Council of 26 Jun. 2013 on common procedures for granting and withdrawing international protection OJ EC 2013 L 180/60.

other Albanian legislation. The integration and family reunification of foreigners granted asylum is actually regulated by Law No. 108, dated 28 July 2013, entitled 'On Foreigners'.[44]

18. Finally, with regard to border control, Law No. 71, dated 7 July 2016, entitled 'On Border Control,' regulates the control and surveillance of the State border, the responsibilities of the Border and Migration Police, cross-border police cooperation, cooperation within the structures of the State Police, and the cooperation with other agencies that have legal obligations related to border security. This law is aligned to Regulation (EU) 2016/399 of the European Parliament and of the Council of 9 March 2016 on a Union Code on the rules governing the movement of persons across borders (Schengen Borders Code).[45] This law respects the fundamental human rights and freedoms established by the Albanian Constitution and the European Convention on Human Rights (ECHR) without impairing the rights of the persons who ask for international protection by respecting the principle of non-refoulement. Border control and surveillance are a power of the MoI.

III. Administrative and Judicial Authorities

19. The Government of Albania has adopted policies pertaining to immigration, asylum, hosting and integration to be implemented by the Ministry of the Interior (MoI), the former Ministry of Labour, Social Affairs and Equal Opportunities actually the Ministry of Social Welfare and Youth (MoSWY), the Ministry of Foreign Affairs (MoFA) and the Ministry of Culture (MoC), depending on the case. The MoI manages administrative procedures related to entry into, residence in, transit through and departure from Albania. It also assesses asylum cases and decides whether or not to grant refugee status to asylum seekers. The MoSWY is responsible for developing a labour migration policy and manages employment relations with non-nationals. The MoFA supervises several agencies relevant to migration, including the National Institute of Diaspora and the MoTCYS plays an important role in student migration. In 2015, Joint Order No. 265, dated 25 May 2015 on Cooperation between the Ministry of Internal Affairs, Ministry of Foreign Affairs and the State Intelligence Service on the treatment of aliens staying regularly in the territory of the Republic of Albania, was adopted.[46]

20. Through the Albanian State Police (ASP), the Department for Border and Migration (DBM) implements immigration and asylum policies in Albania, in compliance with constitutional and legislative dispositions and the guidelines provided

44. The integration and family reunification of foreigners granted asylum was initially regulated by Law No. 9923, dated 3 Jul. 2003, entitled 'On the Integration and Family Reunion of Foreigners Granted Asylum in the Republic of Albania'. *See* http://www.mb.gov.al/files/documents_files/13-11-14-04-05-08ligji_per_te_Huajt.pdf (accessed 13 May 2017).
45. OJ EC 2016, L 77/1.
46. *See* http://www.qbz.gov.al/botime/fletore_zyrtare/2015/PDF-2015/50-2015.pdf. (accessed 13 May 2017).

by the Government. The DBM guarantees the enforcement of RAs and covers the issues of trafficking and smuggling victims or potential victims, including providing humanitarian assistance.

21. The ASP is a centralized police force that operates under the jurisdiction of the MoI. It has twelve regional police directorates, each of which administers at least one police commissariat. Each police commissariat oversees several police stations and police border crossing posts. The Law 'On State Police' creates special sectors for migration and readmission issues in all eight regional departments of the border police. At the majority of border crossing points (BCP) where the readmission procedures take place, specific admission facilities have been set up. The staff has been trained in the reception, interviewing and selection of returned persons.

22. The Border and Migration Police (BMP) monitor and enforce the border. As a unit within ASP, the BMP cooperates closely and continuously with other services of the State Police and other authorities operating at BCPs. According to the law, the BMP has the following specific duties: controlling and surveying the State border in order to protect human lives and health; preventing irregular migration; stopping persons performing illegal activities across the border, including wanted persons fleeing justice; interdicting vehicles and goods entering/exiting illegally; informing the Customs Office of suspected violations of the Customs Code; implementing obligations stemming from international conventions, bilateral or multilateral agreements; organizing meetings with counterpart agencies in other countries regarding the implementation of joint agreements and information exchange to improve the performance of other duties; gathering and processing data in the interest of the service, control and surveillance of the border; implementing control rules and interview procedures at the BCPs; and, implementing measures for entrance, stay, handling and controlling foreigners in the Republic of Albania.

23. According to Law No. 9877 'On the Organization of the Judicial Review System in the Republic of Albania' as amended, the civil court system is organized as follows: District Courts; Appeal Courts; and a Supreme Court. The Law No. 49/2012 'On the Organization and Functioning of the Administrative Courts and Adjudication of the Administrative Disputes' established the specialized courts competent to adjudication administrative disputes. Administrative court system is organized as follows: (i) Administrative Courts of First Instance; (ii) the Administrative Court of Appeal; and (iii) the Administrative College of the Supreme Court.

24. Juridical review proceedings challenge the legal validity of a decision. The court of review is not allowed to examine the evidence with a view to forming its own view on the substance of the case. Judicial review proceedings thus aim to establish whether the tribunal whose decision is being challenged has done something which it had no lawful authority to do. It may have abused or misused the authority which it has or not followed the procedure provided for by statute or in case concerning civil law issues has failed to observe the principle of fairness. As regards the decision itself, judicial review proceedings aim to establish whether the decision is irrational or grossly disproportionate or contains a legal deficiency, for example, whether there or not there is sufficient evidence to support it, whether it has been adopted on the basis of irrelevant facts, or whether there is a misconstruction of the terms of the law which the decision maker is required to apply.[47]

25. Judicial review is not open if there is an appropriate, alternative remedy available. Thus, unless there are exceptional circumstances, an applicant who has failed to use his/her right of appeal cannot start proceedings before a court of law. As a rule, it is not sufficient to show that the right of appeal is a less convenient remedy, for instance because it must be conducted from abroad. The vast majority of judicial review proceedings concern issues of refugee law and human rights.

26. Constitutional amendments adopted in July 2017 launched a comprehensive justice reform process. A cross-cutting justice strategy 2017–2020 and its action plan have been adopted in November 2016. This process in ongoing.

§3. Overview of International Legal Instruments Applicable in Albania

27. As the Communist regime had closed the borders, banned emigration and heavily discouraged all other kinds of migration, Albania needed several years to prepare and implement legislation to meet international standards for migration following the fall of Communism. The new institutional and legislative framework was constructed to meet Albania's new democratic principles and the standards of organizations that Albania had joined. This effort included changes in regulation, law and strategy towards immigration, as well as a new understanding of how institutions and the Albanian Constitution had to deal with immigration issue.

28. The new framework had to not only address new international standards, but also those of organizations of which Albania was already a member and conventions to which Albania was already a party, as the totalitarian regime had never complied with the terms set out in these agreements. The country's aspiration to become a member of the EU has also required various changes to and the inclusion of new definitions in the legislation in order to comply with EU criteria, which is an ongoing process. The most important international agreements with an impact on Albanian immigration legislation include United Nations (UN) Conventions;[48] ILO

47. *See Fjalorth i terminologjisë migratore*, 39 (ONM, Tirana, 2007); *Profili i Migracionit 2016*, 9 (Ministria e Brendshme, Tiranë, 2017); *Migracioni i kthimit dhe ri-integrimi në Shqipëri*, 13 (INSTAT/IOM, 2014); *Return and readmission. The Case of Albania*, 8 (IOM, Tiranë, 2006).

48. *See* for example International Convention on the Protection of the Rights of All Migrant Workers and Members of Their Families, 1990, 1998; International Convention on Social, Economic and Cultural Rights, 1966; International Covenant on Civil and Political Rights, 1966; Convention on the Elimination of All Forms of Discrimination against Women, 1981; Convention on the Rights of the Child, 1990; International Convention on the Elimination of All Forms of Racial Discrimination, 1969; Convention on the Prevention and Punishment of the Crime of Genocide Adopted by Resolution 260 (III) A of the United Nations General Assembly on 9 Dec. 1948; The United Nations Convention relating to the Status of Refugees, 1951; Convention on the Status of Stateless Persons,

Conventions;[49] Council of Europe Conventions and Policy Documents[50] and EU Documents.[51] Albania has ratified and is successfully implementing the majority of

---

1954, and the Convention on the Reduction of Statelessness, 1961; Convention on the Prevention and Punishment of the Crime of Genocide Adopted by Resolution 260 (III) A of the United Nations General Assembly on 9 Dec. 1948; Convention against Torture or Other Cruel, Inhuman, and Degrading Treatment or Punishment, 1987; p Convention on International Organized Crime and its protocols, 2000; Additional Protocol against Trafficking of Migrants through Land, Sea and Air, 2000.

49. Migration for Employment Convention (Revised), 1949 (No. 97) and Migration for Employment Recommendation (Revised), 1949 (No. 86); Convention for the Protection of Human Rights and Fundamental Freedoms, 1950; Migrant Workers Convention, 1975 (No. 143) and Migrant Workers Recommendation, 1975 (No. 151); Private Employment Agencies Convention, 1997 (No. 181); Domestic Workers Convention, 2011 (No. 189).
50. Council of Europe Convention for the Protection of Human Rights and Fundamental Freedoms, 1950; European Social Charter (Revised), 1961, 1996; European Convention on the Legal Status of Migrant Workers, 1977; Council of Europe Framework Convention for the Protection of National Minorities, 1995; Convention on Participation of Foreigners in the Public Life at Local Level, 1997; Council of Europe Convention on Action against Trafficking in Human Beings, 2005.
51. Charter of Fundamental Rights of the European Union, 2000 (OJ C 364/3, 18/02/2000); The EU Radical Equality Directive 2000/43/EC (OJ L 180, 19 Jul. 2000, p. 22–26); Global Approach to Migration and Mobility, 2005 (MEMO/07/549, 05.12/207); Council Directive 2009/50/EC of 25 May 2009 on the conditions of entry and residence of third-country nationals for the purposes of highly qualified employment (OJ L 155, 18 Jun. 2009, p. 17–29); Directive 2009/52/EC of the European Parliament and of the Council of 18 Jun. 2009 providing for minimum standards on sanctions and measures against employers of illegally staying third-country nationals (OJ L 168, 30 Jun. 2009, p. 24–32); Directive 2011/98/EU of the European Parliament and of the Council of 13 December 2011 on a single application procedure for a single permit for third-country nationals to reside and work in the territory of a Member State and on a common set of rights for third-country workers legally residing in a Member State (OJ L 343, 23.12.2011, p. 1–9); Directive 2014/36/EU of the European Parliament and of the Council of 26 Feb. 2014 on the conditions of entry and stay of third-country nationals for the purpose of employment as seasonal workers (OJ L 94, 28.3.2014, p. 375–390); Directive 2014/66/EU of the European Parliament and of the Council of 15 May 2014 on the conditions of entry and residence of third-country nationals in the framework of an intra-corporate transfer (OJ L 157, 27.5.2014, p. 1–22); European Agenda on Migration, 2015 Brussels, 13.5.2015 COM(2015) 240 final; Regulation(EC) No. 810/2009 of the European Parliament and of the Council of 13 July 2009 establishing a Community Code on Visas (Visa Code) (OJ L 243, 15.9.2009, p. 1–58) Directive 2009/52/EC of the European Parliament and of the Council of 18 Jun. 2009 providing for minimum standards on sanctions and measures against employers of illegally staying third-country nationals' (OJ L 168, 30.6.2009, p. 24–31); Council Directive 2009/50/EC of 25 May 2009 on the conditions of entry and residence of third-country nationals for the purposes of highly qualified employment (OJ L 155, 18.6.2009, p. 17–29); Directive 2008/115/EC of the European Parliament and of the Council of 16 December 2008 on common standards and procedures in Member States for returning illegally staying third-country nationals (OJ L 348, 24.12.2008, p. 98–107); Council Directive 2005/71/EC of 12 Oct. 2005 on a specific procedure for admitting third-country nationals for the purpose of scientific research' (OJ L 289, 3.11.2005, p. 15–22); Council Directive 2004/82/EC of 29 Apr. 2004 on the obligation of carriers to communicate passenger data (OJ L 261, 6.8.2004, p. 24–27); Council Directive 2004/81/EC of 29 Apr. 2004 on the residence permit issued to third-country nationals who are victims of trafficking in human beings or who have been the subject of an action to facilitate illegal immigration, who cooperate with the competent authorities' (OJ L 261, 6.8.2004, p. 19–23); Council Directive 2004/114/EC of 13 Dec. 2004 on the conditions of admission of third-country nationals for the purposes of studies, pupil exchange, unremunerated training or voluntary service' (OJ L 375, 23.12.2004, p. 12–18); Council Directive 2003/109/EC of 25 Nov. 2003 concerning the status of third-country nationals who are long-term residents (OJ L 16, 23.1.2004, p. 44–53); Council Directive 2003/86/EC of 22 Sep. 2003 on the right to family reunification' (OJ L 251, 3.10.2003, p. 12–18); Council Framework Decision 2002/946/JHA of

international conventions on migrant workers. Although it is a typical migrant-sending country, Albania has an almost complete legal framework on migrant workers. The complete legal framework is only partly supported by an institutional framework on migrant workers. Particularly, institutional capacities in addressing migrants' rights are limited. The implementation of rights and obligations of foreign workers in the country is guided by the principles of respect for human rights; eliminating discrimination on race, colour, ethnicity, language, culture, economic, sex and gender grounds; transparency of the process; integrity and dignity of foreign workers; the right of foreign workers to appeal to the decisions taken against them; granting the right of family reunion and full rights to their family members.

28 Nov. 2002 on the strengthening of the penal framework to prevent the facilitation of unauthorised entry, transit and residence' (OJ L 328, 5.12.2002, p. 1–3); Council Directive 2000/78/EC of 27 Nov. 2000 establishing a general framework for equal treatment in employment and occupation (OJ L 303, 2.12.2000, p. 16–22); Directive 96/71/EC of the European Parliament and of the Council of 16 Dec. 1996 concerning the posting of workers in the framework of the provision of services (OJ L 18, 21.1.1997, p. 1–6); Directive 2013/32/EU of the European Parliament and of the Council of 26 Jun. 2013 on common procedures for granting and withdrawing international protection (OJ L 180, 29.6.2013, p. 60–95).

Part I. Border Control and Entry

Chapter 1. Organization of Border Control

§1. General

29. The Republic of Albania borders in the North to Serbia and Montenegro and in the Northeast with Kosovo, on the East with the Former Yugoslav Republic of Macedonia, and in the South and South-East with the Republic of Greece. On the West, the Adriatic and Ionian seas form Albania's natural border. The overall length of the border of the Republic of Albania is 1094 km, of which 657 km are a land-border, 316 km a sea-border, 48 km a river-border and 73 km a lake-border.[52] Thus, the importance of border control is significant in Albania, compared to the size and population of the country. On 31 July 2014 the Parliament of Albania adopted the law on 'Administrative and Territorial Division' with eighty-eight votes in favour, receiving as such wide political consensus. Albania has already reorganized the local government structure according to the new territorial map that reduces the number of communes and municipalities. This law entered into force after the local elections held in June 2015. The Administrative Territorial Reform reduced the number of territorial administration organizations at the local level from 365 municipalities and communes to 61 municipalities.[53]Pursuant to the approved government programme, the Minister of State for Local Government has taken all measures to ensure proper support for the implementation of the administrative and territorial reform in Albania.[54]Albania today operates twenty border guard stations and four coast guard stations.[55]

52. Albania can be accessed by air through Mother Theresa International airport, situated 25 km north-west of the capital Tirana. By sea Albania can be accessed through its main ports: Durres port, connecting with Italian ports of Bari, Ancona and Trieste; Vlora port, connecting with Brindisi port; Saranda, connecting the Greek island of Corf. By land Albania can be accessible through: Montenegro (Murriqan and Han i Hotit border crossing points); Macedonia (Qafasan, Blata, Tushemisht, Gorice border crossing points); Kosovo (Morina, border crossing point); Greece (Kapshtica, Kakavija, Tri Urat, Qafe Boti border crossing points).
53. https://www.reformaterritoriale.al/en/.
54. file:///C:/Users/ecanaj/Downloads/Technical%20Criteria%20for%20the%20New%20Administrative-Territorial%20Division%20(2).pdf.
55. . Durres port, Saranda port, Himara port and Vlora Port.

30. Border control is considered an important dimension of the Integration process. Countries in the Balkans region have shown a strong interest to align their policies, legislation and practices with those of the EU. The adoption and implementation of the EU border control policies by Albania confirms its firm commitment in the EU integration process. Albania is seen as a transit country by third-country nationals, and there is a possible rise in irregular transits by third-country nationals. Albania has received strong EU assistance to facilitate the development of its legal framework as well as training and equipment support. In recent years this country has increased its focus on the EU integration process, as is evidenced by certain achievements in the area of border control, or management of irregular immigration. The Albanian border management system is generally in line with EU standards. For this purpose Albania adopted a law on state border control in 2016, as well as some other legal acts on Border and Migration Police (BMP). With the support of the EU experts, Albania managed to link its policies and legislation with two main goals of modern border management – border security and facilitated movement of persons and goods – in an efficient and effective manner.

31. The Albanian Police (The Police) are the main law enforcement institution in Albania. The service is under the control of the Albanian Ministry of the Interior. The Albanian Police Service, a public administration institution, was established to ensure the maintenance of law and order; the apprehension of offenders; the detection of crime and, more generally, for the maintenance of internal peace and security. The Police are organized in a central and local level. The General Directorate constitutes the central level of the Police, while Police Directorates of the regions, the Regional Border and Migration Directorates and their subordinate structures constitute its local level. The structure of the General Police Directorate, its subsidiary structures, including Regional Police Directorates, Regional Border and Migration Directorates,[56] Commissariats, Border and Migration Commissariats, Police Stations and Border and Migration Stations as well as the number of staff members within these structures are appointed by the Minister following recommendations from the General Director.

32. Albania has a 'short history' of the Police as an administrative institution.[57] With the fall of the Communist regime, on 8 June 1991, the National Assembly

56. According to the latest Albanian Progress Report (2016), the overall staffing of the Directorate-General for Borders and Migration, actually, is limited (1,653 employees), in particular against the background of the migration crisis affecting the entire region. Albania needs to ensure appropriate training of its border police staff in compliance with the EU border guard basic training standards, such as the European Border and Coast Guard Agency (Frontex) common core curriculum. *See* https://ec.europa.eu/neighbourhood-enlargement/sites/near/files/pdf/key_documents/2016/20161109_report_albania.pdf, p. 69 (accessed 12 Mar. 2018).

57. From the establishment of the Albanian State (1912) until the year 1944 the main law enforcement body was the gendarmerie. Aside it, the police operated irregularly and had more administrative tasks and tracking responsibilities. On 13 Jan. 1913, the government of Ismail Qemali decided to establish order forces. According to the country's first Constitution, Ch. IX of Organic Status of Albania, Gendarmerie and militia were part of the Armed Forces. The militia was a 'military territorial and sedentary force' which in peacetime supported the gendarmerie operations. After the Congress of Lushnja, the reorganization of the order forces was realised. In early 1921, the paramilitary

adopted Law No. 7492 that depoliticized these forces and on 30 July 1991 the Parliament adopted the Law No. 7504 'On Police Enforcement.' This was the first step towards secession from the worst traditions of the People's Police. Under this law, 'Police Order is an executive armed organ of the Ministry of Public Order (MPO), in the structure óf the Armed Forces of the Republic of Albania', activities of which were based 'in the Constitution and legislation of the Republic of Albania and the principle of legality, objectivity and humanism' After 1992, the Police went through a profound reform. From a repressive instrument of dictatorship it became a State institution for the protection of democratic freedoms and human rights. For the first time, police swept into its ranks many of those politically persecuted by the Communist regime. In 1997 the Police suffered a severe blow when, as a result of a violation of the Constitutional order, most of its stations were burned or destroyed. Albania's integration into the EU sought the implementation of a process of institutional reforms, both economic and social. In this context, Albania has undertaken a series of reforms in view of this integration, and some of them are undertaken in the institution of the State Police.

33. In terms of legislative reform, the most important is the adoption of Law No. 108 dated 31 June 2014 entitled 'On State Police'[58] which clearly defines the separation of the Police from politics, defining a depoliticized police as an institution. An important step was taken with the drafting and approval of a long-term strategy from year 2007–2013, which aims at orienting the State Police service to the citizens. This strategy contained the most important development of the State Police, focusing on the implementation of its strategic priorities and changing the philosophy of policing and management, offering a modern police service.

34. The Border Police are responsible for the control of the border crossing in conformity with the law, as well as for the guarding and controlling of the border. It is part of the State Police. The competence of the Border Police is set out in the Constitution, the Law on State Police, and delimited by standards in international agreements, which regulate border and migration issues and to which Albania is a State party.

The institutions responsible for the handling of various aspects of migration in the Republic of Albania are responsible for implementation of special migration

organization contained: county, district and post commands. The Gendarmerie was indirectly under the jurisdiction of the Ministry of Internal Affairs for peace issues and the Ministry of Justice for the enforcement of court decisions. The gendarmerie was an armed force entrusted with the task of ensuring the State's domestic tranquillity and the implementation of laws and government orders, commended by a general commander, who was the officer of staff proposed by the Ministry of War in agreement with Ministry of Interior, enacted by the High Council. For military issues and for its promotion, discipline, trials, guilt military, the Gendarmerie relied on the Ministry of War, for administrative and quietness issues on the Ministry of Interior; and for justice issues on the Ministry of Justice.

58. https://www.asp.gov.al/images/ligje/ligj/Perpolicineeshtetit.pdf (accessed 11 Apr. 2018).

policies, component part of the overall migration policy according to the definitions in the legal and subordinate legal acts which govern migration policy in the Republic of Albania.[59]

§2. ORGANIZATION

35. Within the framework of immigration management policies, the MoI is responsible for monitoring the movement of individuals across national borders, i.e., the entry, stay, departure and removal of foreigners from Albania. The MoI is also responsible for assessing asylum cases and for deciding whether or not to grant the status of refugee to asylum seekers. The Border Police control whether the crossing of the border is in conformity with the law. They also guard and control the border. The Border Police have the duty to keep under observation the State border, to control periodically the border signs and to implement the obligations in the bilateral agreements on the delimitation of borders concluded with neighbouring countries, to take measures to prevent illegal border crossing, to apply the legal procedures for the detection, verification, documentation and arrest of smugglers, and to seize transportation means which enter or exit through the border with irregular documents.

36. The Border Police are also responsible to verify the necessary data, to check and refuse at the BCPs and at the border foreign citizens and their transportation means that have crossed or are trying to cross the border illegally. If the foreign citizen refuses to go back or has been stopped on Albanian territory and if it is concluded that his/her entry is illegal the foreign citizen is sent to the temporary reception centres for foreigners. It is also the Border Police's responsible to take measures to stop persons who carry out illicit activities across the border as well as the wanted persons; to seize the transportation means which have been used to cross the border illegally and any goods which have been imported into Albania irregularly; to notify the relevant Customs Office if doubts arise or if they (the Border Police) have information that the Code of Customs Duties has been infringed.

37. On the other hand, the Border Police is responsible to take measures to guarantee the fulfilment of obligations deriving from border agreements in order to prevent and to resolve border incidents and to control the applicability of traffic regulations at the border, to assist in the protection of the life and property of the residents in the border area, to take preventive measures against the illegal entering of foreigners and foreign transportation means into the territory of the Republic of Albania. It has to also ensure that asylum seekers or persons granted asylum are not returned or refouled from the territory of Albania in compliance with the provisions of the legislation in force and to receive asylum requests from foreigners made at the BCPs. An asylum request is any statement (verbal, or written or by gesture) of

---

59. *See Migration Profile 2016*, approved by order of Minister of Internal Affairs is published on the official website of the Ministry of Internal Affairs and Albanian State Police at http://mb.gov.al/files/documents_files/EN-_Profili_i_Migracionit_2016-2.pdf.

a foreigner through which he/she makes known that protection in the Republic of Albania is required. In this case, the Border Police will notify the Office for Refugees and UNHCR on the fact of having received an asylum request. These entities will transport the asylum seeker to the respective reception centre. Until this transfer takes place, the Border Police must ensure that the asylum seeker is not returned to the country from which the asylum applicant arrived.

38. The Border and Migration Department directs and controls all subordinate Border and Migration structures. For the purpose of this supervision and the control of the borders, the Republic of Albania is divided into regions, each of which has a Regional Border and Migration Directorate. The number of Regional Border and Migration Directorates, Border and Migration Commissariats and Border and Migration Stations is determined by the Minister on recommendation of the General Director of Police and the Deputy General Director of Border and Migration. It is located in Tirana. The Border and Migration Department supports the Deputy General Director of Borders and Migration Police in the performance of his duties, supervises the performance of subordinated Regional Directorates of Border and Migration and any other subordinate unit reporting directly to it. It exceptionally supervises the performance of any other subordinate border and migration unit. Following the approval of the General Police Directorate, the Border and Migration Department coordinates the implementation of policies and strategies relating to, in particular, the recruitment of Police employees byte Border and Migration Department and its subordinate structures and the training of those employees, the supervision and control of the State borders, the performance of the functions and duties by Border and Migration Department and its subordinate structures and the implementation of international agreements in matters which fall under the competence of the Border and Migration Department and its subordinate structures.

39. The past decade has seen rapid changes in the migration flows in, from and through the countries of the Western Balkans. Regular migration is very important for the country's socio-economic and demographic development. Irregular migration, however, also deserves special attention by the competent authorities. It is an issue of both State security and human security and is usually connected with serious and organized crime and the infringement of human rights. Following visa liberalization for the Western Balkans countries, the region is usually seen as the origin of illegal migration into the EU. During the last few years all eyes were focused on asylum seekers from the Western Balkans countries. However, it is becoming increasingly difficult to ignore the fact that the region is also a transit area for migrants towards the EU. Albania ultimately introduced mobile surveillance units, and green border control, to stop the irregular border crossing to Greece.[60] These measures also contribute towards the combating of trafficking of human beings and

60. *Guidelines for Integrated Border Management in the Western Balkans,* 17, http://ec.europa.eu/enla rgement/pdf/financial_assistance/cards/publications/ibm_guidelines_en.pdf, and the European Age ncy for the Management of Operational Cooperation at the External Borders of the EU (established by Council Regulation (EC) 2007/2004). The technical agreement with Albania was signed in Feb ruary 2009.

drugs.[61] The Total Information Management System (TIMS) was completed in 2012 connecting twenty-four BCPs. As such TIMS is an efficient means to find wanted persons – both domestically and internationally. Albania has advanced in cross-border cooperation through frequent bilateral and multilateral meetings between Albania and Macedonia,[62] Greece and Montenegro, including mobile joint (green) border patrols that are operational along the border with Kosovo, Macedonia as well as with Montenegro. Full liberalization of bilateral and transit transportation with Macedonia, was realized in 2012.[63]

On regional cooperation and good neighbourly relations, Albania continued to play a constructive and proactive role in several regional initiatives such as the South East Europe Cooperation Process, the Adriatic-Ionian Initiative, the EU Strategy for the Adriatic and Ionian Region, the Central European Initiative, the Western Balkans Six and the Regional Initiative for Migration and Asylum. Albania is a committed supporter of the 'Western Balkans six process'. Albania has engaged fully in the Western Balkans Six initiative, particularly the connectivity agenda.[64]

§3. Legal Framework

40. The Albanian legal framework on migrations broadly in line with the EU's *acquis*. Albania adopted a special law for the control and supervision of State borders i.e., Law No. 9861, dated 24 January, 2008 'On state border control and surveillance' and has specially trained immigration police officers. Actually in force is

61. . European Commission, *Albania Progress Report 2005*, 57, https://ec.europa.eu/neighbourhood-enlargement/sites/near/files/archives/pdf/key_documents/2005/package/sec_1421_final_progress_report_al_en.pdf (accessed 14 Jan. 2018).
62. While Macedonia, as part of the Western Balkans, represents a source of illegal migration, it is also a transit route for migrants aiming to reach the EU Member States. The political and social developments in other parts of the world do influence other countries and change migration patterns. Macedonia is part of the so-called 'Balkan route' which operates in the following way: the migrants pass the Turkish-Greek borders, having three options to leave the country: (1) by air (intra-Schengen flight), (2) by sea (intra-Schengen ferry to Italy) and (3) by land (through Bulgaria or through the Western Balkans). The ones who decide to travel through the Western Balkans cross the Macedonian border, usually in the surroundings of Gevgelija and fewer in the surroundings of Bitola, then continue towards Serbia (near to the crossing point of Tabanovce) with an aim to reach the countries of Western Europe. The targeted entry point into the Schengen zone is usually Hungary. *See* M. Lembovska, *Analysis of the national policies and practices dealing with illegal migration and asylum seekers*, 23, http://www.analyticamk.org/images/stories/files/report/14055_illagal_migration.pdf (accessed 13 Mar. 2018).
63. *See* M. Lembovska, *Analysis of the national policies and practices dealing with illegal migration and asylum seekers*, 23, http://www.analyticamk.org/images/stories/files/report/14055_illagal_migration.pdf (accessed 13 Mar. 2018).
64. In March 2015, Albania hosted a Western Balkans Six meeting where countries of the region reviewed the state of play of regional connectivity projects and the implementation of the soft measures on transport and energy identified at the Vienna Conference ahead of the Paris Summit. The meeting also proposed a comprehensive cooperation agenda for the refugee crisis, putting the emphasis on further enhancing the EU-Western Balkans partnership on migration. Work started on establishing the Western Balkans Fund and regional Youth Cooperation Office, both of which will have their headquarters in Tirana. *See* Albania Progress Report 2016 (COM (2016) 715 final), 23, http://ec.europa.eu/neighbourhood-enlargement/sites/near/files/pdf/key_documents/2016/20161109_report_albania.pdf. (accessed 20 Oct. 2017).

Law No. 74, dated 14 July 2016 'On border control'.[65] The system used by border control officers is linked to international systems and the mechanism in place covered every step of the process. The State border police has detailed standard procedures relating to border checks and uses the latest technology, including biometric passport readers. A national electronic registry has been established to record the entry of non-Albanians into the country.[66] Albania believes that effective legislation and strategies are key to combating organized crime and the country has made progress in these areas. In 2009 a law was passed on the prevention of organized crime and human trafficking and in the same year a law was adopted on the jurisdiction of foreign authorities in criminal cases. In 2010 Albania passed a law on the declaration of speedboats in Albanian territory, which also aimed at combating human trafficking. In addition, an action plan was put in place to help fight organized crime and terrorism and to facilitate the exchange of information between law enforcement agencies.

41. Law No. 108/2013, as amended by Law No. 74/2016, regulates nearly all issues regarding the status of foreigners, tending to do so in accordance with the EU's '*acquis communautaire*' and replacing the old legislation with its archaic and dispersed provisions. This reflects the desire to bring Albanian legislation in line with EU standards. The preparation of the new law required the codification of most of the national laws on foreigners and the regulations on asylum and migration. The provisions in the new law generally reflect the standards set out in EU law, as well as the principles of international law and human rights as the provisions governing entry, residence and the deportation of foreigners are a manifestation of the principle of non-refoulement.[67] Law No. 108/2013 provides regime for entry, stay, employment and departure of non-nationals into and from the Republic of Albania. The law stipulates the functions and competences of the State authorities and other entities, be they public or private, Albanian or foreign, carrying out activities in the Republic of Albania which are related to non-nationals who seek to enter, those who enter and stay and those who depart from the Republic of Albania. International agreements concluded with the government of other countries, ratified by law, may provide more favourable, special provisions for the citizens of these countries, which apply with reciprocity.

42. Law No. 74/2016 contains the concepts and conditions relating to work and residence permits of foreigners in Albania. The new Law provided several novelties, including important amendments to the definitions, starting with the concept of 'key personnel' which is defined as the foreigner, who belongs to one of the following categories: business visitors and transferred employees within the company (managers, specialists and graduated interns). Another novelty brought by Law No.

---

65. *See* http://www.qbz.gov.al/botime/fletore_zyrtare/2016/PDF-2016/146-2016.pdf.
66. *See also* http://www.ohchr.org/EN/NewsEvents/Pages/DisplayNews.aspx?NewsID=12587&LangID=E#sthash.YKBdP9cK.dpuf 9 Law No. 108/2013 date 28 Mar. 2013.
67. J.H. Bhuiyan, *Protection of Refugees through the Principle of Non-refoulement*, 99 (Islam R. & Bhuiyan, J.H., eds., Leiden-Boston, 2013).

74/2016 is the definition of the business service providers, defined as natural persons, representatives of a service provider established outside the territory of the Republic of Albania who are seeking temporary access to the Albanian territory, in order to negotiate the sale of services or to enter into agreements to sell services on behalf of the service provider. They do not engage in direct sales to the public and do not receive remuneration from a source within the Republic of Albania.

43. The new regulation on the status of non-nationals is much more detailed in comparison to the old legislation. Finally, with regard to an analysis of systems for immigration and asylum, it is essential to note the efforts that have been made in order to consolidate a broad-based policy for immigration and asylum, both at the level of adopting a suitable legal framework as well as at the level of reinforcing the role of all the elements and interlocutors involved in these processes, in the light of the transversal nature of this phenomenon.

44. In the area of asylum, the institutional and legal framework that has been put in place, the Law on Asylum, is also in line with the EU's standards. In this policy area there is a greater need to have appropriate human and financial resources in order to improve the implementation of the regulatory framework. Problems are mostly related to asylum procedures at reception centres, which are been always conducted in a standardized manner. The most common difficulties concern, in particular, legal issues and an asylum seeker's access to health care, family reunion, social protection, education and housing.[68]

45. Decision No. 513 of 13 June 2013[69]entitled 'On determining the criteria, procedures and documentation for entry, stay and treatment of aliens in the Republic of Albania' establishes the criteria, procedures and documentation for entry and stay and the treatment of non-nationals in the Republic of Albania, the general criteria to be issued a visa, the main documentation requested from all the categories to be issued visa etc. Directive No. 308 of 8 May 2009 entitled 'On providing citizens with biometric passports', as amended by Directive No. 394/4 of 11 November 2011 entitled 'Procedures for providing the Albanian citizens with biometric passports' provides a new procedure to issue biometric passports to Albanian citizens. Accordingly, Albanian citizens who apply for a biometric passport must submit a filled in identification form and two recent passport photos to the Police Commissariat of the district/region where they are resident. The identification form is approved by the Director General of the State Police. A copy of that form is filled in and verified by the police before it is submitted to the civil status office.

The obligation to obtain a visa may be roughly characterized as one of the formal requirements, and some grounds as to the refusal of visas are rather substantial in nature. A visa is a fundamental condition for the entry of non-nationals who are nationals of countries with which Albania has agreed on a visa regime. As a rule,

68. . *See* http://www. qkss.org/repository/docs/Progress_of_Europeanisation_of_the_Security_Sector_in _Albania,_Kosovo_and_ Macedonia_936150.pdf (accessed 12 Apr. 2017).
69. http://www.qbz.gov.al/botime/fletore_zyrtare/2013/PDF-2013/110-2013.pdf (accessed 13 May 2017).

visas are issued upon request by the Albanian diplomatic overseas representations, where the person has appeared in person.

Chapter 2. Right to Enter the Country

§1. Conditions for the Right to Enter

46. The entry of foreign persons to Albania is regulated by the provisions in section 1 of the Law 'On Foreigners'. The entry requirements may be classified in five groups: (i) formal requirements concerning the entry of foreigners; (ii) the categories of foreigners who shall not be permitted to enter Albania; (iii) the ban on entry (iv) the competences of the Minister of the Interior; and (v) procedural guarantees. The last requirement, the absence of a prohibition of entry, can be considered to be a formal requirement. The importance and the composite content of the relevant regulation, however, make it necessary to review this issue separately.

47. The basic requirements to enter Albania are provided for in Articles 6–11 which are found in section 1 of the Law 'On Foreigners' and in Decision No. 513 of 13 June 2013 entitled 'On determining the criteria, procedures and documentation for entry, stay and treatment of aliens in the Republic of Albania'. The formal requirements contain the obligation of entry and exit through border gates with a valid passport or passport substitute documents and the obligation to obtain a visa (Article 6).[70] The entry of foreigners in the Republic of Albania is only permitted at BCPs recognized and defined by law and on the basis of full documentation as accepted by the Albanian authorities.

48. The entry requirements, as provided for in the EU's *acquis communautaire,* are: a valid travel document, an entry visa or residence permit issued by the competent Albanian authorities and sufficient financial resources, as defined by law. What constitutes a valid travel document depends on the nationality of the non-national, as there are different rules that apply to for instance EU citizens and third-country nationals. The non-national intending to enter into, stay in or transit through and depart from the Republic of Albania, except in asylum cases and where otherwise determined by a bilateral or multilateral agreement, must appear in person at a BCP. The valid travel document should be recognized by the Republic of Albania and have a validity period of at least three months before its expiry date.

49. Besides a valid travel document, the non-nationalist required to present the necessary permits for entry and stay in Albania. In practice, this means that the non-national must present either a visa or a residence permit. Visas are required if the non-national comes from a country that is not exempted from the visa requirement and if the stay is of a short nature, i.e., shorter than three months. If the stay is for a longer period, the non-national must present a residence permit granted for the particular purpose of the stay. EU citizens are exempted from these rules. Persons applying for international protection at the border also have the right to enter the territory without one of these permits being granted. Based on a case by case assessment, the non-national may be required to present other, additional documents, as

70. Criteria of entry, stay, exit and transit. *See* L. Ikonomi, *E drejta migratore*, 106 (Tirana, 2014); IOM, *E drejta migratore,* 84 (Tirane, 2009).

approved by a decision of the Council of Ministers. Law No. 108/2013 defines travel document primarily as a passport issued by the authorities of the country of origin of the alien. Secondary legislation provides a list of the information that must be included in the passport in order for it to be considered valid. However, there are also other travel documents that are valid as document for the purpose of entering Albania. Such travel documents include, for instance, diplomatic passports, refugee travel documents.

50. The non-national should not pose a threat to public order and security, national security or the international relations of the Republic of Albania with other countries and there should be no report in the national electronic register stating that the non-national is prohibited from entering Albania. In addition, a non-national must not pose a threat to public health in the Republic of Albania and should not to be a debtor due to administrative measures imposed on him/her, according to the provisions of the law.

51. The Border Police can grant special permission allowing a person to cross the border at other places than at an official BCP or at other times than during the official opening hours of the BCPs. A prerequisite for the issuance of such permission is that such permission does not place any public interest at risk and that there is a valid reason to cross the border outside the designated space or time.[71]

52. The Ministry of Foreign Affairs is the competent authority to visas and verify if the non-national satisfies the entry criteria and should not is refused permission to enter Albania on the basis of provided by the MoI and the National Intelligence Service. Visas can be issued by the Border Police and Immigration authorities in emergency situations, such as a natural disaster, deaths or an illness duly certified. Non-nationals, who can enter Albania without a visa and those who can enter with a visa must demonstrate that they have the financial means necessary, that they have a guarantee, whether natural or legal person where they intend to stay or on whose invitation they are seeking admission to Albania.

53. If the non-nationalist a minor unmarried person, he/she must be accompanied by an adult. If the minor is not accompanied by an adult, he/she can only cross the border at a BCPs if authorized by the parent/s or legal guardian. If minors, preschool pupils enter the country in as a member of an organized group, they must be accompanied by at least one representative authorized by the institution they belong to who must keep a collective nominal list signed by the head of the undergraduate educational establishment.

54. The non-national who is included on the travel document of another person may only enter and leave the Republic of Albania if accompanied by the person in

71. *See* L. Ikonomi, *E drejta migratore*, 105 (Tirana, 2014); IOM, *E drejta migratore*, 107 (Tirane, 2009).

whose document he/she is recorded. A non-national who has more than one nationality must use the same travel document during the stay in and departure from the Republic of Albania as was used to enter the Republic of Albania.

55. Crew members of Albanian or foreign vessels who have been issued an identity document by the port authorities of the country of origin which includes a photograph, have the right to enter into and transit through the territory of the Republic of Albania and stay in the port where they entered the Republic of Albania for 90 days within 180 days without a residence permit. Crew members of an aircraft who have been issued an identify documents by the Civil Aviation Authority of their country of origin which includes a photograph have the right to enter into and leave the territory of the Republic of Albania in conjunction with a flight that is part of their normal engagement without a visa in their travel document.

56. Railway employees engaged in railway shipments of goods or passengers may travel to a border handover crossing point on the train and stay at the border handover crossing point if they can produce an identity document with a photograph as agreed separately in the agreement on railway transit traffic between bordering countries. Residents of border areas, as determined by bilateral agreements recognized by the Republic of Albania, may enter and stay in the Republic of Albania, based on a border document, issued in implementation of the agreement for local cross-border traffic. The staff of international organizations, in the performance of the duties and missions entrusted on them, may enter, stay, transit and leave the Republic of Albania, making use of a laissez passer issued by the organization or any other document which is valid, based on international agreements recognized by the Republic of Albania.

57. Citizens from European Economic Area (EEA) Member States and some other countries can enter Albania without a visa. 'EEA nationals' are nationals of the Member States of the EU together with Lichtenstein, Iceland and Norway (which are parties of the European Economic Agreement). The nationals of the following countries can enter Albania without a visa:[72]

Andorra;
Argentina;
Armenia;
Australia;
Austria;
Azerbaijan;
Belgium;
Bosnia-Herzegovina;
Brazil;
Bulgaria;
Canada;

72. Current lists of visa-requirements can be found at the webpage of the Foreign Ministry of Albania at: http://www.punetejashtme.gov.al/ (accessed 14 May 2018).

Chile;
Croatia;
Cyprus;
The Czech Republic;
Denmark;
Estonia;
Finland;
France;
Germany;
Greece;
Hong Kong (China);
Hungary;
Ireland;
Iceland;
Israel;
Italy;
Japan;
Kazakhstan;
Kosovo;
Latvia;
Lichtenstein;
Lithuania;
Luxembourg;
Macedonia;
Malaysia;
Malta;
Monaco;
Montenegro;
The Netherlands;
New Zealand;
Norway;
Poland;
Portugal;
Romania;
San Marino;
Serbia;
Singapore;
Slovakia;
Slovenia;
South Korea;
Spain;
Sweden;
Switzerland;
Taiwan (China);
Turkey;
Ukraine;
The United Kingdom;

the USA; and
Vatican State.

58. The list of countries[73] whose citizens can enter without a visa due to liberalization of their visa to the Schengen area comprises the following States:

Antigua & Barbuda;
Bahamas;
Barbados;
Brunei;
Costa Rica;
Guatemala;
Honduras;
Macao (China);
Mauritius;
Mexico;
Moldova;
Nicaragua;
Panama;
Paraguay;
Salvador;
Seychelles;
St.
Kitts and Nevis;
Uruguay;
Venezuela.

59. The countries for which Albania, at the time of writing, has imposed visa requirements are: Bahrain; Egypt; Kuwait; Malta; Qatar; Saudi Arabia; Sultanate of Oman; and The United Arab Emirates. Holders of diplomatic passports and providers of services who can enter the Republic of Albania without a visa are the nationals of: Algeria, China, Costa Rica, Ecuador, Egypt, Georgia, Moldova, Russia, South Africa, Thailand, Uruguay and Vietnam.

60. Non-nationals are issued with visas or residence permits depending on their reason to stay in the Republic of Albania. Non-nationals can be granted permission to stay for the purpose of conduction economic activities, a professional or commercial activity, employment, study, family reunification, humanitarian etc. The largest number of non-nationals in Albania is engaged in employment or self-employment. Admission for employment, be it as an employee or employer, is subject to certain common principles: bob-nationals can only work in Albania, as an employer or employee if they have been issued a work permit. An exception is made for special categories of non-nationals in order to facilitate their entry and residence in Albania. The Ministry responsible for issuing work permits is the Ministry of

73. *See* the list available at: http://www.punetejashtme.gov.al/files/userfiles/REGJIMI_I_VIZAVE_PER_TE_HUAJT_02.03.2018.pdf (accessed 14 May 2018).

Labour, Social Affairs and Equal Opportunities. The non-national must specify the reason why he/she would like to be issued a work permit.

61. Albanian law recognizes four types of work permits: Type A (work permit as an employee); Type B (work permit for an independent economic activity); Type C (work permit for a special occasions) and Type D (Continuous Work permit continuous for those who have received successive work permits).

§2. Administrative Procedures and Documents

62. Everyone must, on arrival in Albania, produce a passport or other document establishing his nationality and identity. On examination by an immigration officer, the entrant must furnish such information as may be required to enable the officer to decide whether he requires leave to enter, whether leave enter should be given, and the terms of that leave. The authority granted to an immigration officer to examine the documents of any person who arrives in Albania is set out in Article 6 paragraph 1, letter 'e' of Law No. 108/2013, of 28 March, 2013 entitled 'On Foreigners' that sets out the purpose for which such an examination is conducted, namely to determine whether the person seeking leave to enter:

(a) is or is not an Albanian citizen; and, if not,
(b) may or may not enter in Albania without leave; and if not,
(c) has been given leave which is still in force, or should be given leave and for what period or on what conditions (if any), or should be refused leave.

Documentary evidence to be produced to an immigration officer may include:

(a) a passport or identity card, required frame citizens as evidence of his right to enter;
(b) entry clearance in the form of a visa or entry certificate;
(c) a passport or identity card, required from non-EU citizens.[74]

63. The immigration officer grants leave to enter by written notice, usually in the form of a stamp in the entrant's passport. The stamp gives the date and port of entry, the period for which leave is granted, and any condition imposed on the person who has been granted leave to enter, but does not indicate the rule under which leave has been granted.[75]

74. *Përmbledhje aktesh juridike në fushën e migracionit*, 47 (ACIL/ONM, Tiranë, 2005); IOM, *E drejta migratore*, 85 (Tirane, 2009); European Union, *Albania Progress Report 2013*, COM(2013) final 700 https://ec.europa.eu/neighbourhood-enlargement/sites/near/files/pdf/key_documents/2013/package/al_rapport_2013.pdf (accessed 12 Apr. 2018).
75. *See* L. Ikonomi, *E drejta migratore*, 106 (Tirana, 2014); IOM, *E drejta migratore*, 107 (Tirane, 2009).

64. The procedures for assessing applications for visas and residence permits in Albania are administrative procedures. Thus, these procedures adhere to the general procedural framework created by general norms of administrative justice.

65. Non-nationals, entering the territory of the Republic of Albania in compliance with the requirements defined under Article 6 paragraph 1, letter 'e' and Article 10 paragraph 2 of Law No. 108/2013, dated 28 March 2013 entitled 'On Foreigners', as the case may be, can be requested by the border authorities controlling the BCPs to produce one or some of the following documents: (a) an invitation of guarantor/inviter resident in Albania; (b) a round-trip ticket; (c) accommodation documents based on evidence; (d) a work permit if entering Albania for employment purposes.

66. Evidence of financial resources, Albanian or foreign currency, which can be exchanged at any exchange agencies in the Republic of Albania, or any other kind of payment and instruments that are accepted in business transactions in the Republic of Albania, such as checks, credit cards etc. are necessary. Documentary evidence of financial resources issued by financial agencies in the Republic of Albania, such as contracts of bank accounts, cards of bank deposits etc. either for the intended period of stay, to return to the country of origin or for the period while being transit in a third country, where the alien will be surely admitted or when he(she) proves that will be able to earn such resource lawfully, in the Republic of Albania.

67. The procedural and substantive requirements that have to be satisfied by applicants for particular kinds of visa and residence permits will be examined in relation to the subject group (students, employees, asylum seekers etc.) in the chapters below. This presentation will, hence, concentrate on the general framework and common requirements. Applications for a visa or residence permit must be made by and approved before the arrival in Albania. Thus, a non-national must, in order to be allowed to enter Albania, be able to present a valid travel document and, if requested, a valid visa or residence permit. Obviously, there are exceptions to this rule. Most notably applicants for international protection are not required to apply for a residence permit in advance, as their application is the asylum application made at the border or when in the country. Thus, for applicants for international protection it is sufficient that the application for international protection is filed when arriving in Albania.

68. Foreigners already present in Albania on residence permits granted for the purpose of study, who want to pursue employment, can apply for a residence permit on the basis of employment in Albania after the examination of documentation. The foreign student shall be provided with a work permit for part-time or fixed-term employment, in remunerated activity, if regular university studies are pursued, provided that his/her employer notifies state authorities responsible for the start and termination of employment; the student works up to twenty hours a week.[76]

69. Documentary evidence in support of an application is always required. Depending on the country of origin of the applicant and also the reason for the stay in Albania, the nature of the required documents varies. If, for instance, a residence permit on basis of employment is applied for, proof must be given of the job offer by the employer. Or, if a visa application is filed for the purpose of attending an entry examination to an Albania university, documents must be attached to the application stating that the applicant can indeed take part in the exam. Again, there are exceptions to these rules, which will be considered in more detail in relation to each sub-group of residence permits in the following chapters.

70. At the BCPs or elsewhere, the competent authorities have to carry out the registration of non-nationals who enter or leave the Republic of Albania in accordance with the law based on their travel documents. They also have to record non-nationals, who, for different reasons, are refused permission to enter the territory of Albania and those who enter or have entered the Republic of Albania contrary to the stipulations in Law No. 108/2013 'On Foreigners'.

71. There are two types of border controls that can be undertaken at the Albanian borders: minimum control and rigorous control. All border controls are, as a starting point, carried out as minimum controls. Every person is subjected to a minimal check for the determination of their identity based on their travel document. This minimal check consists of rapid and straightforward verification with the help of the BCIS database and the records on stolen, falsified, lost or invalidated documents. If either information available to the BMP or the information retrieved during the minimum control gives reason for a rigorous control, this can then be carried out.[77]

72. Minimum border controls include the establishment of the alien's identity for purposes of investigating their right of entry, the verification of their travel document and other documents required for entry, to question a person and where appropriate an investigation into the abilities of the driver to drive a vehicle and the safety of the vehicle that is being driven. The BMP must verify that no entry bans or alike are imposed in respect of the foreigner in question.[78] When conducting a minimum border control, the identity of the alien is established, for instance, examining the travel and entry documents presented. Naturally, the assessment of the skills of the non-national as a driver and the safety of a vehicle is only relevant if there is a vehicle involved.

76. *See* Art. 91 para. 1 of the Law No. 108/2013 'On Foreigners' *Përmbledhje aktesh juridike në fushën e migracionit*, 46 (ACIL/ONM, Tiranë, 2005); IOM, *E drejta migratore,* 107 (Tirane, 2009); L. Ikonomi, *E drejta migratore*, 105 (Tirana, 2014).
77. *See* Arts 14 and 15 of Law No. 71/2016, 'On border control'.
78. *Ibid.*

73. The rigorous control includes the above-mentioned regular elements of the border control, as well as an inspection of his or her belongings, property and, where appropriate, the vehicle. The rigorous control is only undertaken if thesis necessary in order to establish the identity of the individual or in order to ensure that that person is not in possession of property acquired by criminal means or other property that cannot be brought across the border. The full check includes the verification of the conditions for border crossing, i.e., the Border and Migration Police check whether the person has a valid travel document for crossing the border, which has not expired, has a visa or a residence permit if that is required by the legislation in force; fully inspect the travel document for any signs of falsification of alteration and its validity; examine the entry/exit stamps on the travel documents to verify by comparing entry/exits dates whether the person has overstayed the authorized period of residence; verify the intended date of departure and the destination of a person as well as the purpose of residence, by checking other additional documents if needed; verify that the person possesses sufficient financial means for the period and purpose of residence and the return to the country of origin or transit to a third country where he/she is authorized to enter or is in apposition as to be able to achieve those financial means in a lawful way; verify that the person, his/her transportation means and items transported do not constitute a risk to public order and security, public health or international cooperation with other countries, by consulting the appropriate records and database.[79]

79. *Ibid.*

Chapter 3. Refusal of Entry

74. At the airports, the Border and Migration Police (BMP) may refuse to grant permission to enter the Republic of Albania for failure to meet the conditions set out in Albanian law. A traveller refused (entry permission) has the right to appeal the refusal order through administrative channels, to the superior structures of the respective BMP authority.

75. According to Article 7 of the Law 'On Foreigners', a non-national is considered to have entered the Republic of Albania irregularly, if he/she crosses the State border outside the place or time designated for the crossing of the State border, avoids border control, or enters the territory of the Republic of Albania when prohibited to enter and stay in the Republic of Albania. The non-nationalist considered to have entered the Republic of Albania irregularly, if he/she enters the territory of the Republic of Albania using the documents of another person, a forged travel document or any other document which is not listed as a document that can be used to enter the territory of the Republic of Albania. A non-national is considered to have entered the Republic of Albania irregularly, if there is no evidence of entry, i.e., an official note made according to the legal procedures in force in the travel document of the alien or in the electronic system used for border controls.[80]

76. A request for entry and residence permission as well as a visa can be refused if the applicant Isa user of narcotics, a chronic user of alcohol, or to persons who have very infectious diseases, makes propaganda for prostitution or other acts which go against the public moral and are punishable by law.[81] Are quest for entry and residence permission as well as a visa can also be refused if the applicant has violated or violates Albanian legislation, works without a work permission or accepts to employ foreigners without a work permit, has left the country supported by public funding or has any other financial obligations towards the Albanian State or citizens, which have not been fulfilled, when they are citizens of a State which is suspected of terrorism against the Republic of Albania, when they have been expelled and try to enter or stay in the Republic of Albania during the time that the expulsion decision expulsion is still in force, if they do not have a passport or other document, as required by Article 9 of the Law 'On Foreigners', which allows them to establish their identity and citizenship, or when they have presented fraudulent documents.

77. According to the Law 'On Foreigners' (Article 9), the Albanian Minister of the Interior can declare a non-national persona *non grata* if this serves them or the interests of the State, the constitutional and legal order, national security and public

---

80. *Përmbledhje e akteve ligjore në lidhje me përzgjedhjen e të huajve. Për policinë e Kufirit dhe Migracionit që merren me të huajt e parregullt*, 3 (Ministria e Brendshme, Tirane, 2008).

81. *See*, in general, J.H. Bhuiyan, *Protection of Refugees through the Principle of Non-refoulement*, 131 (Islam R. & Bhuiyan, J.H., eds., Leiden-Boston, 2013); IOM, *Analysis of Albanian Immigration and Practice as Compared to EU and International Standards. Gap Analysis on Migration Management in Albania,* 43 (IOM, Tirana, 2004).

order. The decision has to be motivated by any of the following reasons: the non-national has committed acts that endanger the sovereignty of the Republic of Albania, its national security, its constitutional order or its public order and security; is a member of terrorist organization or supports and undertakes anarchist actions against the rule of law in Albania; is a threat to the country or threatens the relations of the Republic of Albania with other countries; is suspected of entering and staying in the territory of the Republic of Albania to commit a crime or actions which pose a threat to the Republic of Albania; is involved in organized crime, trafficking in human beings, drugs, or any other illicit trafficking, based on the information received by the institutions responsible for maintaining national security. The non-national is declared persona non grata for a period of no less than five years from the date of the declaration and his/her entry or stay in the Republic of Albania during this period shall be refused.

78. With the exception of those cases where one of the general conditions laid down in Article 10 of this Law applies, the Border and Migration Police shall refuse entry permission at the border if the non-national, is not issued a visa, if the terms subject to a visa was issued have changed or if the terms, which allow for the issuing of a residence permit have changed or the residence permit is cancelled according to the provisions of the Law 'On Foreigners'. The new Law No. 74/2016 added a provision that empowered the Border and Migration Police to refuse entry permission at the border if the non-national enters the territory of the Republic of Albania with the document of another person, a forged travel document or any other document which is not an authorization for entry into the territory of the Republic of Albania.[82]

79. Thus an immigration officer may refuse a person seeking permission to enter Albania if:

(a) false representations were made or false documents were submitted, or material facts were not disclosed, which were relevant to the application for entry;
(b) a change of circumstances since the visa was issued has removed the basis of the holder's claim to admission; and if
(c) refusals justified on grounds of restricted return possibilities; on medical grounds; the existence of criminal records; because the person seeking to enter Albania is the subject of a deportation order; or because refusal would be conducive to the public good.

80. In the case of a refusal to grant entry permission at the border, the BMP issues the non-national an Order of Refusal of entry which, *inter alia*, states the reason/s for that refusal. The procedure to refuse entry permission and the template of the order of refusal of entry has been approved by Instruction of the Minister of the Interior. The non-national, however, has the right to appeal against refusal to grant entry permission. A refusal to grant entry permission is communicated to the

82. *See* Art 10, para. *c* of the Law 108/2013, as amended by the Law 74/2016.

person concerned in a language or form of communication understood by that person. After withholding entry permission the BMP take all measures necessary to return the non-national to his/her country of origin/transit, or to any other country as required by a RA, that the non-nationalist entitled to enter or where he/she can reside.

Part II. Right of Residence: General Provisions

Chapter 1. Short Stay

§1. Conditions for Short Stay

81. Albania has harmonized its legislation so that it is in accordance with the *acquis communautaire* of the EU. It has tightened measures against illegal immigration, in order to prevent it from being a springboard into the EU for migration from European Balkans countries.[83] The Albanian legislation on migration introduces six types of residence permits: short term, family, students, long-term and humanitarian residence permits as well as those issued to victims of human trafficking. A non-national may stay in the Republic of Albania for a short-term period, temporary period or a permanent period.[84] Short-term stays may not exceed a period of 90 days out of 180 days, based on the issued visa or visa-free entry, unless otherwise provided for by law or agreements recognized by the Republic of Albania.[85]

82. Visa policy is one of the EU's justice and home affairs policy fields in which 'communitarisation' is quite advanced. Both the visa procedure and the categorisation of third-countries whose nationals are subjected to visa requirements or waivers to enter the EU for short-term stays without a visa are determined by the relevant EU Regulations. The EU is also competent to determine the visa fees, the documents to be submitted with a visa application and the rights of applicants whose application is rejected. There is actually little scope for Albania to regulate the issuing of short-stay visas (Type C visas) and airport transit visas (Type A visas).[86]

83. . In order to prevent irregular migration via the Western Balkans, at EU level, FRONTEX provides analytical and operational support for the establishment of Coordination points at the Hungarian-Serbian border. There are currently Coordination Points established in Albania (Murriqan) and FYROM (Tabanovce), with the further development of the network to other Western Balkan countries foreseen. *See* European Commission *5th Annual Report on Immigration and Asylum* date 22 May 2014 http://ec.europa.eu/anti-trafficking/sites/antitrafficking/files/5th_annual_report_on_immigration_and_asylum_en_1.pdf (accessed 14 Jan. 2018).
84. *See* Art. 32 of the Law 'On Foreigners'.
85. *See* Art. 32 para. 2 of the Law 'On Foreigners'.
86. *See* European Commission *5th Annual Report on Immigration and Asylum* date 22 May 2014 http://ec.europa.eu/anti-trafficking/sites/antitrafficking/files/5th_annual_report_on_immigration_and_asylum_en_1.pdf (accessed 14 Jan. 2018).

83. According to the Law 'On Foreigners' residence as a tourist or for other comparable temporary purposes that lasts for up to 90 out of 180 days is considered as a short stay. A foreigner who has entered Albania lawfully, and who meets the general conditions for entry and residence as defined in the Law 'On Foreigners', may stay in the country for this period without satisfying any administrative formalities such as registering her/his residence with the authorities or applying for a residence permit.

84. One of the general conditions for entry and residence that a foreigner must meet to be entitled to stay in Albania for a short term, is the possession of a passport or another travel document that is issued by the authorities of the foreigner's country of citizenship or permanent residence, and that is valid throughout his/her entire period of stay in Albania. There are, though, certain exceptions to this requirement. Citizens of the EU Member States as well as citizens of USA may stay in Albania for up to 90 out of 180 days without a valid passport. EU and USA citizens must, however, have an official identity card to prove their identity and their right of residence. Chapter XII of the Law 'On Foreigners' provides more favourable rules for the citizens of the United States of America (USA), who can reside in the Republic of Albania for a period of at least one year without applying for a residence permit. The initial residence permit for citizens of the USA may be issued for a period of five years and they enjoy equal rights as Albanian citizens as regards access to employment.[87] Namely, exemption from the obligation to hold a visa to enter and stay in the Republic of Albania for a period up to 90 days out of 180 days for purposes equivalent to those for which a type 'C' visa is required, as foreseen in Law No. 108/2013 of 28 March 2013 'On Foreigners'. This also applies to citizens of countries who are issued a valid Schengen multiple entry visa, provided that the visa is first used in one of the Schengen zone countries, and to persons who have been issued a valid residence permit by the authorities of one of the Schengen area countries and to persons who have been issued a valid multiple entry visa or a valid residence permit by the authorities of the USA or the United Kingdom of Great Britain and North Ireland, provided that the visa has first been used in these countries. This general rule also applies to foreigners who enter and stay in the Schengen zone countries, without a visa.[88]

85. In addition to the categories of persons already mentioned, asylum seekers are, regardless of their nationality, not required to hold a passport to enter and stay in Albania.

86. The following foreigners are exempted from the visa-requirement.[89] First, regardless of their nationality, persons who hold a residence permit issued by the Albanian authorities which has been issued in accordance with Albanian legislation are not required to hold a visa. Second, certain foreigners are exempted from the

87. *See* Art. 147 of the Law 'On Foreigners'.
88. *See* in particular Art. 6 of the Decision No 513 of 13 Jun. 2013 'On determining the criteria, procedures and documentation for entry, stay and treatment of aliens in the Republic of Albania'.
89. *See* Art. 10 para. 2 of the Law 'On Foreigners'.

visa-requirement on the grounds of their nationality. This exemption is based on treaties or other arrangements concluded between Albania and the States concerned. EEA nationals, for example, can enter Albania without a visa.[90] There are also a number of third countries, or in other words, States other than EU and Nordic States, Switzerland and Liechtenstein and the USA, whose nationals are exempted from the visa-requirement. These third-country nationals may stay in Albania for a maximum of three months within a period of six months following their entry into the Schengen area without satisfying any other formalities than being in the possession of a valid passport. Holders of diplomatic passports and services can also enter the Republic of Albania without a visa.

87. Foreigners may require individual or collective visa. Collective visa are issued to the members of a group of no less than ten people. The Albanian authorities issue the following types of visas: diplomatic visas, which are issued free of charge to diplomats and senior officials,, but also to ministers; a service visa issued to officials or persons arriving in the Republic of Albania within framework for cooperation with Albania's public institutions; tourist visa which are issued to foreigners who visit Albania as a tourist or as a guest, with a maximum period of validity of six months. A foreigner who has been issued a visa cannot exercise economic activity. Work visa are issued to foreign nationals who wish to pursue an economic activity in Albania. A survey visa is issued to foreigners who want to follow special schools (summer schools for example) or courses in the Republic of Albania, the validity of which depends on the duration of the envisaged study. A Medical visa is issued to foreigners who want to visit Albania for medical purposes, for instance medical treatment. A transit visa allows its holder to stay in Albania for only forty-eight hours and does not allow the holder to work or to exercise any other activity in Albania. This visa can be granted with two or more passes. A foreigner can apply fora visa within seventy-two hours of arrival even if he/she is obliged to apply for a visa in the country of origin if there are justifiable reasons why they person has arrived at a BCP without a visa control. This visa is issued by the local police authorities.

88. Foreigners who hold a residence permit that is issued by a Schengen State may stay in Albania for three months. They are exempted from the visa-requirement even if they are citizens of States whose nationals would normally be required to have one. Regardless of their nationality, persons who hold a refugee travel document are not required to hold a visa. Asylum seekers may stay in Albania without a visa while their asylum application is being considered regardless of their nationality.

89. As far as other European countries are concerned, a further general condition for a foreigner's right to enter and short stay in Albania is that the individual concerned does not constitute a danger to public order or security or public health of Albania. An individual, who is regarded to endanger the public order, public

90. Nationals of the Member States of the European Union together with Lichtenstein, Island and Norway, which are parties of the European Economic Agreement.

security, or public health in Albania, if this criterion applies, may be refused entry permission or, once already in the country, be removed from the country by the Albanian authorities.[91]

90. A foreigner who intends to stay in Albania must have secure means of subsistence so that he or she is able to cover the costs of her/his stay there and to return to her/his country of origin. In addition to this, he or she must also be able to establish that he or she actually meets the income requirement and the other conditions for entry and stay. Financial guarantee is the necessary financial amount deposited by the non-national himself or herself, or by the host on behalf of the non-national, in order to cover the costs of living and consequences of any damage that may be caused by an action or omission of the non-national, contrary to the legislation in force for the defined period of stay in the Republic of Albania.[92] According to the Albanian legislation there is no difference between EU citizens and other citizens as far as the required means of subsistence are concerned. It should be noted that in most of the EU Member States EU citizens as well as USA citizens are, usually, not required to possess secure means of subsistence. If, however, such persons become an unreasonable burden on the Albanian's social security system, for instance by resorting repeatedly to social assistance or other comparable social benefits during their short-term stay, they may be removed from the country. Workers, self-employed persons, and job-seekers, who are EU citizens or comparable persons may, however, not be removed from Albania exclusively on this ground.

91. According to the *non-refoulement* principle,[93] that follows from Albania's international human rights obligations and is also recognized in the Albanian Constitution, the European Convention on Human Rights[94] and in the Law 'On Foreigners', and the Law 'On Asylum', no one may be removed from Albania to an area where he or she faces a risk of being subjected to the death penalty, torture, persecution, or treatment that violates the human dignity, or to an area from where he or she could be sent to such an area.[95] The Republic of Albania recognizes and respects its obligation not to return or *refoul* to territory of a person who has benefited from protected as or requested for protection as a refugee or those who fall under the temporary protection regime. Therefore, if there is no country to which an individual can be returned safely, and that is willing to receive him/her, he or she cannot be prevented from entering Albania or removed from that country even if his/her behaviour constitutes a threat to fundamental interest of the Albanian society, or he or she did not meet the other conditions for entry and stay.[96]

---

91. *Përmbledhje aktesh juridike në fushën e migracionit*, 49 (ACIL/ONM, Tiranë, 2005); IOM, *E drejta migratore,* 121 (Tirane, 2009); L. Ikonomi, *E drejta migratore*, 110 (Tirana, 2014).
92. *See* Art. 13 para. 2 of the Law 'On Foreigners'.
93. J.H. Bhuiyan, *Protection of Refugees through the Principle of Non-refoulement*, 131 (Islam R. & Bhuiyan, J.H., eds., Leiden-Boston, 2013).
94. Albania became member of the Council of Europe on 13 July 1995.
95. *See* Art. 10 para. 2 *b)* of the Law 'On Foreigners'.
96. *See* Art. 7 of the Law 'On Asylum' and Art. 10 para. 2 *b)* of the Law 'On Foreigners'.

§2. Administrative Procedures and Documents for Short Stay

92. The entry clearance procedure is, in effect, a kind of pre-entry control, in which an Albanian official, which may also be a visa or entry clearance officer, acts as an immigration officer, applies the Albanian Rules on Immigration. A foreigner who intends to reside in Albania for a short period does not have to undergo any administrative procedures or formalities apart from the regular border formalities. Those who enter Albania from outside the Schengen Area are requested to present their passport or other travel document and a visa at the border unless they are exempted from the visa-requirement. In addition, third country nationals (TCNs) may be asked to produce documents that indicate the purpose of their intended stay and to prove that they meet the requirements for entry and residence. For this purpose they may, for instance, be asked to establish proof that they have sufficient funds to finance their entire stay in Albania.

93. The actual legislation provides for a greater flexibility in the way permission to enter Albania, especially for EU and USA citizens, is granted. Instead of leave to enter, the actual legislation allows for additional ways of giving leave to enter to be specified, e.g., that a visa or other entry clearance is to be treated as leave to enter. This means that holders of a visa, for example, will be able to pass through immigration control with only a quick check to establish their identity and the rightful ownership of the travel document in order to gain entry clearance. Only if this quick check reveals, amongst other matters a change in circumstance, further examination will take place.[97]

94. As a rule entry clearance now equates leave to enter. This means that there are two important dates to consider on a visa or entry certificate, namely, the *effective date* and the *expiry date*. In most cases the effective date will be the date on which the entry clearance is issued. In order to avoid the cost of making an unnecessary application for an extension of stay, an applicant should always confirm his date of travel. The expiry date on a visa or entry certificate reflects the date on which entry clearance and leave to enter are no longer effective. From this date onwards it is no longer permitted to travel to the territory of Albania, and leave to enter will not be granted.

95. The list of travel documents that can be used to enter the Republic of Albania reflects the *acquis communautaire*. According to the migration rules (legislation and administrative and/or judicial practice) in force in the Republic of Albania a visitor in general refers a person living and working outside Albania who wishes to enter or remain in the territory of the Republic of Albania as a tourist. The requirements to be met by a person seeking permission to enter the territory of Albania as a general visitor are not set out in the legislation, but have been developed through administrative and/or judicial practice. In practice a general visitor is somebody who is genuinely seeking permission to enter the Republic of Albania for a limited

97. *See* L. Ikonomi, *E drejta migratore*, 105 (Tirana, 2014); *Përmbledhje aktesh juridike në fushën e migracionit*, 121 (ACIL/ONM, Tiranë, 2005).

period as stated by him/her not extending three month, or not extending six months; who intends to leave the territory of the Republic of Albania at the end of the stated period of the visit as; who does not intend to take up employment, produce goods or provide services in the Republic of Albania; or who does not intend to undertake a course of studies in the Republic of Albania.[98]

96. In addition to these requirements a tourist has to be able to maintain and accommodate him/herself and any accompanying dependants without having to rely on Albania's public funds or by taking up employment. This condition is satisfied if a tourist and any accompanying dependants are maintained or accommodated adequately by relatives or friends. A tourist should also have sufficient resources to cover the cost of the return or onward journey. So, in general, the most important requirement is that he/she *must not* intend to take up employment whilst in the Republic of Albania.

97. According to Decision No. 513 of 13 June 2013 entitled 'On determining the criteria, procedures and documentation for entry, stay and treatment of aliens in the Republic of Albania', in addition to the general documentation, depending on the type of the requested visa (type 'C' visa-tourist in this case), a tourist must submit the following supporting documentation: a round-trip ticket reservation or proof of the availability of personal transportation; documents proving accommodation during the intended stay in the Republic of Albania; documents proving that the applicant has the necessary financial means to live both during the intended stay and to return to the country of origin or residence, or a third country of transit where the applicant will be admitted, or that the applicant has such financial means to entitle him/her to lawfully stay in the Republic of Albania, in compliance with the provisions of this decision.

98. The border control officer at the BCP may ask a non-national who enters the territory of the Republic of Albania according to the specifications in Article 6, point 1 letter 'e' and Article 10 point 2 of Law No. 108/2013 'On Foreigners', on a case by case basis, to present one or some of the following documents: (a) an invitation by the sponsor/host in Albania; (b) a return ticket/reservation; (c) proof of accommodation, supported by evidence; (d) a work permit if entry in Albania is for employment purposes; as well as (e) proof of financial means, either Albanian or foreign currency, exchangeable at an exchange agency in the Republic of Albania or other means of payment, which are accepted as commercial transactions in the Republic of Albania, including cheques, a credit card etc.; (f) proof of financial means provided by a legal person in the Republic of Albania, such as: a bank account contract, savings deposit etc. sufficient to cover the costs of the intended period of stay and for the return to the country of origin or the period of transit in another third country where it is certain that he/she will be admitted, or proof of the possibility to acquire such means in a lawful way in the Republic of Albania to the

98. *See* Art. 1 of the Decision No. 513 of 13 Jun. 2013 'On Determining the Criteria, Procedures and Documentation for Entry, Stay and Treatment of Aliens in the Republic of Albania'. *See Integrimi i refugjatëve në Shqipëri*, 3 (UNHCR, Tiranë, 2004).

amount of EUR 30 per day of stay and EUR 15 for minors; (g) an original international certificate of vaccination when the non-national arrives from a country affected by an epidemic disease or illness, as required by Albanian legislation. The specialized structures of the Ministry of Health (MoH) are duly notified to take the appropriate measures as provide for by law if the person seeking entry permission does not possess this certificate.[99] All documents produced should be assessed in combination with any other evidence, however circumstantial, which may be relevant to the case.

99. All applicants are now routinely required to provide a ten-digit finger scan and a digital photograph when applying for entrance clearance. According to the general rules on immigration that apply in the Schengen Area and Albania alike, the officer checks both the finger scan and the digital photograph. The biometric data are stored on a central government database in Albania and as provided for by the agreement Albania has concluded with the EU Member States.[100]

§3. Legal Position in the Event of Short Stay

100. Everyone within the jurisdiction of the Republic of Albania is entitled to protection of their basic rights, as guaranteed by the Albanian Constitution and the human rights treaties to which Albania is a party. This includes, among others, the European Convention on Human Rights that has a special place in the Albanian legal order.[101] According to Article 15 ECHR the fundamental human rights and freedoms are indivisible, inalienable and inviolable and stand at the base of the entire Albanian juridical order. There are, however, certain exceptions and limitations as to the scope of human rights protection. For example, the full range of economic rights as well as political rights, such as the right to vote, are reserved to

99. *See* Art. 1 of the Decision No. 513 of 13 Jun. 2013 'On determining the Criteria, Procedures and Documentation for Entry, Stay and Treatment of Aliens in the Republic of Albania'.http://www.qbz.gov.al/botime/fletore_zyrtare/2013/PDF-2013/110-2013.pdf (accessed 13 May 2018).

100. E. Canaj, *Lëvizja e lirë e personave në Bashkimin Europian*, 201 (Tiranë, 2014).

101. (1) Normative acts that are effective in the entire territory of the Republic of Albania are: (a) the Constitution; (b) ratified international agreements; (c). the laws; d. normative acts of the Council of Ministers. (2). Acts that are issued by the organs of local government are effective only within the territorial jurisdiction of these organs. 3. Normative acts of ministers and directors of other central institutions are effective within the sphere of their jurisdiction in the entire territory of the Republic of Albania.

According to Art. 17 of Albanian Constitution: 'Limitations of the rights and freedoms provided for in this Constitution may be established only by law, in the public interest or for the protection of the rights of others. A limitation shall be in proportion to the situation that has dictated it. 2. These limitations may not infringe the essence of the rights and freedoms and in no case may exceed the limitations provided for in the European Convention on Human Rights.' *See* https://www.osce.org/albania/41888?download=true (accessed 11 May 2018).

Albanian citizens and specified categories of foreigners who stay in Albania lawfully. According to Article 16 of the Albanian Constitution 'foreigners in the Republic of Albania enjoy the same rights as citizens, with the exception of those rights associated with citizenship'.[102]

101. According to Article 143 of the Law 'On Foreigners' all foreigners in the Republic of Albania enjoy economic, social and cultural rights. Especially in cases of short-term or temporary migration, migrants will often find that they are not in the full focus of attention of government structures. Hence, the authorities are obliged to ensure that non-nationals with a right of residence in the Republic of Albania are integrated into Albanian society. The public institutions cooperate with each other in accordance with their competences, and with the social partners, NPOs and international organizations to promote and implement the programmes designed to integrate foreigners in the society. In accordance with the international obligations and Albanian legislation, foreigners are protected against any form of discrimination. Direct and indirect discrimination by legal persons, be it public or private is prohibited during the entire immigration process.[103]

102. Foreigners who reside in Albania as tourists or for any other temporary purpose are entitled to emergency health care and to an emergency subsistence subsidy. They are, however, excluded from the other public services and benefits. People who stay in Albania temporarily have a limited right to engage in economic activities. They may, for example, pick or harvest berries, fruit or vegetables, or work on a fur farm. Those who arrive in the country on the basis of an invitation or agreement to work as interpreters, teachers, experts, referees, or as professional artists or athletes, may work in Albania without a residence permit for a period that does not exceed three months. Finally, applicants for international protection have the right to pursue gainful employment after they have resided in the country for three months until a final decision on their application has been taken.

§4. Position of Family Members

103. A foreigner and members of his/her family are entitled to enter and reside in Albania for a period not extending beyond three months. In order to be entitled to reside in Albania for a short stay, everyone, this includes each individual member of a foreigner's family, has to satisfy the conditions for short stay personally. Accordingly, each family member must hold a passport and a visa unless he or she

102. According to Art. 16 of Albanian Constitution: 'The fundamental rights and freedoms and the duties accorded to Albanian citizens by this Constitution are also granted to foreigners and stateless persons present in the territory of the Republic of Albania, unless the Constitution specifically attaches the exercise of particular rights and freedoms to Albanian citizenship. 2. The fundamental rights and freedoms and the duties in this Constitution are also granted to legal persons as long as they comply with the general purposes of these persons and with the core of these rights, freedoms and duties'.

103. *See* Arts 143 and 144 of the Law 'On Foreigners'. E.Canaj & G.Bardeli, E drejta e bashkimit familjar ne Bashkimin Europian dhe ne Shqiperi, 145 (UETPRESS, Tirane, 2018).

belongs to one of the categories of individuals who are exempted from the requirements of holding these documents. A foreigner's spouse and his or her children who are under eighteen years of age are, however, not required to hold their own travel documents if their name and date of birth, and with certain exceptions, photograph, are included in the foreigner's passport.[104]

104. In addition to holding the required documents, each person who intends to enter and stay in Albania has to meet the condition of not constituting a danger to public order, public security or public health, and must not be the subject of a valid decision refusing entry permission. Furthermore, the family must have sufficient funds to cover the expenses of each family member's residence in Albania and their return to the country of origin. This condition is designed to prevent as foreigner and any accompanying family members from becoming an unreasonable burden on the social assistance system of the Republic of Albania.

105. According to Albanian legislation *family members* of the foreigner are the spouse; the partner, with whom the foreigner has a stable relationship and which can be substantiated with evidence; minors, unmarried children, who are member of the family, including the children under guardianship and children adopted by court decision or a directly applicable decision based on the international obligations of the Republic of Albania or a decision which must be recognized in compliance with Albania's international obligations. Family members are, as well, the adult children, unmarried, who cannot objectively fulfil their needs due to their health situation; direct descendants, who have been place under the foreigner's or his/her spouse's custody as provided for by the legislation of the country of origin, and who do not enjoy proper family support in their country of origin.[105]

106. A foreigner's family members who meet the conditions for short stay are, during their residence in Albania, entitled to equal treatment as any other foreigner under comparable circumstances.[106]

---

104. E. Canaj, A. Vasjari, *The Right of Family Reunification. Albanian and Kosovo Cases* (G.C. Bruno & B. Venditto &S. Mannelli eds., Rubbettino, 2013) http://www.issm.cnr.it/pubblicazioni/altre_pu bbl/human_mobility/Human_Mobility.pdf (accessed 12 May 2018); E. Canaj, A.Vasjari, *Family Reunification in Albania. A Comparative Study in the Context of Albanian Integration*, 681 (Med iterranean Journal of Social Science, Sapienza, Vol. 4. nr. 6, 2013); E. Canaj, S. Bana, *Il diritto al ricongiungimento familiare nel diritto internazionale e dell'Unione Europea e la sua tutela multi livello*, 87 (Edizioni Nuova Cultura, Italia, 2014); L. Ikonomi, *E drejta migratore*, 106 (Tirana, 201 4).

105. *See* Art. 1, para. 14 of the Law 'On Foreigners'. E. Canaj, A.Vasjari, *Family Reunification in Albania. A Comparative Study in the Context of Albanian Integration*, 682 (Mediterranean Journal of Social Science, Sapienza, Vol. 4. nr. 6, 2013), http://www.mcser.org/journal/index.php/mjss/articl e/view/350; (accessed 13 Mar. 2018); E. Canaj & G. Bardeli, *Bashkimi familjar si një e drejtë the melore në ditët e sotme*, 141 (*Jus&Justicia*, UETPRESS, No. 13, 2016); E. Canaj, *Bashkimi fami ljar në dritën e zhvillimeve të reja europiane*, 75 (*Jus&Justicia*, UETPRESS, No. 7, Tiranë, 2012).

106. *See* E. Canaj, A.Vasjari, *Family Reunification in Albania. A Comparative Study in the Context of Albanian Integration*, 681 (Mediterranean Journal of Social Science, Sapienza, Vol. 4. nr. 6, 2013) http://www.mcser.org/journal/index.php/mjss/article/view/350 (accessed 13 Mar. 2018).

Chapter 2. Residence

§1. Conditions for Residence

107. The Albanian legislation indicates that foreign persons who intend to stay in Albania longer than the visa or visa exemption period or in excess of ninety days are obliged to obtain a residence permit. Therefore, as the main rule anyone who is not an EU citizen, a Nordic citizen or an USA citizen, who intends to reside in Albania for longer than three months must apply for a residence permit. A residence permit can be issued for a period of residence of three or, six months or a year.[107]

108. Permission to stay in Albania on temporarily or permanently is only granted if a foreigner has been issued a residence permit. A permit is evidence that the Albanian authorities have approved an application for permission to reside, work or study during period of validity of that permit. The Law 'On Foreigners' defines residence permit as a permit that is issued upon application to a foreigner for any purpose other than tourism or a comparable purpose for short-term residence, and that entitles its holder to enter Albania repeatedly and to reside there during the validity period of the permit.

109. To be issued a residence permit a foreigner must meet the conditions set out in Articles 4, 5 and 8 of the Law 'On Foreigners'. The Law 'On Foreigners' introduces six types of residence permit that the Albanian authorities can issue to any one intending to reside in the Republic of Albania for a period longer than 90 days within a period of 180 days. Residence permits are issued for short-stays (90 out of 180 days) to family members, students, long-term residents and victims of human trafficking. In addition the Albanian authorities can issue humanitarian residence permits. Residence permit categories are as follows: (a) type 'A' residence permit, which is not renewable, the holder is entitled to reside in the Republic of Albania during the period for which the residence permit is issued; (b) type 'B' residence permit, renewable, issued for a defined period of time, gives holder or entitled to enter, stay and exit the Republic of Albania during the period defined in the residence permit; (c) a type 'C' residence permit is permanent permit and entitles the holder to enter, stay and exit the Republic of Albania; (d) a type 'S' residence permit, renewable, after a period of six months after expiry of the previous type 'S' residence permit, which is issued to seasonal workers, entitles the holder to enter, stay and exit the Republic of Albania within the period of time defined in the residence permit; (e) an 'AL Blue Card' residence permit, renewable, issued for a defined period to the highly qualified workers, entitles the holder to enter, stay and exit the Republic of Albania during the period defined in the residence permit; (f) an 'AL-C Blue Card' residence permit, is a residence permit that is issued for an indefinite period to highly qualified workers and entitles the holder to enter, stay and exit the Republic of Albania.[108]

---

107. *See* L. Ikonomi, *E drejta migratore*, 112 (Tirana, 2014); IOM, *E drejta migratore*, 121 (Tiranë, 2009).

108. *See* Art. 32, para. 1 of the Law 'On Foreigners'.

110. The type of residence permit varies according to the purpose of the stay: engaging in a subordinate professional activity; independent professional activities; research or highly skilled professional activities; study at an institution for secondary education; study at an institution for higher education; unpaid professional internships; attending a programme of volunteer activities; family reunion; as a victim of human trafficking or any other action involving illegal immigration etc. Short-time residence permits, valid for a maximum period of one year, are granted to foreigners who intend to conduct scientific research or establish a business; who possess immovable property; who receive medical treatment, who enter for tourist purposes; or who participate in student exchange programmes. Family residence permits are issued to the spouse, the minor children, and the dependent children of Albanian citizens, foreigners falling within the scope of the Albanian Citizenship Law; foreigners holding residence permits and refugees/ subsidiary status holders, and to a minor child, and any dependent child of the spouse of the above-mentioned people. The maximum period of validity of the first family residence permit is one year and it may be renewed for a validity period of two years. This type of residence permit is only renewed once.[109]

111. Long-term residence permits are granted to foreigners who have resided in Albania with a residence permit for an uninterrupted period of at least five years and to foreigners who satisfy the criteria as determined by the Border and Migration Policies Department. This type of permit grants the holder a very advantageous status i.e., the same rights as those accorded to Albanian citizens with the exception of political rights and some other public rights.

112. As regards residence permits, the Law 'On Foreigners' has recently introduced a so-called Blue Card which is issued to specialized workers. According to Article 33 of the Law 'On Foreigners' there are two types of Blue Card residence permits. The first is an 'AL Blue Card' residence permit, which is renewable and is issued for a defined period of time to the highly qualified workers. This residence permit entitles the holder to enter, stay and exit the Republic of Albania within the period defined in the residence permit. The second is the 'AL-C Blue Card' residence permit, which entitles its holder to stay in Albania permanently and is only issued to highly qualified workers. It entitles the holder the right to enter, stay and exit the Republic of Albania.[110]

113. The introduction of the humanitarian residence permit and the permit for victims of human trafficking (Article 53 of the Law 'On Foreigners') reflects the impact of the developments in the field of International Law and Human Rights on Albanian immigration law. According to this article the Albanian authorities can issue type 'A' temporary residence permits to a foreigner who has lodged an application with the asylum authorities requesting them to grant him/her refugee status. A type 'A' temporary residence permit can also be issued to a victim or potential victim of human trafficking or somebody who is a victim of labour exploitation in

---

109. *See* Art. 34, para. 4 of the Law 'On Foreigners'.
110. *See* Art. 33 paras *d* and *dh* of the Law 'On Foreigners'.

the Republic of Albania. A residence permit is only issued to a victim of labour exploitation if he/she collaborates with the authorities in the criminal proceedings against the employer. The residence permits is issued for the duration of the criminal law proceedings, until the alien receives compensation for being exploited as determined by the authorities in the criminal proceedings. A type 'A' residence permit is also issued to victims of labour exploitation who have collaborated or have agreed to collaborate with justice authorities on the proposal of the State bodies or national security authorities. Finally a type 'A' residence permit is also issued to a stateless person if stateless has been determined by the competent authorities; an abandoned minor, or a minor for whom there is no parental care available, with no legal guardian, or parental custody due to other reasons as well as to a woman who has been pregnant for more than six months.

114. The 2013 amendment to the Law 'On Foreigners' introduced a residence permit that can be issued to foreigners who stay in Albania to conduct voluntary work.[111] The validity of this residence permit may not be longer than the duration of the relevant voluntary work programme for which the residence permit has been requested and issued. The residence permit for voluntary work with a validity period of one year is issued if the intended voluntary work is closely linked with the official voluntary work scheme of the Republic of Albania. Any voluntary work has to be limited in time and the applicant has to fulfil the requirements subject to which a 'residence permit for voluntary service' is issued. Only in exceptional cases, a residence permit may be extended if the duration of the voluntary work programme exceeds a period of one year.

115. Generally, to be issued a residence permit, the applicant must meet both the general requirements which apply to all applicants for a residence permit, and the requirements that are particular to the residence permit that he or she has applied for. Residence permits are always issued on a particular ground, for instance work, study, international protection or as a family member (family reunification).

116. The most important general requirements that have to be satisfied to obtain a residence permit are that the applicant has a valid passport or any other travel document. This requirement is, however, not applied in certain exceptional cases, for instance when the individual concerned applies for a residence permit for the purpose of international protection.

117. Another general condition that needs to be satisfied to obtain a residence permit is that the person concerned does not pose a danger to public order, public security or public health. If an applicant is regarded to pose a danger to these interests, he or she may be refused a residence permit.[112]

A residence permit may also be refused or a residence permit that has been issued may be annulled if the holder has failed to lodge an application in time or to submit the necessary documentation within the specified period of time and fails to give

111. *See* Art. 50 of the Law 'On Foreigners'.

112. *See* Art. 35 para. *c* of the Law 'On Foreigners', as amended by the Law 74/2016.

justified reasons for such omission. This is also the case if holder of a residence permit is unable to prove that he/she fulfils the conditions subject to which the residence permit was issued. In the same way, the residence permit may be refused or a residence permit that has been issued may be annulled if a removal order is issued against the holder of that residence permit. If the holder of a residence permit that is granted for the purpose of family reunion is divorced, this also justifies the annulment of the residence permit. More generally, if the reason for which the residence permit was issued no longer exists, this justifies a decision annulling a residence permit.[113]

118. There are currently 12,519 foreigners staying in Albania who hold a residence permit.[114] The following figures show the breakdown according to the purpose of residence for which a residence permit was applied for: 6,263 applications were made for the purpose of work; 2,783 for family reunion; 652 for study; 2,395 on humanitarian grounds and 426 for other reasons. According to the data in the Electronic Register of Aliens for 2016, Italian and Turkish citizens who come to Albania for employment purposes are predominant in this category. Of the EU immigrants approximately 23% were Italians. Approximately 28% of the labour migrants were Turkish nationals. Data provided by the Ministry of Social Welfare and Youth (National Labour Service) show that the list of foreigners employed in the country in 2016 is followed by citizens of Kosovo (7%), Chinese nationals (6%) and Greeks (5%). Closing the ranks are: Canadians, Egyptians, Macedonians and Indians.[115]

§2. Administrative Procedures and Documents for Residence

119. The regulation on residence permits in particular reflects the impact of EU law on free movement and the right of residence. The non-national who has entered and stays in the Republic of Albania with a long-term type 'D' visa, or the alien who enters Albania without a visa, must lodge an application for a residence permit with the local authority responsible for border and migration.[116] The Ministry of the Interior, after consulting with the State Intelligence Service, is the authority responsible for the procedure of issuing the residence permits. The regional/local State authority is responsible to issue the residence permit to the foreigner.

120. In Albania residence permits are either issued for a fixed-term or permanently. The first residence permit issued to a foreigner is always a fixed-term permit. Fixed-term permits are issued for residence of either a temporary nature

113. *See* Art. 35 of the Law 'On Foreigners'.
114. *See Buletini Informativ nr. 41, Mbi aktivitetin e Strukturave te M.P.B. gjate muajit shkurt 2017,* 37 (Ministria e Puneve te Brendshme, 2014) http://www.mb.gov.al/files/programs_files/17-03-23-11-51-41 Buletin_mujor_shkurt_2017.pdf. (accessed 14 Jan. 2018).
115. file:///C:/Users/ecanaj/Downloads/konf_migracioni_min_financesinstat.pdf (accessed 14 Mar. 2018).
116. *See* Art. 34, para. 1 of the Law 'On Foreigners'.

(temporary residence permits) or a continuous nature (continuous residence permits). The residence permit is issued for a period of (a) three months, six months or a year and may be renewed no more than five consecutive times; (b) two years, and may be renewed once; (c) five years, according to the provisions of the Law 'On Foreigners'; (d) permanently, if the applicant has legally resided for five consecutive years in the Republic of Albania and has ties with or pursues a stable activity in the country.[117]

121. Usually, the first fixed-term residence permit is granted for one year unless it is applied for a shorter period (three or six months). A non-national is issued a temporary residence permit which is valid for the period of stay indicated in the application, but no longer than one year, if the application is lodged for the first time, unless otherwise provided for by law or an international agreements ratified by the Republic of Albania.[118] Under exceptional circumstances it is possible, though, that the first permit issued with a longer or a shorter validity period than one year (*maximum* two years). This is the case, for example, if the permit is issued for the purpose of carrying out a specified work assignment or study that must be completed within a set period.

122. The students, and non-nationals who intend to work in Albania on a temporary basis, as well as beneficiaries of temporary protection, are issued a temporary residence permit. A person who moves to Albania, as we will *see* below, with an intention of working there for a longer period or permanently is issued a continuous residence permit. A continuous residence permit is also issued to refugees and persons receiving subsidiary or humanitarian protection. The duration of validity of the first fixed-term permit may not exceed two years. Neither may it exceed the validity period of the applicant's passport. There are, though, special rules on the validity period of residence permits as regards certain specified categories of foreigners. For instance, the first fixed-term residence permit issued to refugees and beneficiaries of subsidiary protection has a validity period of four years and a person who is a victim of trafficking in human beings is issued a residence permit which is valid for a period of at least six months with a maximum of one year.[119]

123. The holder of a temporary residence permit valid for at least one year is considered a temporary resident of the Republic of Albania only after the registration with the civil registry office of the local governmental unit of the place of temporary residence. Any change of the place of residence must be notified to the responsible authorities in compliance with the national legislation in force.[120]

---

117. *Ibid.*
118. *See* Art. 37, para. 2 of the Law 'On Foreigners'.
119. The application for a residence permit is made by the non-national in person according to the criteria and documentation approved of by decision of the Council of Ministers. The procedure for issuing residence permits is approved of by Instruction of the Minister of the Interior and the Director of the State Intelligence Service.
120. *See* Art. 37, para. 1 of the Law 'On Foreigners' and the Law No. 10129, dated 11 May 2009 'On Civil Registry'.

124. All adults family member of a foreigner who intends to stay in Albania for more than one year and is over the age of eighteen, must file a separate application for a residence permit. Minor children are included in their parents' applications. However, once they themselves become adults (over the age of 18) and are resident in Albania they need to apply for their own residence permit.

125. In comparison with the old legislation, the new regulation setting out the terms forth refusal, non-extension, or cancellation of residence permits is much more detailed and precise. The conditions for the acquisition and the refusal, cancellation, or non-extension of residence permits are regulated for each type of residence permit separately. Nevertheless, the rules on refusal, cancellation and non-extension of a residence permit share certain conditions, for instance not meeting the conditions subject to which a residence permit has been granted or the existence of a deportation decision or an entry ban. Stays outside Albania for a certain period justifies refusal, non-extension, or cancellation of short-term, long-term or family residence permits.

126. The non-refoulement principle is an important safeguard in the procedure to acquire entry permission as well as in cases when deportation is under consideration.[121] Finally, the new legislation emphasizes that non-fulfilment of the conditions as stipulated in Articles 6, 7 and 8 of the Law 'On Foreigners' (on entry into and departure from Albania using official BCPs with valid passports, document checks and foreigners who do not qualify as foreigners who are not permitted entry into Albania) are not be interpreted or implemented in any way that will prevent the application of the rules on international protection. It can be said, therefore, that the regime for international protection is designed to provide an 'extra' favour to foreigners in the field of entry into and stay in Albania.

127. A foreigner must apply for an Albanian residence permit at the police station nearest to the place of residence. The documents must be submitted in support of the application for a residence permit to the local Police Commissariat. The application for a residence permit or the renewal of a residence permit is lodged with the regional authorities responsible for border and migration in person, through the secure online electronic system, or by a legal representative assigned to the applicant according to the law. Residence permit applications made through the secure online electronic system is only possible for the citizens of several countries, amongst others Australia, Andorra, the EU/Schengen Member States, Israel, Japan, Canada, Lichtenstein, San Marino, the Holy City, the USA and New Zealand. The terms for the creation and functioning of this system are laid down in an instruction of the Minister of the Interior.

128. The non-national is issued a residence permit according to the form and content specified in the Decision No. 513 of 13 June 2013 'On determining the criteria, procedures and documentation for entry, stay and treatment of aliens in the

121. J.H. Bhuiyan, *Protection of Refugees through the Principle of Non-refoulement*, 130 (Islam R. & Bhuiyan, J.H., eds., Leiden-Boston, 2013).

Republic of Albania' i.e., in the form of a biometric document. The application for a biometric document residence permit has to be made in person.

129. In addition to the general documentation (*see* paragraphs 119–122), depending on the type of the requested visa, the applicant must submit the following supporting documentation: the invitation by the host and a copy of the identification document of the host attached to the former; a document proving the applicant's professional, commercial activity or capability to pursue such an activity, which is linked to the purpose of the applicant's visa application. In addition, the applicant must submit the copy of the work permit issued by the Albanian labour authorities.[122]

§3. Legal Position of Residents

130. As mentioned above, everyone resident in the Republic of Albania is entitled to protection of their basic rights as guaranteed by the Albanian Constitution and the human rights treaties to which Albania is a party. In addition, according to Article 143 of the Law 'On Foreigners' all foreigners in the Republic of Albania enjoy economic and social rights and the right to protection of their cultural life. The most important right enjoyed by residents (be it short-term or long-term) is their integration into the Albanian society, especially in the economic and social field.

131. According to Albanian law, foreigners who have been issued a residence permit enjoy economic, health-related and social rights, in line with the legislation in force. Foreigners who stay in Albania temporarily have a limited right to engage in economic activities. From a perspective of access to the labour market, holders of a short-term residence permit can engage in subordinate or independent professional activities of a temporary nature.

132. The non-national, who satisfies the requirements, may be employed or self-employed or engage directly in a business activity. In terms of the labour market access, holders of a residence permit can engage in subordinate or independent professional activities that, as a general rule, do not exceed a period of six months or one year. They may also engage in scientific activities in research centres, teach in establishments of higher education or engage in highly skilled activities for a temporary period.

133. According to Articles 39–44, Law 'On Foreigners', a residence permit allows the holder to engage in subordinate or independent professional activities. In addition, a residence permit is a necessary and sufficient condition to receive professional guidance, training, improvement and rehabilitation, without the need for

---

122. *See* Arts 1 and 2 of the Decision No. 513 of 13 Jun. 2013 'On determining the criteria, procedures and documentation for entry, stay and treatment of aliens in the Republic of Albania', available online at: https://www.ilo.org/dyn/natlex/docs/ELECTRONIC/99781/119213/F467343735/ALB-99781.pdf (accessed 11 May 2018).

any additional authorization related to the condition of being a foreign national. The law also ensures equal treatment for foreigners in areas related to labour, such as social security, tax benefits and membership of trade unions.

134. Refugees recognized by the authorities of the Republic of Albania enjoy in compliance with Albanian legislation and pursuant to Section E of the Final Act of the Conference of the Plenipotentiaries, the legal status provided for in the Convention Relating to the Status of Refugees of 1951 and all rights stipulated in any other treaties to which the Republic of Albania is party, as well as the rights accorded to foreigners in general by Albanian legislation. A refugee is, in particular, entitled to a special residence permit and a work permit. Refugees enjoy the right to social assistance to the same extent as an Albanian national and receive any social welfare benefits to which he/she is entitled from the Office for Refugees. In accordance with Article 12 of the Law 'On Asylum' and Article 28 of the Convention Relating to the Status of Refugees of 28 July 1951, the MPO issues refugees, recognized by the authorities of the Republic of Albania, a travel document which bears a return clause. This document can be used to travel to all countries, with the exception of the country of origin, and to return to the Republic of Albania for as long as it is valid.[123]

§4. Position of Family Members

135. A foreigner and members of his/her family are entitled to reside in Albania if they meet the requirements set out in Albanian legislation. A foreigner who is the spouse of an Albanian national is issued a residence permit with a period of validity of no longer than one year when the residence permit is issued for the first time, unless otherwise foreseen by international agreements or by this law. The residence permit may be renewed with a validity period of two years. This rule that applies to the spouse of an Albanian national also applies to the minor, who is unmarried and for who the non-national is the legal guardian. A residence permit is not issued or annulled if it has already been issued if it is proven that the marriage is one of convenience, as set out in Article 59 of the Law 'On Foreigners'.[124]

---

123. *See* Art. 12 of the Law 'On Asylum'.

124. According to Albanian law a 'Marriage of convenience' is considered to be a marriage entered into for the purpose of avoiding the fulfilment of the conditions for entry and stay of non-nationals in the Republic of Albania. A marriage is considered to be a marriage of convenience if one of the following circumstances is found: the spouses, after family reunification, do not maintain their marital union based on no reasons at all; the spouses, after family reunification, do not perform their marital obligations; the spouses never met before their marriage; the spouses fail to provide consistent personal data for one-another; the spouses do not speak a language that they both understand; money was exchanged for the conclusion of marriage, unless the money is dowry, and the spouses come from countries where the presentation of dowry is a custom; and where there is proof of previous marriages of convenience on the part of either of the spouses either in the Republic of Albania or abroad. The non-national is not issued a residence permit for family reunification if a marriage of convenience is established. *See* in general E. Canaj, *The Right of Family Reunification. Albanian and Kosovo Cases*, 95 (G.C. Bruno & B. Venditto & S. Mannelli eds., Rubbettino, 2013) http://www.issm.cnr.it/pubblicazioni/altre_pubbl/human_mobility/Human_Mobility.pdf (accessed

136. The spouse or partner and the child who has reached the age of majority who has been issued a residence permit for the purpose of family reunification has a right to an autonomous residence permit after an uninterrupted period of at least five years residence in the Republic of Albania, provided that he/she has not been issued a residence permit for reasons other than those of family reunification during this period of stay. In the case that the relationship with the spouse or unmarried partner is ended within this five-year period commencing when the first residence permit for the purpose of family reunification was issued, there is no right to an autonomous permit. If the sponsor, the spouse or relatives in the first ascending and descending line pass away there is an entitlement to an autonomous residence permit if they have been issued a residence permit for the purpose of family reunification which is valid for at least three years. An autonomous residence permit is issued if the general requirements laid down in the Law 'On Foreigners' are satisfied or if this is in the best interest of the child. If the children who reach the age of majority are issued a permanent residence permit, the first time application for an autonomous residence permit shall be an application for a permanent residence permit.

137. A foreigner's family members who meet the conditions for residence are, during their residence in the Republic of Albania, entitled to equal treatment as any other foreigner under comparable circumstances.

12 May 2018); E. Canaj, A.Vasjari, *Family Reunification in Albania. A Comparative Study in the Context of Albanian Integration*, 681 (Mediterranean Journal of Social Science, Sapienza, Vol. 4. nr. 6, 2013) http://www.mcser.org/journal/index.php/mjss/article/view/350 (accessed 13 Mar. 2018); E. Canaj, S. Bana, *Il diritto al ricongiungimento familiare nel diritto internazionale e dell'Uni one Europea e la sua tutela multilivello*, 58 (Edizioni Nuova Cultura, Italia, 2014).

Chapter 3. Long-Term Residence

§1. Conditions for Long Term Residence

138. A special five-year long-term residence permit is issued to foreigners who can prove they have been legally living and working in the Republic of Albania during this period. Hence, a non-national is entitled to apply for a permanent residence permit, if he/she has stayed legally for a continuous period and has been resident in the Republic of Albania for at least five years from the moment that the first application for a residence permit was made. The requirements are that the foreigner is over the age of eighteen and he/she has not left the territory of the Republic of Albania for an uninterrupted period of more than twelvemonths.[125]

139. Foreigners have to meet the general criteria set out in the law and the directions of the Council of the Ministers as well as the Border and Migration Police. Immigrants residing in Albania for study or vocational training purposes, foreigners who stay in the Republic of Albania on the basis of temporary protection, or who have lodged an application for residence on this basis and are awaiting a decision on their application, as well as asylum seekers or foreigners who have lodged an application for recognition as a refugee and whose application has not yet given rise to a final decision cannot apply for this permit.[126] The same holds true for foreigners who stay in the Republic of Albania, is temporary by nature, such as seasonal workers or providers of cross-border services, whose residence permit has been officially restricted, or who are resident in the Republic of Albania on the basis of a subsidiary form of protection in accordance with international obligations or national legislation or who have lodged an application to reside on that basis and are awaiting a decision concerning that status.

140. The Ministry of Internal Affairs also issues a permanent residence permit if it is proven that the parents or grandparents of the applicant have Albanian citizenship or if the child was born in the Republic of Albania from parents who have been issued a permanent residence permit. In these cases compliance with the requirements to be issued a permanent residence permit is not required. An application for a permanent residence permit can also be made by a non-national, who has made an investment in the Republic of Albania in excess of a million euros and who can prove that he/she has employed more than ten Albanian citizens for at least one year. The family members and key staff of the investor are also entitled to a permanent residence permit as well.[127]

---

125. *See* Arts 61 and 64 of the Law 'On Foreigners'. *See Buletini Informativ nr. 41, Mbi aktivitetin e Strukturave te M.P.B. gjate muajit shkurt 2017,* 26 (Ministria e Puneve te Brendshme, 2014) http ://www.mb.gov.al/files/programs_files/17-03-23-11-51-41Buletin_mujor_shkurt_2017.pdf. (acces sed 14 Jan. 2018).
126. *See* Art. 62 of the Law 'On Foreigners'.
127. *See* Art. 65 of the Law 'On Foreigners'.

141. Albanian legislation recognizes a residence permit issued to a long-term resident of another country. In fact, based on a bilateral or multilateral agreement in force in the Republic of Albania as well as the principle of reciprocity, the long-term resident of another country may lodge an application for a long-term residence permit in the Republic of Albania, if he/she fulfils the general conditions set out in the law 'On Foreigners' irrespective of the reason why a long-term resident wishes to stay in the Republic of Albania. The entry and residence conditions that apply to a long-term resident of another country who wishes to stay in the Republic of Albania in a bilateral or multilateral agreement to which the Republic of Albania has become a party applied on the basis of reciprocity to long-term residents in the Republic of Albania who wish to reside in the territory of another Contracting Party.[128]

142. As a general rule, if a foreigner, a long-term resident of another country, wishes to remain in Albanian for a period longer than three months, he/she is entitled to a residence permit if he/she is not employed by a supplier of cross-border services or is not a supplier of cross-border services, but works as an employee or as a self-employed person; or pursues a study or a vocational training; or presents a credible reason for wanting to reside in Albania. These foreigners must have sufficient means of subsistence and as well as adequate accommodation.[129]

143. The entry and residence conditions that apply to long-term residents of another country are specified in Articles 66 and 67 of the Law 'On Foreigners'. A long-term resident of another country may, according to the conditions laid down in Article 66 of the Law 'On Foreigners', may enter and stay in the Republic of Albania for 90 days within a period of 180 days without having been issued a visa for a residence permit may be applied for within sixty days from entry if he/she meets the following requirements; (a) has a valid travel document and long-term residence permit in the country which is party to an agreement concluded with the Republic of Albania on the mutual movement of long-term residents; (b) has documentation to prove that he/she has guaranteed normal accommodation in the Republic of Albania; (c) provides evidence of stable financial means which are sufficient to maintain him/her and any accompanying family members; (d) has a sickness insurance that covers all risks as provided for by the legislation in force; and (e) has a valid work permit if an economic activity is to be pursued; or (f) has sufficient financial means to exercise a self-employment activity, in addition to the necessary permit to exercise this activity; or (g) provides evidence of being registered with an educational or vocational training institution recognized by the Republic of Albania in the case of studies or vocational training.[130]

---

128. *See* Art. 66 of the Law 'On Foreigners'.

129. *See* L. Ikonomi, *E drejta migratore*, 113 (Tirana, 2014); IOM, *E drejta migratore*, 85 (Tirane, 2009); *Fjalorth i terminologjisë migratore*, 7 (ONM, Tirana, 2007); *Analiza e mangësive mbi legjislacionin dhe praktikën shqiptare të emigracionit krahasuar me standartet europiane dhe ato ndërkombëtare*, 22 (ONM, Tiranë, 2004).

130. *Buletini Informativ nr. 5, Mbi aktivitetin e Strukturave të M.P.B. gjatë muajit shkurt 2014*, 27 (Ministria e Punëve të Brendshme, 2014).

144. The Law 'On Foreigners' recognizes other special circumstances in which the Albanian authorities issue a foreigner a permanent residence permit. For instance if it is proved that the parents or grandparents of the non-national are Albanian, or a child was born in the Republic of Albania of parents who have been issued a permanent residence permit by the Albanian authorities. A child is issued a residence permit without consideration whether he/she satisfies the conditions subject to which the residence permit is normally issued.

145. After obtaining a residence permit, a foreigner has the right to invite his family members if they have been issued with residence permit in the country where the alien was a long-term resident.

146. When a foreigner who has been issued a long-term residence permit by another country is granted a right to remain in the Republic of Albania under a bilateral or multilateral agreement, the Albanian authorities are obliged to notify the country of former residence of the long-term resident of their decision to grant residence permission to that foreigner.

147. The right to remain as a long-term resident of another country may be refused or annulled for reasons of public order or public safety, taking into consideration the seriousness and nature of the offence committed and the harm that may result if that person remains on Albanian territory. A residence permit issued to long-term residents of another country and any accompanying family members under the conditions set out in Article 67 of the Law 'On Foreigners' may be annulled or its renewal may be refused and their removal from the country may be ordered if it is proven that the residence permit has been obtained fraudulently or by using forged documents or if the holder of the residence permit does not reside in the Republic of Albania according to the conditions in this law. As regards the obligation to readmit a long-term resident in the case of an annulment of or refusal to renew his/her residence permit, the country that initially issued a long-term resident status to the foreigner is obliged to readmit that person.

§2. Administrative Procedures and Documents for Long-Term Residence

148. There are some specific documents that have to be submitted by long-term residents of another country who apply for a type 'B' residence permit, in addition to the general criteria. Namely: a copy of the work permit or a certificate of registration for work and a certificate of registration with the taxation office where they will run their activity as a self-employed person. If exempted from this obligation by law a certificate of declaration of employment with the respective employment office has to be submitted. A copy of the residence permit of the long-term resident issued by the other country must also be submitted.[131]

131. *Ibid.*, 26.

149. The application for the residence permit of a long-term resident of another country must be submitted to Albanian authorities no later than three months after the date of entry into Albanian and must be accompanied by the documents which prove that the applicant meets the conditions, as well as a document that proves the long-term resident status granted by another country and a valid travel document (or certified copies of those documents). The decision on the application for a residence permit must be made within this period of three months. This period may be extended for a further period not exceeding three months if the application did not include all the aforementioned documents or if the case is unusually complex. An applicant is notified of any decision to extend the period for processing the application. If a decision is not taken within six months, the application for a residence permit is to be classed as approved.[132]

150. A family member of the non-nationals, who has been issued a residence permit according to the requirements of Article 67 of the Law 'On Foreigners, seeking family reunification must submit: a valid travel document and a copy of the first page of that document; a copy of the residence permit of the sponsor already resident in the Republic of Albania; a certified copy of the family member's long-term residence permit issued by the authorities of the country of former residence and evidence of family ties with the long-term resident in the other country prior to their arrival in the Republic of Albania. hereto be admitted as a family member the following conditions apply: a sickness insurance covering all risks according to the legislation in force and certificate of vaccination against the diseases covered by the Albanian vaccination programme and proof of sufficient and stable financial means to prevent the family from becoming a burden on the Albanian social assistance system or proof that the long-term resident has sufficient financial resources to prevent the family from becoming such a burden.

151. If the family members of the long-term resident who has been issued a residence permit by the Albanian authorities according to the conditions Article 67 of the Law 'On Foreigners' does not reside in the country where the sponsor was a long-term resident, he/she has to apply for family reunification. As a general rule, this application falls under the regime for family reunification in Section V of the Law 'On Foreigners'.

132. *See Përmbledhje aktesh juridike në fushën e migracionit*, 122 (ACIL/ONM, Tiranë, 2005); L. Ikonomi, *E drejta migratore*, 116 (Tirana, 2014); *Integrimi i refugjatëve në Shqipëri*, 59 (UNHCR, Tiranë, 2004); IOM, *E drejta migratore*, 85 (Tirane, 2009); *Fjalorth i terminologjisë migratore*, 7 (ONM, Tirana, 2007); *Analiza e mangësive mbi legjislacionin dhe praktikën shqiptare të emigracionit krahasuar me standartet europiane dhe ato ndërkombëtare*, 78 (ONM, Tiranë, 2004).

152. According to the provisions of the Decision No. 513 of 13 June 2013 'On determining the criteria, procedures and documentation for entry, stay and treatment of aliens in the Republic of Albania', the procedure to grant long-term resident status should not be longer than six months. If a residence permit is annulled or if a request to have a residence permit refused, this decision can be appeal in an administrative court.[133]

§3. Legal Position of Long Term Residents

153. The legal position of a long-term resident in Albania is very strong, especially under the new regulations. This type of residence permit grants the holder a very advantageous status as they enjoy the same rights as those enjoyed by Albanian citizens with the exception of political rights and some other public rights. During their stay, long-term residents not only enjoy the same rights as Albanian citizens, but are also entitled to the same benefits and advantages as Albanian nationals enjoy. Long-term residents enjoy economic rights, health-related and social rights under the same conditions as Albanian nationals, in line with the legislation in force in Albania. The key problem in the Republic of Albania as regards the fulfilment of these rights seems to be how this legal position can actually be enjoyed in practice.

154. Long-term resident holders also enjoy the same rights as Albanian nationals do with regards to: access to professional work as either a self-employed person or employee; the protection by the law regulating employment and work conditions, including dismissal and remuneration; access to education and vocational training; the recognition of professional diplomas, certificates and other evidence of formal qualifications; access to social security, social welfare and social protection services; tax exemptions or reductions; access to health care; and the freedom to move freely within the whole of Albanian territory.[134]

§4. Position of Family Members of Long Term Residents

155. Albanian legislation provides for general rules applicable to family reunion. Members of the applicant's family who can qualify for family reunion are: the spouse; partner, who is in a partnership of a stable and proven nature; minors, unmarried children, who are a member of the family, including the children under guardianship and children adopted by a court decision, a directly applicable decision based on the international obligations of the Republic of Albania or a decision which must be recognized in compliance with Albania's international obligations,

133. *See* L. Ikonomi, *E drejta migratore*, 120 (Tirana, 2014); *Integrimi i refugjatëve në Shqipëri*, 5 (UNHCR, Tiranë, 2004); IOM, *E drejta migratore*, 84 (Tirane, 2009); *Fjalorth i terminologjisë migratore*, 39 (ONM, Tirana, 2007); *Analiza e mangësive mbi legjislacionin dhe praktikën shqiptare të emigracionit krahasuar me standartet europiane dhe ato ndërkombëtare*, 22 (ONM, Tiranë, 2004).

134. *See* Art. 70 of the Law 108/2013 as amended by the Law 74/2016.

as well as adult children, unmarried, who cannot objectively be considered able to fulfil their needs due to their health situation; direct descendants, under the sponsor's or his/her spouse's custody, according to the legislation of the country of origin, and who do not enjoy proper family support in their country of origin qualify as family members of a long-term resident. Unmarried partners are to be treated, to the extent applicable, equally as spouses with respect to family reunification.[135] When a minor who has entered the Republic of Albania for family reunification purposes, reaches the age of majority, he/she has the right to apply independently of the other family members for a residence permit. In case of polygamous marriages, an application for family reunification can be made for only one of the spouses and the children born from that spouse.

156. To be issued a residence permit as a family members of a long-term resident, who has been issued with residence permit according to the requirements of Article 55 of the Law 'On Foreigners', a family member must submit the following documents: a valid travel document and a copy of the first page of that document; a copy of the residence permit of the sponsor who is already resident in the Republic of Albania; a certified copy of the family member's long-term residence permit issued by the authorities in the country of the previous residence; if necessary, evidence of being a family member of the long-term resident in the other country prior to the arrival in the Republic of Albania; a sickness insurance that covers all risks according to the legislation in force and a vaccination certification for the diseases covered by the Albanian vaccination programme; proof of stable financial means sufficient not to have to resort to the Albanian social assistance system or proof that the long-term resident has sufficient financial resources not to become a burden on the Albanian social assistance system.[136]

157. Constituting a serious threat to public order or public security justifies the cancellation of a long-term residence permit. The grounds for granting resident permits for humanitarian reasons or to victims of human trafficking are related to the termination of the reason why these permits were issued in the first place.

158. The legal positions of family members, who hold a permanent residence permit or a long-term resident's EU residence permits, or a permanent right of residence, is similar to that of the other long-term residents.

---

135. *See* Art. 69 para. 2 of the Law 'On Foreigners'.
136. IOM, *E drejta migratore*, 86 (Tirane, 2009); *Fjalorth i terminologjisë migratore*, 39 (ONM, Tirana, 2007); *Analiza e mangësive mbi legjislacionin dhe praktikën shqiptare të emigracionit krahasuar me standartet europiane dhe ato ndërkombëtare*, 78 (ONM, Tiranë, 2004); *Përmbledhje aktesh juridike në fushën e migracionit*, 47 (ACIL/ONM, Tiranë, 2005); L. Ikonomi, *E drejta migratore*, 120 (Tirana, 2014).

Part III. Right of Residence for Specific Categories of Persons

Chapter 1. Nationals with Preferential Treatment

159. This chapter addresses the right to reside of different categories of migrants related to their right to enter and stay in Albania. There are at least three groups of persons who are given preferential treatment in terms of the right to reside in Albania. These groups are citizens of the EU Member States, of the Schengen Area and citizens of USA. Considering that in all the provisions of the Albanian legislation the first two categories are regulated together,[137] in this chapter we will consider them together as well. Special provisions concerning USA citizens are found in Section III paragraph E of Decision No. 513 of 13 June 2013 'On determining the criteria, procedures and documentation for entry, stay and treatment of aliens in the Republic of Albania'.

§1. EU Citizens

160. EU citizens enjoy, as mentioned, special treatment regarding the right to enter and reside in Albania. The rule is that all EU citizens have the right to move freely within, reside in and work in the Republic of Albania. The only condition is that an EU citizen has a valid passport or identity card to enter the country and the only obligation is that the EU citizen and any accompanying family members must not become an unreasonable burden on the social assistance system of Albania. EU citizens and their family members are allowed to enter Albania without further formalities. Nevertheless, if a family member comes from a country for which the EU has imposed a visa-requirement, Albania can require that family member to present a visa, unless the family member can present a residence card issued by the authorities of an EU Member State. EU citizens and their family members can be denied entry permission by the Albania authorities if justified for reasons of public order and safety, and on grounds of public health.

161. EU citizens and citizens of the Schengen countries as well as their family members haves the right to stay in Albania after three months if the EU citizen is employed or self-employed in Albania, if he or she has sufficient means of support

137. *See* Arts 39, 41, 43, 44, 47, 48, 49, 51, 52, 71, 72 and 84 of the Law 'On Foreigners'.

from other sources than work or if he or she is enrolled as a student in Albania and has sufficient means of support not to be dependent on Albanian social assistance. An EU citizen is also entitled to reside in the territory of Albania for a period extending three months if he is a qualified person as long as he/she remains a qualified person. His family member(s) have the same right.

162. If the stay in Albania is for the purpose of studies, only the spouse and minor children qualify as family members. Upon successful completion of the study, an EU citizen, if registered with an employment office based on an employment contract, may apply for a residence permit for employment purposes.[138]

163. EU citizens and Schengen countries citizens are exempted from the obligation to be issued a work permit. Nationals of one of the EU Member States and the Schengen countries who are staying legally in the Republic of Albania and who are entitled to employment as well as Albanian citizens, except where employment relates specifically to the holding of Albanian citizenship, pursuant to the Albanian legislation are excused from the obligation of provision with work permits and work registration certificate.[139] In this case, the Republic of Albania due to general provisions and the obligation under the Stabilization and Association Agreement (SAA) has expanded the standard of equal treatment for EU member states. Indeed they enjoy equal rights with the Albanian citizens in the field of employment and self-employment.

164. EU citizens who have resided in Albania continuously for five years have the right to a permanent residence permit. This also includes the family members of EU citizens who have resided with the EU citizen in Albania for a period of five years.

165. If the EU citizen (sponsor) dies, the family member's right of residence is affected even if the family member himself or herself is an EU citizen. In fact, in the case of the sponsor's death, the spouse and relatives in the first ascending and descending line, who have resided in the Republic of Albania with a residence permit for the purpose of family reunification with a validity period of at least three years are entitled to apply for an autonomous residence permit if they fulfil the general requirements laid down in the law or if this is to be considered in the best interest of the child. If the family member's right to residence in Albania is based on a marriage to an EU citizen and the spouse is an EU citizen him/herself, the right of residence as a family member is lost in the event of a divorce. The general rule on autonomous residence permits apply here as the legislation does not provide for special rules for EU citizens.

166. Non-EU citizens who have been issued a residence permit by an EU Member State as a long-term resident third-country national enjoy the right to move

138. The difference between EU citizens and other non-nationals can be seen in different provisions of the Law 'On Foreigners', in particular, *see* Art. 52, para. 5 of the Law 'On Foreigners'.
139. *See* Art. 72 of the Law 'On Foreigners'.

freely within the Union.[140] EU long-term resident status holders who apply for a residence permit in Albania within three months of their arrival in that country are granted permission for a fixed term or a continuous stay, depending on the reason for their stay in Albania. The residence permit issued depends on the reason for the stay in Albania. Family members accompanying an EU-long-term resident status holder are issued the same residence permit as the sponsor according to Albanian law.

167. As a general rule deportation of EU citizens from Albania can be carried out if an EU citizen constitutes a major concern for Albania's public safety, order or health. In all instances of deportation, a general assessment of the situation must be carried out.

§2. USA Citizens

168. USA citizens enjoy certain special rights in terms of residence in the Republic of Albania. Bilateral agreements have been signed between the Republic of Albania and the USA regarding the transfer of USA citizens. Chapter XII of the Law 'On Aliens' and Section III paragraph E of Decision No. 513 of 13 June 2013 'On determining the criteria, procedures and documentation for entry, stay and treatment of aliens in the Republic of Albania' provide special provisions for citizens of the USA, granting them more favourable treatment than other foreigners.

169. The more favourable treatment enjoyed by the citizens of the USA on the one hand allows them to reside in the Republic of Albania for a period of at least one year, without applying for a residence permit and the issuing of an initial residence permit that is valid for a period of five years. Citizens of the USA who stay in the Republic of Albania for one year without a residence permit may re-enter and stay in the Republic of Albania without residence permit, if they reside outside the territory of the Republic of Albania for three months in a fifteen month period of stay in the Republic of Albania.[141]

170. The period of validity of the first residence permit issued to an USA citizen is linked to the requested purpose of stay for which evidence has to be presented which is specified in the decision. If citizens of the USA satisfy the criteria, they may apply for permanent residence permit, after staying as residents for five uninterrupted years in the Republic of Albania.[142]

---

140. *See* Council Directive 2003/109/EC of 25 Nov. 2003 concerning the status of third-country nationals who are long-term residents, OJ EC 2003, L 16/44.

141. *See* Art. 147 para. 1 of the Law 'On Foreigners' and s. E para. 1 of the Decision No. 513 of 13 Jun. 2013 'On Determining the Criteria, Procedures and Documentation for Entry, Stay and Treatment of Aliens in the Republic of Albania'.

142. *See* paras 2 and 3 of s. E of the Decision No. 513 of 13 Jun. 2013 'On determining the Criteria, Procedures and Documentation for Entry, Stay and Treatment of Aliens in the Republic of Albania'.

171. The citizens of the USA enjoy equal rights as the Albanian citizens as regards access to the Albanian labour market. As a general rule this also includes equal rights as regards self-employment. Usually, family members of USA citizens living in Albania are granted family residence permits without having to satisfy the requirement that the sponsor must have sufficient financial means to support them.

Chapter 2. Students

172. The right to education is one of the basic human rights which are recognized in the Albanian Constitution. The right to education is granted to Albanian citizens, all foreigners and stateless persons resident in the Republic of Albania alike. Section IV of the Law 'On Foreigners' deals with the residence permit for specific categories in the Republic of Albania. The right to remain in Albania as a student is regulated in Article 52 of the Law 'On Foreigners'. Foreigners, who have enrolled as a student with an educational institution in Albania, are issued a temporary residence permit if their study will lead to a degree or a vocational qualification.

173. A residence permits can also be issued to a student for other types of studies, for instance a study that does not directly lead to a degree or vocational qualification, but aim at deepening the knowledge in a particular field of expertise already acquired through a previous study by the student. However, if there are no special grounds, a residence permit is generally only issued to students studying at a university or an educational institution in Albania equal to a university.

174. According to Article 52 of the Law 'On Foreigners' there are two main types of student. First of all, an adult student also referred to as a general student. A student is considered to be an adult student if, on arriving in the Republic of Albania that person is older than 18 and enrols for post-18 education. Second, a child student. This category of students covers children aged between 4 and 17 who wish to enter the Republic of Albania for the purpose of attending education. It is the first category of students that will be discussed in this chapter as the second category of students falls outside the scope of this monograph.[143]

---

143. The Albanian education system has three levels: pre-school, school and extra-curriculum education. In turn, school education is divided into three levels: primary, secondary and higher. Pre-school, although not compulsory, it is open to all children from 3 to 5 years of age inclusive. Primary school is universal, compulsory and free. It spans nine years and is divided into three cycles, the first cycle lasts four years, the second two years and the third three years. Educational and training courses aim to provide children with a differentiated education. They enable them to conclude their compulsory schooling and obtain a certificate at the end of the 2nd and 3rd cycles plus a 1st or 2nd level professional qualification certificate. On successful completion of primary education, the pupil receives a diploma. Upon request, a diploma can also be issued on the successful completion of any cycle. Secondary school: Any pupil who successfully completes primary school has the right to attend secondary school; Secondary education lasts three years and is organized in a differentiated way. Its courses are oriented on working life or for the continuation of studies (they all contain technical, technological and professional training components in the Albanian language and culture, suitable for several courses). On the successful conclusion of secondary school the pupil receives a certificate that confirms the training acquired and, in the case of courses mainly oriented for working life, the qualification obtained relevant to specific professional activities. Higher Education encompasses universities and polytechnics and is organised in three cycles: studies leading to a BA; studies leading to an MA; and studies leading to a Doctorate. Higher education has three levels: BA – 180 ECTS credits with a normal duration of six semesters of student work. However, a programme may continue up to 240 ECTS credits, with a normal duration of seven or eight semesters of study, as a result of Albanian and EU legislation or of consolidated practice in leading higher education institutions in Europe. MA – 90 to 120 ECTS credits and a normal

175. Albanian legislation provides that to qualify for entry permission, a general student must meet the following requirements. First of all, there must be no justification to refuse entry permission under the general grounds for refusal.[144] Second, a general student must provide evidence that he/she has been accepted by an educational institution as a student. As a general rule, a confirmation must be obtained from a sponsor that a student has been registered as a student by an educational institution. In addition, a general student must provide evidence that he/she has sufficient knowledge of the language of the education or training he/she will be attending (usually Albanian or English and sometimes Italian or Turkish). The documentation that can be used by general students is listed in Section C, point 4, paragraph *c)* of Decision No. 513 of 13 June 2013 'On determining the criteria, procedures and documentation for entry, stay and treatment of aliens in the Republic of Albania'.[145]

176. A general student who has been admitted as a student by an educational institution or who attends training or participates in professional internships is issued a residence permit with a validity period no longer than one year when issued as a first time permit (i.e., temporary residence permit). This residence permit can be extended every year for another year until the completion of the studies or internship. If the duration of the study programme is less than one year, the period of validity of the residence permit corresponds with the duration of the study programme.[146]

177. A general student must provide evidence that he/she has sufficient financial means to secure a living in the Republic of Albania during the period of study. This is the general rule. The amount of the available funds that the applicant will have to provide documentary evidence for depends on the duration of the course. After finishing one study programme, a general student may wish to attend another course. In these circumstances the Albanian legislation has no specific regulation, but the case fall under the general rule.

178. In accordance with Article 52 of the Law 'On Foreigners', a general student has to provide evidence that progress is being made, as provided for by law or administrative practice in order to have a residence permit renewed. No further details are given in this regard.

---

duration of three to four semesters of student work. The universities award the following degrees: BA – 180 to 240 ECTS credits for a normal six to eight semester course of student work; MA – 300 to 360 ECTS credits for a normal ten to twelve semester course of student work, in the event that it will lead to exercising a specific professional activity. The duration of the course is fixed by EU legislation and is the result of stable, consolidated practice within the EU. *See* for more at www .arsimi.gov.al.

144. *See* Art. 10 of Law 108/2013.

145. *See*, in particular, s. C, point 4, para. *c)* of Decision No. 513 of 13 Jun. 2013 'On Determining the Criteria, Procedures and Documentation for Entry, Stay and Treatment of Aliens in the Republic of Albania': 'For students and school pupils: Document of admission with the education establishment in Albania: *i.* Proof of financial resources sufficient for living for the duration of stay in Albania. ii. Proof of proficiency of language'.

146. *See* Art. 52 paras 1 and 2 of the Law 'On Foreigners'.

179. A residence permit issued to a general students entitles him/her to take up employment for a limited number of hours After completing their first year of study, general students are entitled to pursue an economic activity as an worker or self-employed person outside the study period, for a maximum of twenty hours a week, or the equivalent in days or months per year. A student cannot, however, fill a full-time, permanent vacancy. As a general rule self-employment is also permitted if the number of hours during which the student pursues an economic activity does not exceed the time limit of twenty hours a week or the equivalent in days or months per year.[147] A general student is issued a work permit for part-time or fixed-term paid employment, when attending a regular university study, provided that his/her employer notifies the State's authorities, responsible for the registration of the start and termination of employment.[148] EU citizens and Schengen country citizens are exempted from the obligation to be issued with a work permit.

180. Upon successful completion of his study if the former student is issued a work permit, and if the EU citizen is registered with an employment office based on an employment contract, the residence permit may be renewed for employment purposes. Half of the period of stay for study purposes is taken into consideration when calculating the period of residence.[149]

181. A work permit can be issued to special categories, with a validity of up to one year to a pupil or student, who wants to take up an economic activity under an agreement for student exchange and who participates in an job exchange programme during the summer holiday.[150]

182. The family members of a student can join him/her in or enter the territory of Albania as long as the general grounds for refusal do not apply and, if when applying for leave to remain, the family member does not qualify as an illegal entrant. A family member can either be the spouse or civil partner of a general student who has leave to remain in the Republic of Albania as a general student or is, in the process of being granted entry clearance or leave to remain as a general student. For EU citizens, the general rule is that a family member can also be the partner of a general student if they have been in a relationship similar to a marriage for a period of at least two years.

183. A marriage or civil partnership must be an existing relationship at the time the application is made. The spouses and civil partners must intend to live with each other throughout the general student's stay in Albania. A family member may not intend to remain in Republic of Albania beyond any period of leave granted to the genera; student. There must be evidence that the general student has sufficient financial means, as set out in the general rules for the admission of family members, to maintain him/herself and any accompanying family members.

---

147. *See* Art. 52 para. 4 of the Law 'On Foreigners'.
148. *See* Art. 91 para. 1 of the Law 'On Foreigners'.
149. *See* Art. 91 para. 2 of the Law 'On Foreigners'.
150. *See* Art. 101 para. 1, point *ii)* of the Law 'On Foreigners'.

184. If the application is successful, the spouse or the partner is granted entry clearance and leave to remain for a period which expires on the same day as the leave to remain granted to the general student expires. Leave to remain is granted subject to the conditions that the general student does not have recourse to public funds and that the family has registered with the police, if this is required.

185. A general student can also be accompanied by a child. If the accompanying family member is a child, the requirements that need to be satisfied are usually the same as those that apply to the spouse and the civil partner. This means that the child must not fall under the general grounds justifying a refusal to grant permission to remain and must not qualify as an illegal entrant. The applicant must be the child of the parent who has been granted leave to enter or remain as a general student or who is in the procedure to be granted entry clearance or leave to remain as a general student. The child must be under the age of 18 on the date the application is made and must not be married or in a civil partnership; must not have formed an independent family unit, and must not be leading an independent life. He/she may not intend to stay in Albania beyond any period of leave granted to the general student who is the parent of the child.

186. If the application is successful, a child is granted entry clearance and leave to remain for a period which expires on the same day as the leave granted to his/her general student parent. This permission to remain is granted subject to conditions that there is no recourse to public funds and that the family is registered with the police if this is required.[151]

151. See *Analiza e mangësive mbi legjislacionin dhe praktikën shqiptare të emigracionit krahasuar me standartet europiane dhe ato ndërkombëtare*, 45 (ONM, Tiranë, 2004); *Fjalorth i terminologjisë migratore*, 12 (ONM, Tirana, 2007); L. Ikonomi, *E drejta migratore*, 131 (Tirana, 2014); *Integrimi i refugjatëve në Shqipëri*, 49 (UNHCR, Tiranë, 2004); IOM, *E drejta migratore*, 107 (Tirane, 2009).

Chapter 3. Researchers

187. The mobility of researchers is a key element in the acquisition and transfer of knowledge. A researcher is a scholar who can, or will in time through learning and experience, demonstrate: specialized knowledge or expertise, possesses conceptual and intellectual capacities, such as the ability to identify and frame key problems, who can think critically and analytically, and who can generate and communicate interesting and original insights; academic skills, such as the ability to produce high-quality written scholarly work and research papers – clearly composed so that the argument, and the evidence that supports it, can be grasped by the intended audience (whether specialist or more general, a conference delegate or a reader with time to reflect); research skills, such as the ability to use sources effectively, gather and organize information, analyse text, data and theory; personal attributes, such as the ambition and ability to work to high standards, can take initiative and responsibility, is well organized in one's procedures and balanced in one's judgments, can collaborate well with others where appropriate, and can take on board and incorporate constructive criticism; social skills, such as the ability to liaise with students, colleagues and academics from other institutions in an effective and appropriate way, is able to adjust to different circumstances as required by academia and can integrate into the larger community of scholars.[152]

188. After signing the Stabilization and Association Agreement (SAA) in 2006 Albania has promoted and facilitated the entry and residence of researchers from other countries. It has developed a regime of general respect for this category of 'migrants' and their right to conduct research or scientific research. A purpose of the Law 'On Foreigners' was to introduce a special procedure governing the entry and residence of other nationals coming to Albania to carry out a research project for a period of more than three months. Hence, the aim is to facilitate as much as possible the admission to and mobility of researchers in the Republic of Albania. The Republic of Albania has become a subscriber to the EU's *Horizon 2020* and *Erasmus+* programmes which create opportunities and benefits that favour scientific research and have clearly resulted in closer scientific collaboration between local and foreign researchers. These innovative initiatives are financially supported by the Ministry of Education and Sports.[153]

189. According to Article 3 paragraph 30 of the Law 'On Foreigners' 'Researchers and experts' are used to refer to migrants with specialized knowledge who are essential for the service and research sections and have a high qualification level as

---

152. *See Analiza e mangësive mbi legjislacionin dhe praktikën shqiptare të emigracionit krahasuar me standartet europiane dhe ato ndërkombëtare*, 46 (ONM, Tiranë, 2004); *Fjalorth i terminologjisë migratore*, 13 (ONM, Tirana, 2007); L. Ikonomi, *E drejta migratore*, 131 (Tirana, 2014); *Integrimi i refugjatëve në Shqipëri*, 50 (UNHCR, Tiranë, 2004); IOM, *E drejta migratore*, 108 (Tirane, 2009).

153. *See*, in particular, http://www.arsimi.gov.al/al/newsroom/lajme/konferenca-per-prezantimin-e-broshures-se-programit-erasmus.

required for the activity performed by an enterprise or research institution employing them. This provision does not apply to applicants for asylum or subsidiary protection or to those who fall under a temporary protection scheme, nor to doctoral students conducting research relating to their theses as students or third-country nationals whose expulsion has been suspended for reasons of fact or law, and researchers seconded by a research organization to another research institution in a Member State of the EU.[154] It also does not apply to EU citizens, Schengen country citizens, and when there is a special regime in place as provided for by an international agreement.

190. An applicant is considered to be a researcher if he/she comes to Albania to study at a university after completing a master degree and wishes to obtain a licentiate degree, a doctor's degree or to conduct post-doc research and receives a scholarship or salary from an official sponsor, such as a university or a research institute. Lecturers, researchers or foreign specialists in the field of scientific research, coming to the Republic of Albania within the framework of a bilateral governmental agreement or an agreement between educational institutions themselves are considered to be 'researchers'. The official sponsor which pays the salary or provides the scholarship can be Albanian or foreign.

191. Article 51 of the Law 'On Foreigners' provides the conditions subject to which a residence permit for scientific research is issued. The Ministry of the Interior will issue a 'residence permit for scientific research' with a validity period of no longer than one year if the applicant has concluded an agreement for this purpose with an Albanian institution and meets the general conditions to be issued with a residence permit as set out in Article 39 of Law 'On Foreigners'. These researchers are issued a visa type D/AP.[155]

192. Article 72 of the Law 'On Aliens' provides an exemption from the obligation to apply for a work permit or a work registration certificate. Lecturers, researchers or foreign specialists conducting scientific research, coming to the Republic of Albania within the framework of a bilateral governmental agreement or an agreement concluded between educational institutions are not need a work permit or business registration certificate.

193. The Law 'On Foreigners' does not specify any other conditions that researchers or foreign specialists conducting scientific research in Albania have to satisfy. Therefore the general rules that apply to general students also apply to them. The family members of a researcher can join him/her or enter the territory of Albania if the general grounds to refuse entry permission do not apply to them and if,

154. They are covered by Directive 2004/114/EC on the conditions of entry and residence of third country nationals for the purposes of studies, vocational training or voluntary service, *OJ EC* 2014, L 375/12.

155. *See Analiza e mangësive mbi legjislacionin dhe praktikën shqiptare të emigracionit krahasuar me standartet europiane dhe ato ndërkombëtare*, 2 (ONM, Tiranë, 2004); *Fjalorth i terminologjisë migratore*, 13 (ONM, Tirana, 2007); L. Ikonomi, *E drejta migratore*, 131 (Tirana, 2014); *Integrimi i refugjatëve në Shqipëri*, 45 (UNHCR, Tiranë, 2004); IOM, *E drejta migratore*, 58 (Tirane, 2009).

when applying for leave to remain, they do not qualify as an illegal entrant. A family member is either the spouse or the child of a person who has been granted leave to enter and remain in the Republic of Albania as a researcher, a lecturer or foreign specialist conducting scientific research, or who is in the process of applying for entry clearance or leave to remain as a researcher.

194. If the application is successful, the spouse or the child is granted entry clearance and leave to remain for the same period as the leave granted to his/her spouse or parent. This permission is granted subject to the conditions that there is no recourse to public funds and that the family is registered with the police if this is required.[156]

---

156. F. Tashko, *Marrëdhëniet Individuale të punës, Komentar* 10 (Tiranë 2006); L. Ikonomi, *E drejta migratore*, 138 (Tirana, 2014); IOM, *E drejta migratore*, 56 (Tiranë, 2009); *Përmbledhje aktesh juridike në fushën e migracionit*, 48 (ACIL/ONM, Tiranë, 2005).

Chapter 4. Labour and Economic Migration

§1. Labour Employment

195. In this chapter the conditions governing entry to and residence in the Republic of Albania for the purpose of working, conducting business or investing. Nationals of other countries who wish to work, conduct business and invest in Albania will be considered.

196. Today, many countries are characterized by ageing and shrinking populations. In order to ensure their economic growth and maintain their welfare system, they have implemented a series of measures to reduce the demographic effects, amongst which providing channels for legal migration. As these countries try to attract the same group of people, mainly highly skilled professionals and low-skilled workers, increasing competition between States can be observed. In particular, high-skilled professionals are targeted by receiving societies. High-skilled workers are encouraged to stay for longer periods or even enticed to settle permanently in their host-State by providing them with rights and benefits, facilitating their stay, and making them the target of integration policies.

197. All throughout the twentieth century, Albania has been a migrant sending nation. For Albanians, the twentieth century definition of international migration meant Albanians immigrating to other countries, especially other European countries. Yet, recently, international migration has also come to mean the reception of foreigners into Albanian society. It was only after the 1990s that foreigners gradually began entering Albania.

198. If an Albanian business wants to employ a foreigner it will have to use the domestic law routes for entry dealt with in this chapter. A general visitor is prohibited from working in Albania. A student is restricted as to what work he may do and how many hours he/she can work, as discussed in the previous chapter. But the following people may freely carry out any of these activities: (i) anyone admitted for settlement; (ii) anyone given limited leave to remain with a view to settlement, e.g., spouses, civil partners and those in a non-marital relationship; (iii) refugees and those granted humanitarian protection and (iv) anyone admitted as the dependant of someone with limited leave to remain in Albania who has not been prohibited from taking up employment, such as the dependants of exceptional talent, intra-company transfer workers or temporary workers or crew members of vessels.

199. The right to work in Albania enjoyed by a non-national is first of all specified in several provisions in the Albanian Constitution[157] and developed in provisions in other laws. The conditions for issuing a permit for temporary employment

157. *See* Art. 16 of the Albanian Constitution where: 'The fundamental rights and freedoms and the duties set out in this Constitution for Albanian citizens are also enjoyed by foreigners and stateless persons in the territory of the Republic of Albania, unless the Constitution specifically attaches the exercise of particular rights and freedoms to Albanian citizenship'; Article 49 which specifies that:

are specified in Articles 39–40 of the Law 'On Aliens'. According to these provisions migrants have right to work in the Republic of Albania on a temporary basis in accordance with Albanian immigration rules. Free movement of workers is regulated in Title V, Articles 46 and 48, of the SAA. These provisions establish the principle of national treatment thus allowing workers, who are third-country nationals legally employed in an EU Member State to take up employment in Albania under the same conditions as apply to Albanian if the State of which that non-nationals has signed a bilateral agreement with Albania that includes working conditions, salary or dismissal. As discussed in the previous chapter (Part III Chapter 1§2) EU citizens and USA citizens enjoy more favourable treatment.[158]

200. The following categories of workers are covered by the rules discussed in this chapter: an employed person; a self-employed person; crew members employed on a vessel registered in the Republic of Albania; and highly qualified workers.

201. The authority responsible for border and migration issues 'residence permit for an employed person' if the applicant satisfies the conditions and submits the necessary documentation providing evidence that the requirements to be issued a 'residence permit for an employed person' are satisfied. The residence permit for an employed person is issued on the basis of the work permit. When a 'residence permit for employed person' has been issued, the holder is obliged to notify the competent authorities of any change in circumstance that lead to the issuing of that residence permit in the first place and must request for approval of those authorities if a change is related to: (a) the name and address of employer, the address of place of residence and/or place of work; or (b) the employment contract. These provisions do not apply to EU citizens or Schengen country citizens.

202. A temporary residence permit is issued which is valid for the period of stay indicated in the application, but that is no longer than one year if the application is lodged for the first time and unless otherwise provided for by law or international

---

'Everyone has the right to earn the means of living through lawful work that he has chosen or accepted himself. He is free to choose his profession, place of work, and his own system of professional qualification. 2. Employees have the right to social protection' and Art. 59 that states: '1. The State, within its constitutional powers and the means at its disposal, and with a view to supplement private initiatives and responsibilities, aims at: a. employment under suitable conditions for all persons who are able to work.' *See* in general K. Çela, *E drejta e Punës*, 15 (Ilar, Tiranë, 2011); Zh. Çuçi, *Sistemet e mbrojtjes shoqërore*, 36 (Ilar, Tiranë, 2007); F. Tashko, *Marrëdhëniet Individuale të punës, Komentar* 12 (Tiranë 2006); Çela, K & Haxhi, P, *E Drejtë e Krahasuar e Punës*, 74 (Iliar, Tiranë 2002).

158. *See* Art. 30 para. 4 of the Law 'On Foreigners': '4. The conditions in points 2 and 3 of this Article and the conditions in international agreements shall not apply to EU citizens and Schengen country citizens.' Art. 41 para. 4: '4. The conditions in points 2 and 3 of this Article and the conditions in international agreements shall not apply to EU citizens and Schengen country citizens.' Article 43 para. 2: '2. Citizens of European Union and Schengen countries shall be exempted from the conditions in this Article.' Article 44, para. 4: 'EU citizens and Schengen country citizens shall be exempted from the obligation to be issued a work permit.

agreements ratified by the Republic of Albania. So, the limited period of leave to remain is initially one year but may be extended for two years and can be followed by an application for settlement.

203. An applicant must fulfil and demonstrate that the general requirements have been met. An employee must present a certified copy of the document proving that he/she is employed, show that he/she generates sufficient income to provide sufficient means of subsistence for him/herself and any accompanying family members and present a copy of the work permit issued by the competent Albanian authority.[159] An application for a residence permit or an extension of a residence permit will be turned down if the applicant does not satisfy the general conditions for residence he/she is an illegal entrant, or if he/she is in the territory of Albania in breach of immigration rules. A period of overstaying that is no longer than one month is ignored. Recourse to public funds will always justify withdrawal of temporary leave to remain. As a general rule, a worker who has spent a continuous period of five years in Albania can make an application for settlement.

204. The authority responsible for border and migration may revoke or annul a 'residence permit for an employed person' which is obtained fraudulently. The Albanian authorities may also revoke or annul a 'residence permit for an employed person' if the holder of the residence permit no longer satisfies the conditions set out in Article 40 and Article 39, point 3, letters *a*, *b*. A 'residence permit for an employed person' may not be revoked or annulled for public health reasons if the holder suffers from a disease or becomes incapable of working after the residence permit has been issued. A 'residence permit for an employed person' may not be cancelled because of changes in the internal labour market. Unemployment in itself is not a sufficient reason to annul a 'residence permit for an employed person', unless in the period of unemployment exceeds one of the following periods: three months within a twelve-month period for the holder of a 'residence permit for an employed person', who has lawfully exercised activities as an employed person for at least for three years'; and six months within a twelve-month period for the holder of a 'residence permit for an employed person', who has lawfully exercised activities as an employed person for more than three years.

205. A migrant worker must submit evidence that demonstrates that he can support himself in the Republic of Albania. If there are family members who accompany a migrant worker to Albania, there must be evidence that each or together, they have savings to support themselves. This falls under the general regime for family reunification in the territory of the Republic of Albania (*see* paragraphs 132, 150 and 151).

206. If a migrant worker changes employment, either within the organization or moves to a new organization, he/she needs to apply for an extension of the residence permit issued to him/her. The migrant worker will state that he/she has a new

---

159. K. Çela, *E drejta e Punës*, 15 (Ilar, Tiranë, 2011); Zh. Çuçi, *Sistemet e mbrojtjes shoqërore*, 36 (Ilar, Tiranë, 2007); F. Tashko, *Marrëdhëniet Individuale të punës, Komentar* 10 (Tiranë 2006).

job and will also have to provide evidence that he/she will have sufficient means of subsistence. The migrant worker may perform supplementary work if this is in the same profession or at the same professional level as the main employment. In addition the migrant worker may also do voluntary work in any sector, provided that he/she is not paid and does not receive any other payment for his/her work with the exception of a reasonable reimbursement of any expenses made.

207. Family members of a migrant worker have the right to join or accompanied the migrant in/to the territory of Albania if they are his/her spouse, the civil partner, unmarried partner or a child under the age of 18. A family member has to obtain a residence permit and a subsequent extension as the migrant. He or she may be able to apply and to obtain a settlement as the migrant as well. The provisions are exactly the same as for the migrant family member. The regime for the two other categories of residence permits is as follows. Residence permits are issued to crew members, employed by the owner of a vessel registered in the Republic of Albania, who perform their activity as employed persons for more than 90 days within a period of 180 days, and those who perform their activity as employed persons with a foreign vessel, but who, due to the specifics of the nature of the activity, remain in an Albanian port for more than 90 days within 180 days. As a general rule, citizens of EU Member States and Schengen countries citizens are exempted from the provisions of this article.

208. For highly qualified work the authority responsible for border and migration affairs only issues the 'AL Blue Card' residence permit to a highly qualified worker who has been issued a special work permit for highly qualified worker and meets the conditions required to be issued with the 'AL Blue Card' residence permit. The 'AL Blue Card' residence permit for highly qualified workers is issued for a two-year period and it may be renewed for an additional three-year period. If the work permit for the highly qualified worker is issued for a period of validity of less than two years, the validity of the 'AL Blue Card' residence permit equals that of the period of validity of the work permit plus an additional three months. The holder of the 'AL Blue Card' residence permit must notify the competent authorities of any changes in the employment relationship. EU Member State citizens and Schengen country citizens are exempted from the obligation to hold a work permit.

209. No residence permit for highly qualified work 'AL Blue Card' is issued to: applicants for international protection and people residing in Albania under a temporary protection scheme; refugees, and people who have applied for the refugee status as long as no final decision has been taken with regard to their application; people who have applied with the Border and Migration authorities of the Republic of Albania for, or have been issued a residence permit as a researcher, for the purpose of a study/research project; people who enjoy the status of long-term residents and exercise their right to stay in the Republic of Albania for the purpose of performing an economic activity as an employed or self-employed person; people who have entered the Republic of Albania, based on the commitments assumed by Albania under an international agreement, which facilitates the entry and temporary stay of several categories of legal and natural persons, related to investments; people whose expulsion order has been suspended for legal reasons.

§2. Seasonal Workers and Temporary Workers

210. In this paragraph we'll consider the juridical regime of the special categories of migrant workers in the territory of Albania i.e., seasonal workers and temporary workers. Seasonal workers are migrant workers who wish to work in the Republic of Albania for a short period. A residence permit for seasonal employment is issued if the requirements to qualify as a seasonal worker are satisfied. A residence permit issued for the purpose of seasonal work is valid for a period of no longer than six months within one calendar year, with right to renewal for up to five consecutive years, provided that period between issuing the consecutive residence permit exceeds a six months period.[160] Seasonal workers can be accompanied by their family members.[161]

211. In the context of the movement of workers, seasonal workers are of great importance to the Republic of Albania, from both an economic and a social point of view. This is reflected in the legislation on the basic rights in Article 47 of Law No. 108/2013 on residence permit for seasonal employment of foreigners. With the adoption of the Law 'On Foreigners' in March 2013, any employee or self-employed person who is a national of an EU Member State can acquire a certificate of registration from the labour office. This is a significant labour market liberalization, not seen before the adoption of the Law 'On Foreigners'. Requests for permission to remain for the purpose of seasonal work are also decided on the basis of bilateral agreements that Albania has concluded with other countries. The criteria for the issuing of a seasonal work permit are further specified by Decision No. 934, dated 26 December 2012 of the Council of Ministers 'On determining the number of workers with temporary contracts, for 2013, for the central government units' as amended by Decision No. 355, dated 24 April 2013 of the Council of Ministers.

212. According to Article 47 of the Law 'On Foreigners' the Albanian authority issues a residence permit for seasonal employment if the applicant meets the requirements for being issued with a residence permit with a validity period of no longer than six months within a calendar year, with right to renewal up to five consecutive years, provided that the interruption from one residence permit to the other exceeds a six month period. This provision does not apply to EU citizens and Schengen country citizens, or if there is a special regime provided for by an international agreement.

---

160. *See* Art. 47 para. 10 of the Law 'On Foreigners'.

161. M. Blecher & J. Dine, *Komentar i Ligjit nr. 9901, 14 Apr. 2008, Për tregtarët dhe shoqëritë tregtare* 61 (Guttenberg, 2009); F. Galgano, *E drejta tregtare* 54 (Luarasi University Press Tiranë, 2009); A. Malltezi, *E drejta shqiptare e shoqërive tregtare*, 49 (Tiranë, Mediaprint, 2011); Law No. 9723, 5 Mar. 2007, 'National Registration Center' www.qkr.gov.al; A. Malltezi, J. Rystemaj & L. Pelinku, *Aspekte të së drejtës së biznesit në Shqipëri*, 17 (Tiranë, 2014).

213. The Albanian authorities can issue a residence permit to unremunerated trainees. This residence permit has a maximum validity period of one year. A residence permit for the purpose of completing an unremunerated traineeship is issued, if the intended activity will improve the skills and qualifications of the trainee and it is strictly limited in time. In exceptional cases, a residence permit may be extended.[162]

214. Seasonal workers are not allowed to reside in Albania permanently. They must return to their country of origin upon completion of their work contract. An employer can only apply for another seasonal work permit for the same worker if the mandatory six month period has expired (*see* paragraph 211).[163]

215. The Albanian authorities may issue a 'residence permit for youth exchange programme' with a maximum validity period of one year if the intended activity is closely linked with a youth exchange programme or mobility scheme, as defined in a bilateral or multilateral agreement to which the Republic of Albania is a party. A 'residence permit for youth exchange programme' is issued for a limited period. In exceptional cases, a 'residence permit for youth exchange programme' can be extended if this is provided for in the agreement.[164]

216. The residence permit that is issued to facilitate youth exchange and mobility is a novel category that was introduced by the Law 'On Foreigners'. The mobility scheme has to be defined in a bilateral or multilateral agreement to which the Republic of Albania is a party. There is a list of countries especially drawn up for this purpose. The number of youth exchange places is usually capped by the Albanian Government for each individual scheme. Once the limit is reached, no further applications are considered. To be eligible for admission under an exchange or mobility scheme the applicant has to be between the age of eighteen and thirty when entry clearance is granted. To be admitted, the applicant must not have been issued permission to reside in the Republic of Albania for this purpose in the past. A residence issued for the purpose of participating in a youth exchange programme or mobility scheme is limited in time – one year – and can only be extended in exceptional circumstances. A person can be granted leave to remain for this purpose once.

217. Practice has shown that a young foreign national who resides in the Republic of Albania for the purpose of participating in a youth exchange scheme may do whatever work he/she likes. It is not permitted to setup a business, exercise a sport professionally or work as a trainee doctor. An employer is, therefore, free to employ a youth mobility participant.

---

162. *See* Art. 48 of the Law 'On Foreigners'.
163. A. Malltezi, J. Rystemaj & L. Pelinku, *Aspekte të së drejtës së biznesit në Shqipëri,* 18 (Tiranë, 2014); F. Galgano, *E drejta tregtare,* 54 (Luarasi University Press Tiranë, 2009); A. Malltezi, *E drejta shqiptare e shoqërive tregtare,* 49 (Tiranë, Mediaprint, 2011); M. Blecher & J. Dine, *Komentar i Ligjit nr. 9901, 14 Apr. 2008, Për tregtarët dhe shoqëritë tregtare* 61 (Guttenberg, 2009); Law No. 9723, 5 Mar. 2007, 'National Registration Center', available at: www.qkr.gov.al.
164. *See* Art. 49 of the Law 'On Foreigners'.

218. In the same way, according to Article 50 of the Law 'On Foreigners', a residence permit is issued for the purpose of voluntary service that has a validity period of no longer than one year. To be issued a 'residence permit for voluntary service' the intended activity must be listed on to a voluntary service scheme that has been recognized by the authorities of the Republic of Albania. The validity of a 'residence permit voluntary service' is directly related to the duration of the relevant voluntary service programme for which a residence permit is requested. In exceptional cases, a residence permit may be extended, if the voluntary service programme runs beyond that year. Article 50 of the Law 'On Aliens' does not apply to EU Member State citizens, Schengen countries citizens, and where a special regime is foreseen by international agreements.

219. The voluntary service must relate directly to the purpose of the sponsoring organization and be performed in accordance with a voluntary service scheme that has been recognized by the authorities of the Republic of Albania. Besides the condition that the worker is not paid or otherwise remunerated for his work, a residence permit issued for the purpose of voluntary work does not entitle the holder of that document to take up a permanent position. The migrant must comply with the conditions of leave and depart when his residence permit expires.

§3. Independent Economic Activities

220. 'Independent economic activities' or 'business person' issued to identify migrant workers who are engaged in an economic activity as a self-employed person. According to Article 41 of the Law on 'On Foreigners' a residence permit is issued to a self-employed person if the submitted documentation provides evidence that that person satisfies the requirements (*see* paragraph 220) to be issued a 'residence permit for a self-employed person'. The residence permit that is issued to a self-employed person authorizes that person to exercise the activity in accordance with the specifications on the work permit. These specifications concern the purpose of the intended employment, the region where self-employment is authorized and the time frame during with the economic activity can take place.

221. The main condition that has to be satisfied to qualify as a self-employed person is that the migrant does not have recourse to the public funds. Additionally a self-employment migrant may not take up any other employment than working for the business or businesses that he has established, joined or taken over. Self-employment also precludes working as a professional sportsperson (including as a sports coach). Like some other categories of workers, a self-employment migrant, who has spent a continuous period of five years working in the Republic of Albania, may request a permanent residence permit. A self-employment migrant who is an entrepreneur can apply for permission to settle in the Republic of Albania before he/she has worked there for five years if he/she creates several jobs for other persons.

222. After a 'residence permit for self-employed persons' has been issued, the holder of that document is obliged to notify the competent authorities of any change in the conditions for which the permit was issued and request for its approval if the change is related to (a) *the* name and address of residence or the place where the work is performed and (b) the activities for which the self-employed person has received authorization to conduct them.[165]

223. Article 41 of the Law 'On Foreigners' concerning self-employment migrants and the provisions of international agreements do not apply to EU Member State citizens or Schengen countries citizens.

224. The application form for a residence permit for a self-employed person specified the documents that have to be submitted with the application form. If the documents are genuine, the application procedure will proceed. If the documents are found to be false, the application is refused, whether or not the documents are essential to the application. The Albanian authorities may revoke or annul a 'residence permit for a self-employed person' which is proven to have been obtained fraudulently. The authorities may also revoke or annul a 'residence permit for a self-employed person' if there is a change in the grounds on which the residence permit is issued.

225. A residence permit issued to a self-employed person may not be revoked or annulled for public health reasons if the holder suffers from a disease and becomes incapable of working after the residence permit has been issued. A residence permit for a self-employed person may not be cancelled because of changes in the internal labour market after it has been issued. Financial difficulties experienced by the self-employed person do not qualify as a sufficient reason to revoke or annul a 'residence permit for a self-employed person', unless the period during which the holder of the residence permit fails to cover his/her costs of living as defined in a decision of the Council of Ministers, exceeds the following periods: three months within a twelve-month period for the holder of the 'residence permit for a self-employed person', who has lawfully exercised activities as self-employed person for at least for two years'; and six months within a twelve-month period for the holder of the 'residence permit for a self-employed person', who has lawfully exercised activities as employed person for longer than two years.

165. *See* Art. 41 para. 2 of the Law 'On Foreigners'. *See*, in general, M. Blecher & J. Dine, *Komentar i Ligjit nr. 9901, 14 Apr. 2008, Për tregtarët dhe shoqëritë tregtare* 63 (Guttenberg, 2009); F. Galgano, *E drejta tregtare,* 54 (Luarasi University Press Tiranë, 2009; A. Malltezi, *E drejta shqiptare e shoqërive tregtare,* 56 (Tiranë, Mediaprint, 2011); M. Blecher & J. Dine, *Komentar i Ligjit nr. 9901, 14 Apr. 2008, Për tregtarët dhe shoqëritë tregtare* 61 (Guttenberg, 2009); Law No. 9723, dated 5 Mar. 2007, 'National Registration Center' www.qkr.gov.al; A. Malltezi, J. Rystemaj & L. Pelinku, *Aspekte të së drejtës së biznesit në Shqipëri,* 30 (Tiranë, 2014).

§4. Investment Activities

226. Albania has a liberalized economic and legal framework and conditions for conducting business. It has, in particular, constantly improved mechanisms designed to attract Foreigner Investment (FI). Foreign investment means every kind of investment in the Republic of Albania made directly or indirectly by a foreign investor. Foreign Direct Investment (FDI) is a new economic concept that has rapidly increased in importance. Driven by technological change, global competition and market liberalization, foreign direct investment plays a key role in the process of global economic integration with effects in both the host countries and in the investing economies. The effects generated in host countries are an increasing level of diversity and economic growth. FDI also has significant importance for political and social developments.[166]

227. As it is well known, FDI brings the necessary capital into the Republic of Albania, increases the productivity of its economy through the transfer of knowledge and technology, affects the opening of new markets for trade, increases the competitiveness of the Albanian economy, reduces the current account deficit, increases employment and, above all, affects the welfare of the population positively. Like any government, the strategic priorities of the Albanian government are to increase foreign investments as it contributes towards the economic development of the country. Attracting these investments requires well defined policies and strategies aimed at a continuous improvement of the legal and institutional framework, economic stability and sustainable growth, the improvement and modernization of the infrastructure and the improvement of the business climate and investment environment. There is no legal framework for investment activities in the Law 'On Foreigners'. There are, however, several laws in force in the Republic of Albania that regulate foreign investments. Important laws are: the Law No. 7764 dated 2 November 1993 'On foreign investment', as amended by the Law No. 10316, dated 16 September 2010, the Law No. 9901, dated 14 April 2008, 'For entrepreneurs and trading companies' and the Law No. 9663, dated 18 December 2006 'On Concessions', as amended by the Law No. 9995, dated 22 September 2008, the Law No. 10157, dated 15 October 2009 and by the Law No. 10281, dated 20 May 2010.[167] This legal framework is in accordance with the *acquis communautaire* of the EU.

166. *See* in particular A. Malltezi, *E drejta shqiptare e shoqërive tregtare,* 56 (Tiranë, Mediaprint, 2011); M. Blecher & J. Dine, *Komentar i Ligjit nr. 9901, 14 Apr. 2008, Për tregtarët dhe shoqëritë tregtare* 63 (Guttenberg, 2009); 65; A. Malltezi, J. Rystemaj & L. Pelinku, *Aspekte të së drejtës së biznesit në Shqipëri,* 19 (Tiranë, 2014).

167. In addition, there are several decisions of the Council of Ministers of the Republic of Albania, e.g., Decision No. 27, of 19 Jan. 2007 of the Council of Ministers 'On approval of rules for the evaluation and award of concessions', as amended by Decision No. 104, dated 28 Feb. 2007, No. 87, of 16 Jan. 2008, Decision No. 544, of 1 May 2008, Decision No. 448, of 16 Jun. 2010 and Decision No. 469, of 16 Jun. 2010 of the Council of Ministers.

In this section we will consider the bilateral investment agreements concluded by the Republic of Albania with forty-four countries across the world.[168]

228. According to the Law No. 7764, dated 2 November 1993 a 'foreign investor' in the Republic of Albania is: (a) a person who is a citizen of a foreign country; (b) a person who is a citizen of the Republic of Albania, but who has always resided abroad; (c) any legal person (entity) created under the law of a foreign country who directly or indirectly seeks to commit or is committing to an investment in the Republic of Albania in accordance with the law; or who has made investments in accordance with the laws in force since 31 July 1990; and any 'Community society' in the meaning of Article 49 of the Stabilisation Association, approved by Law No. 9590, dated 27 July 2006 'On ratification of the Agreement Stabilization and Association Agreement between the Republic of Albania and the European Community Member States'.[169]

229. The Albanian Investment Development Agency (AIDA) is founded and operates on the basis of Law No. 10303, dated 15 July 2010 'On the creation and organization of Albanian Investment Development Agency'. AIDA's main objectives are to attract foreign investment, to increase the competitiveness of the Albanian economy through the support for small and medium sized enterprises, as well as innovation. The direct contribution of AIDA to the economic development becomes evident when considering the facilitation and support of direct investments in Albania, the increasing competitiveness of Small and Medium Enterprises (SMEs) and the encouragement and support to exports of goods and services. AIDA offers foreign and domestic investors, comprehensive support for their investment projects. Its qualified staff assists not only with market analysis to help establish potential sectors for investment, but also with advice on finding suitable properties and locations, as well as helping to identify new and existing projects. AIDA also provides aftercare services which aim to address successfully the demands of foreign investors after they have successfully completed projects.[170]

230. All sectors of the Albanian economy are open to foreign investment and there is no need to apply for prior authorization by the government. There is no restriction in terms of the share of foreign investors in companies: even a 100% foreign ownership is possible and foreign investments cannot be expropriated or nationalized directly or indirectly.

231. The general rules on residence for independent workers also apply to investors. The family members of investors enjoy the same rights. Special rules apply as set out in paragraph 226, if the State provides legal protection.

---

168. *See* A. Malltezi, *Koncesionet në Shqipëri. Nga e drejta private në të drejtën publike*, 52 (Mediaprint, 2013); T. Dobi, *Investimet e huaja përballë pushtetit local si aktor kryesor në administrimin e tokës bujqësore, një betejë e humbur*, 73 (*Jus&Justicia*, No. 5).
169. *See* L. Ikonomi, *E drejta migratore*, 140 (Tirana, 2014).
170. *See* for further information www.aida.gov.al.

Chapter 5. Humanitarian Reasons

§1. Humanitarian Grounds

232. The introduction of a humanitarian residence permit and a permit for victims of human trafficking (Articles 53 and 54) on the one hand, reflect the impact of the developments in the field of International Law and Human Rights. The categories of foreigners who can obtain a 'humanitarian residence permit' are determined largely by considering the process of international protection, the impossibility or great difficulty of expelling a foreigner from the country, and other probable necessities in respect to extraordinary circumstances. Therefore the non-*refoulement* principle constitutes an important guarantee for those issued a 'humanitarian residence permit', both on entry and in cases of deportation. It can be said, therefore, that the international protection regime provides 'extra' protection to foreigners in the field of entry into Albania.

233. According to Albanian legislation, as mentioned before in paragraph 81, the authorities can issue both humanitarian residence permits, and residence permits for victims of human trafficking. Both residence permits are a temporary permit type 'A', which are limited. They may not be issued for a period in excess of six months and cannot be renewed. A residence permit issued for these reasons only serves the purpose of residence in Albania and does not allow the holder to re-enter the territory of the Republic of Albania if the holder leaves the country.

234. The grounds for granting resident permits for humanitarian reasons or to victims of human trafficking are specified in Articles 53, 54 and Article 34 of the Law 'On Foreigners' as well as in other Albanian laws concerning humanitarian issues. These grounds are specified in paragraph 1 of Article 53 of the Law 'On Foreigners': if the asylum seeker has submitted an application to the asylum authorities to be recognized as a refugee; is a victim or potential victim of trafficking; has been subjected to conditions of labour exploitation in the Republic of Albania and collaborates in criminal proceedings against the employer, until the end of the process and until the alien receives the compensation determined by the process; has collaborated or agrees to collaborate with justice authorities on the proposal of the state bodies or national security authorities; has been determined as a stateless person by the competent authorities; is an abandoned minor, or is under no parental care, legal guardianship, or escort for other reasons or is a woman pregnant more than six months.

235. A non-national who is issued a temporary residence permit, according to point 1 of Article 53 of the Law 'On Foreigners' enjoys the right to stay and move within the territory of the Republic of Albania. He/she has to collaborate with the competent bodies to establish his/her identity, but the lack of evidence which proves his/her identity is not sufficient to justify a refusal to issue the temporary residence permit. A holder of a humanitarian residence permit is entitled to health care, financial assistance and support, as provided for by law.

§2. UNACCOMPANIED MINOR CHILDREN

236. The general definition describes an 'unaccompanied minor' as a minor who is not a national of a State who enters the territory of that State (in this case in the territory of the Republic of Albania) unaccompanied by an adult who is responsible for him/her and for as long as he/she is not been taken under the care of such a person, or a minor who is left unaccompanied after entry to the territory.[171]Unaccompanied children are considered to be children younger than 18 years who have been separated from both parents and other relatives and who are not being taken care of by any adult as defined in the law. States must take particular measures to ensure that asylum procedures provide appropriate protection to unaccompanied children. There are several Conventions[172] providing special protection to unaccompanied children in international law, most of them have been ratified by Albanian since 1991. The Albanian legislation recognizes the principle of the best interests of the child (Article 106 of the Law 'On Foreigners') which must be the primary consideration in any measure which affects or might affect a child's human rights.[173]

237. According to the Law 'On Foreigners' unaccompanied minors are considered 'Vulnerable Persons' just like disabled people, elderly people, pregnant women, single parents with minor children, as well as persons who have been subjected to torture, rape or other forms of severe psychological, physical or sexual

171. *See* Art. 3 para. 31 of the Law 'On Foreigners' which states that 'Unaccompanied minor' shall mean an alien, minor who enters the territory of the Republic of Albania unaccompanied by an adult who is responsible for him/her and for as long as he/she is not been taken under the care of such person, or a minor who is left unaccompanied after that entry to the territory of the Republic of Albania.'. *See also* Art. 1 para. 1 of the Law 'On Asylum'.

172. These include, at a global level, the *Geneva Convention relating to the status of refugees* of 1951, read together with its Additional Protocol of 1967 (*Geneva Refugee Convention*); the *American Declaration on the Rights and Duties of Man* (ACHR); the *Convention on the Elimination of All Forms of Discrimination Against Women* (CEDAW); the *Convention on the Rights of the Child* (CRC) and its Protocols; the *Convention on the Rights of Persons with Disabilities* (CRPD); the *International Convention for the Elimination of All Forms of Racial Discrimination* (ICERD); the *Convention against Torture and Other Cruel, Inhuman or Degrading Treatment or Punishment* (CAT); and the *International Convention for the Protection of All Persons from Enforced Disappearance* (CPED) the *International Convention on the Protection of the Rights of All Migrant Workers and Members of Their Families* (ICRMW) the *Arab Charter on Human Rights* (ArCHR) etc. These treaties are supplemented by many other global and regional treaties and standards.

173. *See*, in particular, Art. 106 of the Law 'On Foreigners' which states that: 'At the moment of enforcement of the removal of the alien from the territory, it shall be considered in the best interest of the child, vulnerable persons, family life and health situation of the alien who is subject to removal from the territory.'; Article 125 of the Law 'On Foreigners' which, in the case of detention specifies that 2. The minor may only be detained in the closed centre if it is his or her or his/her family best interest or, in premises separated from those for the adults.'; Article 16 para. 5 of the Law 'On Asylum' that specifies: 'In accordance with the relevant international instruments which the Republic of Albania is party to, as regards unaccompanied minor asylum seekers under 16 years of age, the latter shall not be held in prison-like conditions, only as an absolute last resort measure. Instead special arrangements will be made that are suitable for children.'

violence.[174]The situation of unaccompanied minors, whether seeking asylum or not, warrants special consideration, due to both their vulnerability to exploitation and abuse and to their incapacity to cope with systems and institutions designed to address adult migration.[175] Under Albanian legislation and practice children enjoy particular protection against discrimination and children's rights must be and are protected without discrimination of any kind, including discrimination due to their nationality, immigration status or statelessness. In addition, in any decision concerning children the primary consideration is the best interests of the child.

238. Unaccompanied minors, in particular, are unlikely to spontaneously file an application for asylum, and procedures must therefore ensure that as soon as it becomes known that the child may have a well-founded fear or be at risk of persecution, they are referred to an asylum procedure. The unaccompanied or separated child will need the assistance of an appointed adult familiar with his or her background, who is competent and able to represent the child's best interests (a guardian or legal representative), and should be given access to a qualified legal representative free of charge. Applications made by unaccompanied or separated children must be given priority and decisions must be rendered promptly and fairly. The procedure must take into consideration the need of the child to express his or her views freely and always be, as the principal standard of consideration, in the best interest of the child.

239. An unaccompanied minor who, in exceptional cases, is the subject of a detention order, must be accommodated in a State social centre opened specifically for this purpose or at another centre based on cooperation with international organizations dealing with children, victims of trafficking in human beings or other categories of persons in need. The minor may only be detained in a closed centre if it is in his or her or his/her family's best interest or, in premises separated from those for the adults. The opinion of a social worker or psychologist must be taken into consideration when detaining a minor in a closed centre. In cases of doubt concerning the age of the detained minor, the Albanian authority may request the specialized State institutions to run a Deoxyribonucleic Acid (DNA)-test in order to verify his/her age. In respect of tracing, the use of DNA tracking systems should not create additional obstacles to family reunification, requires prior informed consent of the applicant, and should be used only when necessary (*see* paragraphs 150–151: 205). If the doubts concerning the age of a detained person remain even after the verifications and expertise, it shall be presumed that the person is a minor.[176]

240. As regards family reunification the State should provide, as it considers appropriate and in cooperation with any other entity, protection and assistance to a

174. Article 3 para. 25 of the Law 'On Foreigners' states that 'Vulnerable Persons' shall mean minors, *unaccompanied minors*, disabled people, elderly, pregnant women, and single parents with minor children, as well as persons who have been subjected to torture, rape or other forms of severe psychological, physical and sexual violence.' (emphasis added).

175. Th. Kaime, *The Normative Framework for Children's Rights in Refugee Situations*, 401 (Islam R. & Bhuiyan, J.H., eds., Leiden-Boston, 2013).

176. *See* Art. 125 of the Law 'On Foreigners'.

refugee child and trace the parents or other members of the family of any refugee child in order to obtain information necessary for reunification with his or her family.[177] In cases where no parents or other members of the family can be found, the child shall be accorded the same protection as any other child permanently or temporarily deprived of his or her family environment for any reason.[178] As set out in Albanian legislation, tracing is an essential component of any search for a durable solution and should be prioritized except where the act of tracing, or the way in which the tracing is conducted, is contrary to the best interest of the child or could jeopardize fundamental rights of those being traced. In any case, in conducting tracing activities, no reference should be made to the status of the child as an asylum seeker or refugee.

241. Family reunification in the country of origin is not in the best interest of the child and should, therefore, not be pursued if there is a 'reasonable risk' that such a return would lead to the violation of fundamental human rights of the child. The existence of such a risk must be indisputably documented when granting refugee status or in a decision of the competent authorities on the applicability of the *non-refoulement* obligation.

§3. VICTIMS OF TRAFFICKING IN HUMAN BEINGS

242. Human Trafficking[179] is a crime under international law. Both the Council of Europe Convention on Trafficking in Human Beings (Council of Europe Trafficking Convention) and the Protocol to Prevent, Suppress and Punish Trafficking in Persons Especially Women and Children, supplementing the United Nations Convention against Transnational Organized Crime (UN Trafficking Protocol), as well

177. Th. Kaime, *The Normative Framework for Children's Rights in Refugee Situations*, 421 (Islam R. & Bhuiyan, J.H., eds., Leiden-Boston, 2013).
178. *See ExCom, Conclusion No. 84 (XLVIII) on Refugee Children and Adolescent,* UNHCR, 48th Session, 1997, para. (b)(i). *See also, Guidelines on Policies and Procedures in dealing with Unaccompanied Children Seeking Asylum,* UNHCR, February 1997.
179. Human trafficking is 'the recruitment, transportation, transfer, harbouring or receipt of persons, means of the threat or use of force or other forms of coercion, of abduction, of fraud, of deception, of the abuse of power or of a position of vulnerability or of the giving or receiving of payments or benefits to achieve the consent of a person having control over another person, for the purpose of exploitation', Art. 3, *UN Trafficking Protocol;* Art. 4, *Council of Europe Trafficking Convention:* 'Exploitation shall include, at a minimum, the exploitation of the prostitution of others or other forms of sexual exploitation, forced labour or services, slavery or practices similar to slavery, servitude or the removal of organs'; 'The consent of a victim of trafficking in persons to the intended exploitation [. . .] shall be irrelevant where any of the means' described in the definition have been used. The Human Rights Committee finds that human trafficking is a violation of Arts 3 (gender equality), 8 (forced labour) and 24 (children rights) ICCPR: *Concluding Observations on Greece,* CCPR, UN Doc. CCPR/CO/83/GRC, 25 Apr. 2005, para. 10. The Committee against Torture finds that 'human trafficking for the purpose of sexual and labour exploitation' falls under the practices prohibited by Art. 16 (cruel, inhuman or degrading treatment or punishment) of the *Convention against Torture and Other Cruel, Inhuman or Degrading Treatment or Punishment* (CAT): *Concluding Observations on Spain,* CAT, UN Doc. CAT/C/ESP/CO/5, 9 Dec. 2009, para. 28. *See also, Conclusion No. 90 (LII) General,* ExCom, UNHCR, 52nd Session, 2001, para. (s).

as the acquis communautaire of the EU require States Parties to criminalize the practice in their national law. Trafficking can entail multiple violations of the human rights of trafficked persons, including the prohibition on slavery, servitude and forced or compulsory labour, and the right to liberty.[180] Human Trafficking is a crime under Albanian legislation as well. The Government of Albania has taken significant steps to improve efforts to identify and protect victims of trafficking.[181]

243. A trafficked person is someone who has been recruited, transported, transferred, harboured or received, by means of the threat or use of force or other forms of coercion, of abduction, of fraud, of deception, of the abuse of power or of a position of vulnerability or of the giving or receiving of payments or benefits to achieve the consent of a person having control over another person, for the purpose of exploitation.[182] The recruitment, transportation, transfer, harbouring or receipt of a child for the purpose of exploitation is considered 'human trafficking' even if this does not involve any of the means previously listed.[183]

244. According to Article 54 of the Law 'On Foreigners', the Albanian authorities issue a type 'A' temporary residence permit with a three-month validity period to any person, regardless of his/her will to collaborate with the criminal justice authorities, if there are reasonable grounds to believe that that person is a victim or potential victim of trafficking, identified as such by the authorities responsible for identification and referral of victims of trafficking. This residence permit is issued to the victim or potential victim of trafficking in order to allow him/her to recover, and to be treated because of the physical and mental conditions, as well as to allow the person to take a well-informed decision whether or not to cooperate with the criminal justice authorities.

245. The victim or potential victim of trafficking enjoys all the rights and services entitled to the victims of trafficking according to the Albanian legislation in force during the recovery and reflection period.

246. The residence permit issued for the recovery and reflection period may be revoked if it is established that the victim or potential victim of trafficking has acquired or claimed this status unfairly, has actively restored the relationship, either voluntarily and/or on his/her own initiative, with the persons suspected of trafficking in human beings, or if it is considered that his/her stay in Albania constitutes a

---

180. *See* K. Touzenis, *Trafficking in Human Beings, Human rights and transnational criminal law, developments in law and practices*, 23 (UNESCO, Migration Studies 3, 2010); *Id. Irregular Migration, Migrant Smuggling and Human Rights: Towards Coherence, 19* (International Council on Human Rights Policy, Geneva, 2010).

181. N. Tota, *Trafikimi i qenieve njerëzore. Aspekte penale juridike, krahasuese dhe kriminologjike*, 61 (UETPRESS, Tiranë 2018).

182. *Ibid.*, 17.

183. *See*, in general, Arts 5 and 9–11, *UN Trafficking Protocol;* Chs II and IV, *Council of Europe Trafficking Convention. See also*, Art. 6 CEDAW; Arts 34 and 35 CRC; *General Recommendation No. 19, Violence Against Women,* CEDAW, U.N. Doc. HRI/GEN/1/Rev.9 (Vol. II), 1989, paras 13–16 and 24(g).

threat to national security. The decision to revoke residence permit for the period of recovery and reflection is communicated to the victim or potential victim of trafficking in writing and in a language that he/she understands, and informing him/her of the reasons for the cancellation, unless there are national security reasons.

247. The local department responsible for border and migration, issues a type 'B' residence permit to victims of trafficking in the Republic of Albania, identified as such by the authorities responsible for the identification and referral of victims of trafficking, in either one or the other, or in both of following situations: (a) the competent authority deems that his/her stay is necessary because of the social and personal situation; (b) the competent authority deems that his/her stay is necessary for the purpose of collaboration with the criminal justice authorities during criminal investigation or proceedings.

248. A residence permit cannot be issued subject to the condition that the victim has sufficient financial means to cover expenses during the period of stay and may not be refused because the victim or potential victim of trafficking cannot provide the required identification documents.

§4. Others

249. Several international instruments, all of a regional nature, provide a definition of 'refugee' that is broader than that in the *Geneva Refugee Convention* and, therefore, offer protection which is complementary to that of the Geneva Convention.[184] In EU law, the *EU Qualification Directive* grants complementary protection (known in the Directive as 'subsidiary protection') to people facing 'serious and individual threat to a civilian's life or person by reason of indiscriminate violence in situations of international or internal armed conflict'. All these situations, while not reflecting treaty obligations for Albania, have been endorsed and implemented in Albanian legislation. In fact, Albanian legislation has to meet all the criteria of the SAA and other issues in the context of the envisaged accession to the EU, in particular those relating to the human rights.

250. As we have mentioned in the first Chapter (paragraph 16), in order to harmonize the Albanian legislation with the EU Directive the Albanian legislator adopted Law No. 121/2014 'On asylum in the Republic of Albania' which forests

184. *See*, for example, Art. 1(2) of the *OAU Convention Governing the Specific Aspects of Refugee Problems in Africa* (OAU Refugee Convention) which extends refugee protection 'to every person who, owing to external aggression, occupation, foreign domination or events seriously disturbing public order in either part or the whole of his country of origin or nationality, is compelled to leave his place of habitual residence in order to seek refuge in another place outside his country of origin or nationality'. In the Americas region, the *Cartagena Declaration* at para. III includes in the refugee definition 'persons who have fled their country because their lives, safety or freedom have been threatened by generalized violence, foreign aggression, internal conflicts, massive violation of human rights or other circumstances which have seriously disturbed public order.' *See Migration and international Human Rights Law. A practitioner's Guide*, 80 (ICJ, 2014).

out the conditions and procedures for granting and cancelling refugee status, supplementary protection and temporary protection in the Republic of Albania, as well as the rights and obligations of asylum seekers, refugees and persons enjoying temporary and supplementary protection, the right to family reunification. The conditions for the integration of refugees and persons under subsidiary protection in the Republic of Albania are also set out in this legislative act. Article 1 paragraph 12 of the Law 'On Asylum' defines a 'complementary form of protection' as a form of protection given to a person, who, even though does he/she not meet the refugee criteria, as expressed in this section of this Law, shall not be subject of any deportation order or expulsion decision, issued by the competent authorities of the Republic of Albania, based on the reasons set out in the European Convention 'On protection of human rights and fundamental freedoms' of 1950, and the UN Conventions against torture, on civil and political rights and any other international instrument to which Albania is signatory party.

251. According to Article 15 of the Law 'On Asylum' a person who enjoys a complementary form of protection benefits from all the rights granted by this law to refugees in accordance with the 1951 Convention, with the exception of being issued a Travel Document.[185]

185. *See* L. Ikonomi, *E drejta migratore*, 141 (Tirana, 2014).

Chapter 6. Asylum

§1. Conditions

252. Albania, as mentioned in the first Chapter (paragraph 17), has ratified the Geneva Refugee Convention of 1951 with its Additional Protocol of 1967.[186] Asylum seekers or refugees are the migrants who enter a country, whether regularly or irregularly, in order to escape persecution in their country of origin.[187] The Convention provides a quasi-universal definition of refugee in Article 1A. 2 according to which a refugee is a person who 'owing to well-founded fear of being persecuted for reasons of race, religion, nationality, membership of a particular social group or political opinion, is outside the country of his nationality and is unable or, owing to such fear, is unwilling to avail himself of the protection of that country; or who, not having a nationality and being outside the country of his former habitual residence as a result of such events, is unable or, owing to such fear, is unwilling to return to it.' To comply with the obligations in the SAA, Albania has amended the Law on Asylum and its policies. The main legal act acknowledging the right to asylum or temporary protection for foreigners who are in need of international protection, refugees or other persons that is currently in force in Albania is Law 'On Asylum' No. 121/2014 dated 18 September 2014, which is partially approximated with several Directives of the Council and European Parliament. The conditions and procedures for granting and cancelling asylum, supplementary protection and temporary protection that apply in the Republic of Albania are in the Law 'On Asylum', which also specifies the rights and obligations of asylum seekers, refugees and persons enjoying temporary and supplementary protection, the right to family reunification. This is also where the conditions that apply to the integration of refugees and persons under subsidiary protection in the Republic of Albania can be found.[188] In 2016, Decree of the Council of Ministers (DCM) No. 206, dated 16 March 2016 'On establishment, composition, organization and functioning of the National Commission for Asylum and Refugees' was adopted. This Commission was staffed in 2017.

253. The Albanian legislation on asylum recognizes a range of rights enjoyed by refugees. It guarantees a certain number of rights, which reflect protection standards guaranteed by human rights law, and differ according to the situation of the refugee in Albania, his or her legal presence or recognition of refugee status. It is

186. *See* in general Wallace-Janeczko, *The concept of asylum in international law,* 158 (Islam R. & Bhuiyan, J.H., eds., Leiden-Boston, 2013).

187. The international right to seek asylum was first recognised in the *Universal Declaration of Human Rights* which states in Art. 14.1 that 'everyone has the right to seek and to enjoy in other countries asylum from persecution'. While not enshrining a right of asylum, the *Geneva Convention relating to the status of refugees* of 1951, read together with its Additional Protocol of 1967 (*Geneva Refugee Convention*), contains a set of rights and entitlements that follow from the recognition of refugee status. *See* Islam, R., *The origin and evolution of international refugee law*, 13 (Islam R. & Bhuiyan, J.H., eds., Leiden-Boston, 2013).

188. *See Albania – Migration Profile* 34 (IOM, Min. e Brendshme, 2016), http://www.mb.gov.al/files/documents_files/Profili_i_Migracionit_2016 (Eng). pdf (accessed 20 Feb. 2018).

important to stress that a determination by the State to 'grant' refugee status is not a determination of the status, but only its formal recognition.[189] Therefore, a refugee enjoys this status before the State provides the refugee with the relevant documentation or ensures that the status is affirmed under domestic laws and procedures. However, the protection actually enjoyed by virtue of this right is limited until the State determines that the refugee's situation fulfils the definition of refugee in both the Refugee Convention and Albanian legislation.[190]

254. Furthermore, whenever international human rights law affords more protection than the Refugee Convention, international human rights law should prevail and the provisions of Albanian legislation are interpreted in the light of the rights under international human rights law.

I. Refugee Status

255. A person satisfies the definition of a refugee from the moment he/she meets the criteria of Article 1A.2 of the Geneva Refugee Convention. Article 2 of the Law 'On Asylum' No. 121/2014 specifies that a refugee is a foreigner who owing to a well-founded fear of being persecuted for reasons of race, religion, nationality, membership of a particular social group or political opinion, is outside the country of his/her origin and is unable, or owing to such a fear, is unwilling, to avail himself of the protection of that country; or who, not having nationality and being outside the country of his/her former habitual residence as a result of such events, is unable, or owing to such fear, is unwilling to return to it.[191]To be recognized under the Albanian legislation as a refugee the following criteria apply: (1) a well-founded fear of persecution; (2) the persecution must be for reasons of race, religion, nationality, membership of a particular social group or political opinion; (3) the person must be outside the country of his or her nationality or, if stateless, outside the country of

189. *See* Islam R., *The origin and evolution of international refugee law*, 13 (Islam R. & Bhuiyan, J.H., eds., Leiden-Boston, 2013).

190. *See* L. Ikonomi, *E drejta migratore*, 132 (Tirana, 2014); IOM, *E drejta migratore*, 85 (Tirane, 2009).

191. Moreover, the law provides for the principle of non-refoulement according to which: (1) The Republic of Albania recognizes and respects the obligation of authorities not to return, extradite or remove from the territory those persons who have been granted or applied for the right to asylum or other forms of protection in these cases: (a) to a country where their life or freedom would be threatened on basis of race, religion, nationality, membership in a particular social group or political opinion; (b) to a state where there is reason to believe that an asylum seeker may be at risk to be subjected to torture or to inhuman and degrading punishment or any other treatment provided by the European Convention for the Protection of Human Rights and Fundamental Freedoms, interpreted by the European Court or in treaties/international conventions to which Albania is a party; (c) to a state where there is reason to believe that an asylum seeker may be subject to enforced disappearance; (d) to their country of origin, if foreigners were given a form of protection, in accordance with the provisions of this law; (e) to a third country, which may return or send the person to a country specified by the letters 'a', 'b' and 'c', of this article.

his or her former habitual residence; and (4) the person must be unable or, owing to such fear, unwilling to seek the protection of the country of nationality or habitual residence.[192]

256. For all refugees present on Albanian territory, regardless of their means of entry or status, the Albanian Law 'On Asylum' recognizes, the prohibition of non-discrimination on the basis of race, religion or country of origin in the application of the Refugee Convention; the freedom to practice religion and the freedom as regards the religious education of children equal to that accorded to nationals; the obligation to issue an identity card and a residence permit; and protection in accordance with the principle of *non-refoulement.*

257. Any refugee granted protection in the Republic of Albania enjoys, in compliance with Albanian legislation and pursuant to Section E of the Final Act of the Conference of the Plenipotentiaries of the 1951 Refugee Convention, the legal status as provided for in that Convention and all rights stipulated in other relevant international treaties that the Republic of Albania is party to, as well as the rights accorded to foreigners in general by Albanian legislation, as defined by the Law 'On Foreigners'.[193]

258. As a general rule, the following rights are enjoyed by same group of people: the right to primary education on an equal basis with nationals of the State; property rights; and the right to access secondary and tertiary education which are equated to the level of protection afforded to non-nationals. A limited number of rights under the Albanian legislation on asylum are accorded to refugees who are lawfully present on the State's territory, albeit not necessarily 'resident' or with a durable status, such as might be the case for students or visitors. These rights are: the right to self-employment and the right to freedom of movement, which are enjoyed on an equal basis with foreign nationals; and the same procedural rights in the case of expulsion decisions, which apply to the refugee. The majority of rights recognized are applicable to refugees who are 'lawfully staying' in the State of refuge, ensuring them a situation of stable and durable residence. These rights are: the right to travel documents, which is a right particular to refugees; and the right to equal treatment as nationals in respect of the right to public relief and assistance and labour and social security rights. Furthermore, the following rights are to be enjoyed on an equal basis with foreign nationals: the right of association, which is limited to non-political and non-profit making associations and trade unions; the right to engage in wage-earning employment and in liberal professions; and the right to housing as well as the right to access to courts.[194] Albanian language courses as well as civil education and professional training courses are provided for by law. Similar

192. G.S. Goodwin-Gill & J. McAdam, *The Refugee in International Law*, 392 (Oxford, Oxford University Press 2010); A. Edwards, *Human Rights, Refugees and The Right 'To Enjoy' Asylum*, 299 (17 *Int'l J. Refugee L.* 293 2005); Bhuiylan J.H., *Refugee Status Determination: Analysis and Application,* 37 (Islam R. & Bhuiyan, J.H., eds., Leiden-Boston, 2013).

193. *See* Art. 12 of the Law 'On Asylum'.

194. *See*, in general, A. Parashar, *Human Rights of Refugees,* 378 (Islam R. & Bhuiyan, J.H., eds., Leiden-Boston, 2013).

rights are also provided to persons granted subsidiary protection status. However, the application of the previous legal enactments (in particular in as far as access to employment and documents are concerned) was hampered by the absence of the necessary by-laws. So the authorities also had to adopt the necessary by-laws, as provided for by Article 86 of Law No. 121/2014 so that a refugee's access to education, employment, housing and health is guaranteed in practice.[195]

259. A foreigner in the Republic of Albania is denied the right of asylum if there are serious reasons to believe that he/she has committed a crime against peace, a crime of war or against humanity, as defined in the international conventions; he/she has committed a serious non-political crime outside the Republic of Albania; or if he/she has been guilty of acts contrary to purposes and principles of the UN.[196]

260. As regards the obligations of the refugees, Albanian legislation provides that any asylum seeker or refugee has to respect the Albanian Constitution, laws and other legal acts of the Republic of Albania. No asylum seeker or refugee in the Republic of Albania is allowed to engage in any activity, which could disturb the public order, pose a threat to national security or undermine the relations of the Republic of Albania with other countries. No asylum seeker or refugee may act against the principles and purposes stemming from UN Treaties and Conventions acceded to by the Republic of Albania.[197]

261. In the Republic of Albania, a refugee enjoys, in compliance with Albanian legislation and pursuant to Section E of the Final Act of the Conference of the Plenipotentiaries, the legal status as provided for in the Geneva Refugee Convention of 1951 and all rights stipulated in other relevant international treaties to which the Republic of Albania is a party, as well as the rights accorded to foreigners in general by Albanian legislation. In particular, he/she is entitled to have a special residence permit and a work permit. He/she enjoys the right to social assistance to the same extent as an Albanian national. The social welfare benefits he/she is entitled to are paid out by the Office for Refugees.

262. The Albanian MPO issues refugees a travel document which bears a return clause in accordance with Article 28 of the Geneva Refugee Convention of 28 July 1951. This document can be used to travel to all countries, with the exception of the country of origin, and to return to the Republic of Albania for as long as it is valid.[198]

195. *See* Arts 48–62 of the Law 'On Asylum'.
196. *See* Art. 9 of the Law 'On Asylum'.
197. *See* Art. 11 of the Law 'On Asylum'.
198. *See* Art. 12 of the Law 'On Asylum'.

II. Subsidiary Protection Status

263. There are circumstances when persons in need of protection fall outside the definition of refugee in the *Geneva Refugee Convention.* These circumstances include people who are victims of the indiscriminate effects of violence in conflict situations, or persons who cannot be expelled from the country of destination in the light of the international human rights law principle of *non-refoulement*, but who do not satisfy the refugee definition. There are situations where neither international human rights law nor the *Geneva Refugee Convention* requires States to provide protection, but where the State has developed a system of protection for 'humanitarian' or 'compassionate' reasons, such as serious health risks or destitution by extreme poverty in case of return.[199] Different terminology is used in different national legislation, such as 'discretionary forms of protection' or 'complementary forms of protection'. In Albanian legislation the terminology used is 'Subsidiary protection'.

264. As the general rule stated for refugees, subsidiary protection is denied if: there are serious reasons to believe that the applicant has committed a crime against peace, a crime of war or against humanity, as defined in the international conventions; he/she has committed a serious non-political crime outside the Republic of Albania; or he/she has been guilty of acts contrary to purposes and principles of the UN.

III. Temporary Protection

265. Since the adoption of the Geneva Refugee Convention, the Albanian legislator has included an array of other forms of protection for people who do not satisfy the definition of 'refugee' under that Convention and for people who wish to apply for or are potentially able to qualify for asylum, but for whom the circumstances of entry to the State of refuge does not allow them to access immediately the ordinary Refugee Status Determination Procedure (RSDP), as in the case of a mass influx of asylum seekers, in both the Law 'On Asylum' and the Law 'On Foreigners'. The terminology 'temporary protection' is used in Albania to identify the legal regime including other forms of protection, such as that provided to people fleeing war or other crises. According to Article 3 of the Law 'On Asylum', 'temporary protection' is a special protection procedure, which provides immediate and temporary protection to displaced persons in the event of a mass influx, who are unable to return to their country of origin, in particular if there is also a risk that the asylum system will be unable to process this influx without adverse effects for its efficient operation, which is in the interest of these persons.

---

199. *See Complementary Forms of Protection: Their Nature and Relationship to the International Refugee Protection Regime (*UNHCR, Doc. EC/50/SC/CRP.189 June 2000,), paras 7–9. *See also*, R. Mandal, *Protection Mechanisms Outside of the 1951 Convention* ('Complementary Protection')', 8 (*UNHCR Legal and Protection Policy Research Series,* Department of International Protection, UNCHR, UN Doc. PPLA/2005/02, June 2005).

266. Temporary protection constitutes, in the words of UNHCR and as specified in Albanian legislation'a specific provisional protection response to situations of mass influx providing immediate emergency protection from *refoulement*', without formally according to refugee status. In situations of mass influx, additional protection is necessary, not because of a 'deficiency' of refugee protection, but due to factual circumstances, which may prevent a State from providing immediate access to the ordinary procedure for asylum. In these situations, the principle of *non-refoulement* in both refugee and international human rights law obliges a State to grant some form of temporary protection, until the persons concerned can access the refugee status determination procedure.[200]

267. Albania has to provide this protection regime to comply with its commitment to observe the *non-refoulement* principle both under international refugee law and international human rights law. It is a kind of 'interim protection' for people who may prima facie qualify as refugees, but whose conditions of arrival mean that they cannot apply for protection immediately through an ordinary application for refuge protection. Applicants for temporary protection should, in particular, 'not be penalized or exposed to any unfavourable treatment solely on the ground that their presence in the country is considered unlawful; they should not be subjected to restrictions on their movements other than those which are necessary in the interest of public health and public order' (Article 6 of the 'Law on Asylum').

268. According to Article 13 of the Law 'On Asylum', an asylum seeker who has been granted Temporary Protection on Humanitarian Grounds on an individual basis by the competent authorities of the Republic of Albania, enjoys the rights granted by this law to refugees in accordance with the 1951 Convention relating to the Status of Refugees, except with respect to the issuance of a travel document.

269. As regards the rights of those enjoying temporary protection, Article 14, entitled 'Rights of Asylum Seekers granted Temporary protection prima facie owing to situations of large-scale influx of persons', of the Law 'On Asylum' states that a person granted temporary protection enjoys the rights granted to refugees, unless otherwise provided for by the National Commission for Refugees, as specified in Article 32 of the Law 'On Asylum'.

---

200. *See* Art. 2(a), *Council Directive 2001/55/EC of 20 Jul. 2001 on Minimum Standards for Giving Temporary Protection in the Event of a Mass Influx of Displaced Persons and on Measures Promoting a Balance of Efforts between Member States in Receiving such Persons and Bearing the Consequences Thereof,* Official Journal EU 2001, L 212 /12 ('EU Temporary Protection Directive'); J.H. Bhuiyan, *Protection of Refugees through the Principle of Non-refoulement*, 123 (Islam R. & Bhuiyan, J.H., eds., Leiden-Boston, 2013).

§2. PROCEDURES

I. Asylum Procedure

270. Asylum claims are dealt with by the Albanian Law 'On Asylum'. This chapter only offers on outline of the procedure. Anyone in the Albanian territory can make apply for asylum, whatever his/her immigration status is. He/she may be someone who has arrived without a visa or with forged documents or someone who has obtained limited leave to enter for a different reason (e.g., as a visitor), an overstayer, or even an illegal entrant. The asylum application can be made on entry or after entry in the territory of the Republic of Albania.

271. The Albanian Law 'On Asylum' defines an applicant for asylum as a person who makes a request to be recognized as a refugee under the Geneva Convention on the basis that it would be contrary to Albania's obligations under that Convention for him/her to be removed from or required to leave Albania, or otherwise makes a request for international protection. To be granted asylum, or the status of a refugee, a claimant must meet the requirements, as set out in Article 1A of the Geneva Convention.

272. As set out in the Law 'On Asylum', an asylum applicant is granted asylum in the Republic of Albania if he/she is in the territory of Albania or has arrived at a port of entry in Albania and there are no reasonable grounds for regarding him as a danger to the security of the Republic of Albania and the applicant has not been convicted by a final judgment of a particularly serious crime, constitute a danger to Albanian society. In addition, protection is granted if refusing the application would mean that the applicant, in breach of the Geneva Convention, would be required to return to a country in which his life or freedom would be threatened on account of his race, religion, nationality, political opinion or membership of a particular social group.

273. According to Article 21 of the Law 'On Asylum', applicants wishing to claim asylum in the Republic of Albania have to address the competent authorities, at the border or within the territory of the Republic of Albania, and file an asylum request with them. In the alternative they can address the Office for Refugees directly and file an asylum application with that office. If the asylum application is made with the police authorities, the applicant is immediately referred to the Office for Refugees in Tirana in order to be registered as an asylum applicant and where he/she can file his/her asylum application.

274. The police authorities who refer the asylum seeker to the Office for Refugees as well as the Office for Refugees are responsible for taking all necessary steps to establish the identity of an asylum seeker. The Directorate of the Criminal Police assists these authorities in establishing the identity of the asylum seeker and preserves and keeps the data in separate files in order to ensure the safety of an asylum seeker.[201]

275. An asylum application is made in writing in Albanian or in one of the UN' official languages, if made with the Office for Refugees. The application must state, besides the applicant's identity, the asylum seeker's reasons for seeking protection on the territory of the Republic of Albania. The applicant must fear persecution, but the claim is rejected if there is no real risk or reasonable likelihood of the fear of persecution materialising. The main issue is that is considered is the credibility of the claimant's testimony that he has a genuine fear for persecution (the subjective test). The Office for Refugees may rely on information on the conditions in the country from which the applicant is fleeing to show that there is insufficient basis for the fear (the objective test). As a general rule, persecution includes an act of physical or mental violence, including an act of sexual violence; a legal, administrative, police, or judicial measure which, in itself, is discriminatory, or which is implemented in a discriminatory manner; and prosecution or punishment which is disproportionate or discriminatory.

276. The asylum seeker must provide all necessary bio-data to and fill in the forms presented by the Office for Refugees. A Refugee Status Determination Information leaflet is provided to the asylum seeker at the time of the submission of his/her application for asylum. If the asylum seeker so desires, the Office for Refugees can assist him/her to contact a pro bono lawyer, an expert on refugee matters or UNHCR. If the asylum seeker does not have sufficient command of the Albanian language a qualified interpreter is engaged so that he/she can communicate freely during all phases of the procedure, as provided for by this Law. An asylum seeker can choose another interpreter, albeit at his/her own expenses.[202] According to Article 24 of the Law 'On Asylum', a female interpreter is engaged for the hearing, if this is possible, if the application is made by a female asylum seeker.

277. An applicant is obliged to cooperate with the authorities by clarifying the facts presented by him/her, particularly: to provide the necessary information, verbally or in writing, as requested by the relevant authorities; to observe any official orders which require him/her to report with or present him/herself to the competent authorities or institutions, as requested; to present and hand in all documents relevant to the procedure which are in his/her possession to the authorities responsible for the implementation of the rules and procedures envisaged in the Law 'On Asylum'; to keep the Office for Refugees informed of any change of address without delay. An asylum seeker is informed that the information provided by him/her will

201. *See* Art. 22 of the Law 'On Asylum'.
202. *See* Arts 23 and 25 of the Law 'On Asylum'.

serve as the basis for decision taking and that it should, therefore, be true, accurate and as detailed as possible and that all information provided will remain confidential.[203]

278. An asylum seeker has to explain the facts underlying his/her well-founded fear of persecution or the occurrence of human rights violation, and provide the necessary data comprising of information on the place of residence, itinerary, stopovers in other countries and asylum claims filed in other countries, as well as any other data necessary to decide on his/her the case. A hearing is not public and the confidentiality of a hearing is guaranteed vis-à-vis the asylum seeker. A hearing can only be observed by representatives of the central or local government and a UNHCR representative.

279. In some cases applicants may be able to provide some documentary evidence to support their claims, such as newspaper or Internet articles, passports or identity cards, political party membership cards, arrest warrants, photographs or medical reports. Obviously the applicant may find it difficult to provide evidence of events in his home country and many statements may be unsupported. According to UNHCR's Handbook, statements should not necessarily be rejected for this reason. If an applicant's account appears credible, he/she should, unless there are good reasons to the contrary, be given the benefit of the doubt. Unsupported statements need not, however, be accepted if they are inconsistent with the general account put forward by the applicant.

280. An asylum seeker is interviewed in connection with his/her asylum application by staff members of the Office for Refugees. According to Article 24 of the Law 'On Asylum', a female asylum seeker, if this is possible, is interviewed by a female staff member. If this hearing cannot be carried out on the same day as the application is made, the asylum seeker is informed immediately of the date of the hearing which cannot take place later than twenty-one days from the day when the asylum seeker filed his/her asylum application with the Office for Refugees. An asylum seeker may be accompanied, counselled or represented by a lawyer during the hearing. Representation by a lawyer does not exempt an asylum seeker from responding to questions directed to him/her personally.

281. The Office for Refugees has to document all important data provided by the asylum seeker. When the asylum application is completed with all the necessary data provided and forms filled out, the Office for Refugees provides an asylum seeker with a document that certifies his/her identity and the receipt of the asylum application and that also ensures compliance with the principled of non-refoulement, in accordance with the Law 'On Asylum'. The Office for Refugees conducts a hearing, verifies the facts provided by the asylum applicant and completes the necessary documentation before reaching a decision on the application for

203. *See* Art. 24 of the Law 'On Asylum'. *See* L. Ikonomi, *E drejta migratore*, 116 (Tirana, 2014); IOM, *E drejta migratore*, 89 (Tiranë, 2009).

asylum. The file, if this is deemed necessary and when requested by the Office for Refugees, may contain a recommendation provided by UNHCR regarding the asylum application.

282. The Office for Refugees bases its decisions on the relevant refugee definition provided for in Articles 4, 6, 8 and 9 of the Law 'On Asylum'. When taking a decision, the Office for Refugees may not transfer the burden of proof to the asylum seeker, but must grant him/her the benefit of the doubt where appropriate. It must take any recommendation presented by UNHCR into consideration. The Office for Refugees is obliged to take a decision within thirty days after the hearing of the asylum seeker and provide the asylum seeker and UNHCR with a copy of the decision without delay, but in any case no later than five days from the date that the decision was taken. The decision of the Office for Refugees is given in writing and is motivated.[204]

283. The asylum seeker is allowed to stay in the Republic of Albania until the final decision concerning his/her asylum application is taken.

II. Review of the Decision Rejecting the Application for Asylum

284. If an asylum application is accepted, the Office for Refugees informs the asylum seeker of the conditions of under which refuge is granted. If an asylum application is turned down, the Office for Refugees informs an asylum seeker of this refusal in a written, motivated and individualized decision which spells out the right to lodge an appeal and the appeal-related timeframe. If the Office for Refugees fails to serve a decision within the five day timeframe, starting from the asylum seeker's hearing date, the Office for Refugees' silence is treated as an implicit rejection of the application.

285. The Office for Refugees may declare an asylum application 'abusive' or 'manifestly unfounded'. As a general rule this happens when it has been established that the claim made by the asylum seeker is clearly fraudulent, in the sense that the applicant deliberately attempts to deceive the authorities or if the claim made by the asylum seeker is not related in any manner to the criteria for granting asylum as specified in Chapter I of the Law 'On Asylum'. Asylum is denied to any foreigner who arrives from a third country that is party to the 1951 Convention/1967 Protocol who cannot establish a well-founded fear of persecution for at least one of the reasons contained in Article 1A of the aforementioned Convention, a Human Rights violation or a threat of refoulement in the meaning of Articles 4 and 6 of the Law 'On Asylum', and if he/she can lawfully return to that country where his/her application for refugee status is examined in accordance with international standards.

286. In cases where the Office for Refugees considers an asylum application to be 'abusive' or 'manifestly unfounded', Albanian law provides for an accelerated

204. *See*, in particular, Art. 27 of the Law 'On Asylum'.

appeal procedure. If, during the first instance stage of the accelerated procedures, the Office for Refugees does not serve its decision within a ten day timeframe, an application is automatically transferred to the normal Refugee Status Determination Procedure. If this is the case, an asylum seeker is granted a period of seven days, starting on the day he/she receives the decision of the Office for Refugees, to lodge an appeal. The National Commission for Refugees handles this appeal with priority in order to reach a final decision within the shortest possible period of time. The National Commission for Refugees may decide on the information contained in the files, if it deems it unnecessary to conduct a hearing with the asylum seeker.[205]

287. The right of appeal is dependent on the outcome of the application. An appeal against a decision of the Office for Refugees has to be addressed to the National Commission for Refugees within fifteen days from the date that the asylum seeker receives the decision.

288. A request for appeal must contain a motivation why the decision should be considered as unfounded as well as any other complementary data and documents, which were not presented to the Office for Refugees in first instance. The Office for Refugees passes the whole file concerning the asylum seeker who has appealed its decision on to the National Commission for Refugees. The registration of an appeal request suspends the decision of the Office for Refugees. The asylum seeker is permitted to remain on Albanian territory while the appeal is pending.

289. Before taking a decision, the National Commission for Refugees conducts a hearing with the asylum seeker in accordance with Article 26 of the Law 'On Asylum', if it cannot take a positive decision based on the information contained in the file. The National Commission for Refugees adheres to the same principles as those which determine the procedure followed by the Office for Refugees. The National Commission for Refugees adopts its decision at the latest forty-five days after the day the appeal was filed. The motivated decision of the National Commission for Refugees is delivered to the asylum seeker by the Office for Refugees. The decision of the National Commission for Refugees is final.[206]

290. An applicant whose asylum claim has been rejected can be expelled when the decision is final. The asylum seeker is removed from the territory as provided for in Article 106 of the Law 'On Foreigners'. The Office for Refugees informs, without delay, the competent authorities of any final, negative decision in asylum matters.[207]

---

205. *See* Art. 28 of the Law 'On Asylum'.
206. *See* Art. 29 of the Law 'On Asylum'.
207. *See* Art. 30 of the Law 'On Asylum'.

III. Unaccompanied Minor Asylum Claimants

291. Under Article 22 of the Geneva Convention, States must take particular measures to ensure that asylum procedures provide appropriate protection to children.[208] Albania provides appropriate protection to unaccompanied children as follows.

292. Albanian legislation on migration and asylum recognizes the principle of the best interests of the child which must be the primary consideration in any measure which affects or might affect a child's human rights. As there are no special provisions in the Law 'On Asylum' regarding asylum claims made by unaccompanied minors, protection offered to them is based on the general rules and the general provisions concerning migrants and refugees.

293. As unaccompanied minors, in particular, are unlikely to spontaneously file an application for asylum this must be accounted for in procedures that must ensure that, as soon as it becomes known that a child may have a well-founded fear or be at risk of persecution, he/she is referred to an asylum procedure. The unaccompanied or separated child usually needs the assistance of an appointed adult familiar with his or her background who is competent and able to represent the child's best interests (a guardian or legal representative). In Albania an unaccompanied minor is usually given access to a qualified legal representative free of charge, as provided for in Articles 32, 53 of the Law 'On Asylum'.

294. As a general rule applications made by unaccompanied or separated children are given priority over those made by adults and decisions are usually rendered promptly and fairly. The asylum application of an unaccompanied minor must be handled immediately. In as far as possible, children who are members of a family must be kept together.[209] The procedure accommodates for the need of the child to express his or her views freely, and the principal standard of consideration is the best interest of the child.[210]

295. In addition, Article 16, paragraph 5 of the Law 'On Asylum' states that in accordance with the relevant international instruments which the Republic of Albania is party to, as regards unaccompanied minor asylum seekers under sixteen years of age, the latter are not to be held in prison-like conditions, unless this as an absolute last resort measure. Instead special arrangements are to be provided that are suitable for children.[211]

---

208. *See* the General Comment on States' obligations towards unaccompanied or separated children of the Committee on the Rights of the Child.
209. *See* Art. 16 of the Law 'On Asylum'.
210. *See* Art. 17 of the Law 'On Asylum'.
211. *See Analiza e mangësive mbi legjislacionin dhe praktikën shqiptare të emigracionit krahasuar me standartet europiane dhe ato ndërkombëtare*, 46 (ONM, Tiranë, 2004); L. Ikonomi, *E drejta migratore*, 152 (Tirana, 2014); IOM, *E drejta migratore,* 95 (Tirane, 2009).

IV. Safe Country of Origin and Safe Third Country

296. Albanian legislation allows the asylum authorities to decide on the basis of the 'safe country of origin' and 'safe third country' concepts. A list of 'safe countries of origin' and 'third safe countries' is adopted annually by the asylum administration. These lists are used extensively in first instance decisions. Both the 'safe third country' concept and the 'safe country of origin' concept are incorporated in the Law 'On Asylum', but are not defined.

297. The 'safe country of origin' principle allows Albania to deny asylum seeker access to the asylum system on the grounds that human rights are so well protected in their country of origin that persecution severe enough to cause people to flee never occurs there. The principle is different (though not unrelated) to the 'safe third country' rule under which asylum seekers can be turned away at the EU's external borders or sent back to 'safe' countries through which they have passed, where they are expected to lodge their asylum application. However, in Albania the 'safe country of origin' and 'safe third country' concepts are applied as a rebuttable presumption that can be contested by asylum seeker in each and every individual case.[212]

298. By definition of Albanian law, all Member States of the EU are considered to be 'safe third countries'. In addition, Albanian law provides for the possibility to draw up a list of other 'safe third countries'. To qualify as a 'safe third country', the application of the 1951 Refugee Convention and of the European Convention on Human Rights has to be 'ensured' there.

299. Albanian law refers to the EU common list of 'safe countries of origin' as the only source applicable for considering a country of origin as safe, as provided for in the SAA and in compliance with other obligations in the context of Albania's future accession to the EU.

300. Applications of asylum seekers from 'safe countries of origin' are considered as manifestly unfounded, unless the applicant presents facts or evidence which justifies the conclusion that they he/she may be persecuted in spite of the general situation in that country. Although this is not required by law, applications made by nationals of 'safe countries of origin' are prioritized by the Office for Refugees.

§3. Legal Position

301. A refugee is normally granted a period of five years leave to remain in the territory of the Republic of Albania. According to the Albanian immigration rules,

212. H. Lambert, *Safe Third Country in the European Union: An Evolving Concept in International Law and Implications for the UK*, 318 (Journal of Immigration, Asylum and Nationality Law Vol 26, 2012); M. Foster, *Responsibility Sharing or Shifting? 'Safe' Third Countries and International Law* 64 (Canada's Journal on Refugees, 25/2, 2008); G.S. Goodwin-Gill & J. McAdam, *The Refugee in International Law*, 392 (Oxford, Oxford University Press 2010).

it is usually known as a residence permit valid for five years. After completing the five year period for limited leave to remain, a refugee can apply for settlement.

302. A refugee's status can be reviewed which may lead to that status being withdrawn, cancelled or revoked. Such a step does not in itself affect the person's leave to remain but, in practice, it will normally result in curtailment of any limited leave to remain or revocation of any indefinite leave to remain, and in action being taken to remove the person from the territory of the Republic of Albania.

303. Special rules in the Albanian Law 'On Asylum' give the National Commissioner for Refugees the power to initiate a procedure for the cessation of refugee status with the Office for Refugees, if there are good reasons to believe that the refugee concerned falls under the cessation clause, as stipulated by Article 8 of this law.[213]

304. In addition, foreigner whose asylum claim has been rejected finally can be expelled, subject to provisions in the Albanian Law 'On Foreigners'. The Office for Refugees must inform, without delay, the competent authorities of any final, negative decision in asylum cases.[214]

§4. Position of Family Members

305. Family Reunification helps to create socio-cultural stability facilitating the integration of the migrant in the territory of the host-State. Family reunification is a recognized reason for immigration in many countries. Family reunification means that the presence of one or more family members in a certain country enables the rest of the family to immigrate to that country as well. As mentioned in paragraph 133 the purpose of the new Albanian legislation is to create a complete legal framework, that is in accordance with the EU rules on family reunification, in particular, Directive 2003/86/EC which regulates family reunification of migrants (workers, self-employers etc.) within the territory of the EU. The intention here is to examine the conditions, the beneficiaries and the procedures for family reunification of refugees and asylum seekers who are in Albanian, in particular the Albanian Migration and Asylum Legislation, Law 'On Foreigners' and Law 'On Asylum in the Republic of Albania'.[215]

---

213. *See* Art. 18 of the Law 'On Asylum'.
214. *See* Art. 30 of the Law 'On Asylum'.
215. L. Ikonomi, *E drejta e migracionit*, 59 (Tiranë, 2011); A. Aliu & H. Gashi, *E drejta familiare* 96 (Prishtinë, 2007); A. Anastasi, *E drejta kushtetuese e krahasuar: raste nga praktika kushtetuese dhe leksione për studentët e drejtësisë*, 36 (Tiranë, 2009); R. Cholewinsky, *Family Reunification and Conditions Placed on Family Members: Dismalting a Fundamental Right*, 35 (European Journal of Migration and Law, 2002); S. Bariatti, *La famiglia nel diritto internazionale privato comunitario*, 89 (Milano, 2007); Mandro A., *E drejta familjare*, 63 (Tiranë 2009); A. Mandro, V. Mecaj T. Zaka & A. Fullani, *E drejta familjare* (Tiranë 2006); S. Omari *E drejta familjare*, 77 (Tiranë 2008).

306. In Albania where the Law 'On Asylum' guarantees the right to asylum to the spouse, children under younger than 18 and to any other relative under the legal custody of a refugee provided that they reside together in Albania. Any person older than 18 cannot be granted asylum by application of the principle of family unity according to paragraph 1 of Article 6 of the Law 'On Asylum', unless he/she is a dependant of his refugee parent(s) who has/have been granted the status of refugee in the Republic of Albania. This child must lodge an individual application if he/she desires to be granted refugee status by the Albanian authorities (Article 6 of the Law 'On Asylum'). In the case of divorce, separation or the death of the family member who has been granted refugee status, the family members who have obtained asylum in accordance to paragraph 1 of Article 6 of the Law 'On Asylum', shall continue to enjoy protection in Albania. The same also applies to children who enjoy protection in accordance with the principle of family unity when they reach the age of 18.[216]

307. This section examines the rights granted to family members who are reunited with a refugee in Albania. The rights enjoyed by family members included: the right of residence; the right to take up employment as a worker or as a self-employed person; the right to education and the right to social benefits. Albanian legislation specifies the basic rights that family members can claim and the Law 'On Asylum' specifies that all family members enjoy the same rights and have to comply with the same obligations as a refugee. Once the Albanian authorities have accepted the application for asylum it should facilitate the effective exercise, i.e., entry into the territory. Any administrative formalities should, at this point, be as few as possible and without costs. The right of residence is the most obvious right to be conferred on family members, other than the right of entry. All legal instruments explicitly mention this right albeit in different wording: 'the right of residence is granted to', 'have the right to remain permanently in the territory of', 'be issued with a residence document' etc. Admission is, however, limited to those family members who will actually cohabit with a refugee. The validity of the first residence permit issued to family members is five years.

308. An important question in this respect is in how far the right of residence of the family members depends on the relationship with a refugee. Can family members, for instance, remain in Albania after a divorce (in the case of spouses), or when reaching the age of adulthood (in the case of descendants)? In the case of divorce, separation or the death of a refugee, the family members who have obtained permission to stay in Albania with a refugee in accordance to paragraph 1 of Article 65

216. *See*, in particular, E. Canaj, A.Vasjari, *Family Reunification in Albania. A Comparative Study in the Context of Albanian Integration*, 681 (Mediterranean Journal of Social Science, Sapienza, Vol. 4. nr. 6, 2013) http://www.mcser.org/journal/index.php/mjss/article/view/350 (accessed 13 Mar. 2018); L. Omari & A. Anastasi, *E drejta kushtetuese*, 35 (Tiranë, 2008).

of the Law 'On Asylum', can remain in Albania. The same applies to children who have been reunited with a refugee in accordance with the principle of family unity when they reach the age of 18.[217]

309. Besides the right of residence, family members, or at least the members of the nuclear family can claim a set of rights. The most important one is the right to take up an employment, which is clearly closely linked to the right of residence of family members. Therefore, it is limited or even absent when the right of residence is limited. It is in the interest of the host State, i.e., Albania, to allow persons, legally residing in their territory to take up employment. Family members, who are accepted for the purpose of family reunification, are treated in the same way as the sponsor is as far as human rights and fundamental freedoms and rights in other international agreements ratified by the Republic of Albania are concerned. Thus Albania respects the principle of reciprocity and non-discrimination, like Albanian citizens. This is mentioned as a general principle in Article 2 of the Law 'On Foreigners'.[218]

310. Family members also enjoy the right of free movement on the territory of Albania expressively mentioned in Article 67 of the Law 'On Asylum'. The last remark regarding a family member's rights concerns the right to access to education and social advantages. EU law provides that the family members of EU citizens and TCNs enjoy the right to access to education (primary or secondary) and vocational training and social advantages. This is, however, not explicitly provided for in Albanian legislation. A comparison of Albanian legislation on family reunification with that of the Member States of the EU shows that there are not only similarities between these legal regimes, but that there are also a lot of differences.[219] In Albania the categories of family members of foreigners are limited to the spouse/partner and minor children. As an extra condition, the law requires that the spouse and the children live with the sponsor. Albania law does not provide for the right to family reunification for de facto partners. An interesting point concerns the age of majority of the children. This is specified to be 18 years old, while it was mentioned that the minor children should not be married. However, it is not specified whether reference had to be made to the general rules of private law, or to the law of the State of which the foreigner is a national. Union law on family reunification, for EU citizens provides that children must be under 21. Albanian law is not in accordance with the rules of family unit of EU citizens, but it is in line with the general regime for family reunification of third-country nationals that are in the territory of the EU, which states the majority age limit to be 18 years.

---

217. *See Integrimi i refugjatëve në Shqipëri*, 45 (UNHCR, Tiranë, 2004); L. Ikonomi, *E drejta migratore*, 145 (Tirana, 2014); IOM, *E drejta migratore,* 122 (Tiranë, 2009).

218. L. Ikonomi, *E drejta migratore*, 129 (Tirana, 2014).

219. *See* E. Canaj & S. Veliu, *Implementing European rules into Albanian legislation. The right of Family Reunification*, 35 (UETPRESS, Tirane, 2017); E. Canaj, A. Vasjari, *Family Reunification in Albania. A Comparative Study in the Context of Albanian Integration*, 681 (Mediterranean Journal of Social Science, Sapienza, Vol. 4. nr. 6, 2013) http://www.mcser.org/journal/index.php/mjss/article/view/350 (accessed 13 Mar. 2018).

Part IV. Loss of Right of Residence

Chapter 1. Conditions under Which the Right of Residence Might Be Lost

311. In this chapter we will consider when the right of residence might be lost. As we set out in the paragraph 77 of the previous chapter visas and residence permits are granted for many different reasons. Usually, the validity of a residence permit or visa is related to the reason why the permit is granted. The ground for which the residence permit has been granted also determines the period of validity of a permit. In the Republic of Albania most residence permits are initially granted as temporary permits. They are granted for a specified period, and must, on expiry of this period, be renewed if the holder wishes to stay and/or continues to stay in Albania. It is in the stage of renewal of a residence permit that an assessment whether the conditions for the granting of the residence permit still are met, is undertaken.[220]

312. In most of the cases the loss of the right of residence is connected to a negative decision on an application for renewal of a fixed-term residence permit, not to the withdrawal or cessation of a residence permit that has been issued to the holder of that permit. Obviously, decisions regarding the renewal of residence permits and decisions on the withdrawal or discontinuation of the right to reside, as well as issues relating to the refusal of entry permission, must be compatible with the rule of law and the right to legal security as a legal subject.[221]

313. It is clear that issues regarding immigration and the right to stay in Albania are issues that are linked to sovereign concerns regarding national security and other issues of public interest. Thus, the rules on the loss of the right of residence include, despite the requirements posed by the rule of law, a fairly broad margin of appreciation for the decision maker. It is for the decision maker to use these margins appropriately.[222]

---

220. L. Ikonomi, *E drejta migratore*, 132 (Tirana, 2014); G. Appave, *Emerging Legal Issues in International Law on Migration*, 390 (R., Opeskin, Perruchoud & J., Redpath-Cross, eds., Cambridge, 2012); R., Opeskin, Perruchoud & J., Redpath-Cross *Conceptualising International Migration Law*, 14 (Opeskin, B., Perruchoud, R. & Redpath-Cross, J., eds., Cambridge, 2012); N. Klein, *International Migration by Sea and Air*, 260 (Opeskin, B., Perruchoud, R. & Redpath-Cross, J., eds., Cambridge, 2012).
221. IOM, *E drejta migratore*, 184 (Tiranë, 2009).
222. L. Ikonomi, *E drejta migratore*, 57 (Tiranë, 2014).

314. Decisions regarding immigration and, in particular, the right to stay are often described as 'administrative act' as they are, in reality, an administrative route. The most common grounds for administrative removal are that a person has remained beyond the period specified in his limited leave to remain (i.e., the *overstayers)* or has violated a condition subject to which leave to remain was granted. A person who wishes to extend his stay in Albania should apply for an extension before his/her visa or residence permit expires. Loss of the right of residence is traditionally connected with amendments of the period of the validity of residence permits. However, the right to stay in Albania can also be changed if the permit for a short stay – a visa is amended. Anon-national who has only been issued a visa to stay in Albania can clearly not be said to reside in Albania. Any alteration concerning the validity of the permit for short stay affects his/her right in the same manner as for holders of residence permits.[223]

315. In the Law 'On Foreigners' there is no specific section that lists the grounds which justify that a visa or a residence permit is revoked or annulled. Rules on revoking and annulling visa and residence permits are found in different sections of the Law 'On Foreigners'. Articles 28 and 29 of the Law 'On Foreigners' concern the validity of visas that have been issued; Articles 35, 40, 42, 46 of the Law 'On Foreigners' concern the annulment, revoking temporary residence permits; Article 60 of the Law 'On Foreigners' concerns the annulment of a residence permit obtained for the purpose of family reunification and Articles 63, 64 and 68 of the Law 'On Foreigners' concern the refusal to issue and the annulment of a permanent residence permit.[224]

316. First, the rules concerning revoking of visas do not apply to the initial granting of visas. A visa can be revoked if it becomes apparent that the holder cannot produce a valid travel document or documents substantiating the purpose of stay in Albania when entering the country. Further, a visa can be revoked when the conditions for the granting of the visa are no longer present. A visa can be annulled if it is established that, at the moment of entry and during the stay, the holder no longer meets the conditions based on which the visa was issued, or if the purpose for which the visa was issued has changed or is no longer valid. A visa may be annulled at the request of the holder or his/her host in the Republic of Albania.[225] This means that if the circumstances why the visa was granted change before the holder enters Albania, a new visa must be applied for. If for any reason, notwithstanding the fact that a visa has been issued, the holder of that visa is refused permission to enter Albania, the visa is revoked as a result of the refusal to grant permission to enter. Finally, if the holder of a visa issued for a particular reason cannot present the required evidence of a valid health insurance, a visa can be revoked.[226]

---

223. IOM, *E drejta migratore*, 185 (Tiranë, 2009).
224. *Ibid.*, 181.
225. *See* Art. 28 para. 4 of the Law 'On Foreigners'.
226. L. Ikonomi, *E drejta migratore*, 57 (Tirana, 2014).

317. The annulment of a visa is the automatic consequence of the withdrawal or revocation of a visa, but can also be the result of an incorrectly granted visa or if it was granted by mistake by the authorities. In practice, an annulment is carried out by marking the visa.[227] According to Article 28 of the Law 'On Foreigners' a visa may be annulled by the Albanian embassies or consular posts abroad or consular posts of the Ministry of Foreign Affairs in the Republic of Albania if a visa has been issued in breach of the legal provisions in force; the applicant has presented false information or forged documents to be issued; the visa has been issued erroneously to the person; the holder is declared persona non grata after the date of the issuing of the visa or the holder, repeatedly, fails to comply with the rules set by the customs authorities and the authority responsible for border and immigration concerning the crossing of the Albanian border.[228]

318. A visa may be refused if the applicant is the subject of an entry ban, presents a false travel document or fails to prove the purpose of the intended stay or does not fulfil the requirements for the entry and stay or fails to provide proof of secure means of support for the duration of stay in the Republic of Albania and the return to the country of origin or habitual residence. A visa is also refused if the applicant has exceeded the time limits of stay in the Republic of Albania is considered to be a threat to public security or public health, fails to establish the authenticity of the submitted statements, or cannot guarantee that he/she will leave the territory of the Republic of Albania within the time limit indicated in the visa which is being applied for.[229]

319. The situations in which a foreigner loses the right of residence are connected with the withdrawal of a residence permit or with situations in which a residence permit is not renewed. Expulsion, which is different from a refusal to grant entry permission, concerns removals from Albania in cases where the non-national has resided legally, with the required residence permit and with proper registration of his/her in Albania, or in cases where the non-national continues to stay in Albania after the validity of a residence permit has expired and the registered right to stay or any other legal grounds for residing in Albania no longer exists.

320. A foreigner can, according to the Law 'On Foreigners', be expelled if a residence permit is no longer valid. Residence in Albania then becomes illegal and expulsion is automatically permitted. In addition, the loss of the rights of residence makes residence irregular and justifies an expulsion measure.

321. The Law 'On Foreigners', states that the loss of the right of residence justifies an expulsion measure if the person has failed to lodge an application for the extension of residence permission or to complete the necessary documentation by

227. *See* Art. 28 para. 2 of the law 'On Foreigners' which states that 'The annulment of the visa shall be immediately made known to the alien and a stamp stating 'ANNULLED' shall be affixed to the visa in the travel document of the alien.'.
228. *See* Art. 28 para. 1 of the law 'On Foreigners'.
229. *See* Art. 29 para. 1 of the Law 'On Foreigners'.

the specified date, or fails to give reasons justifying such omission, or is unable to prove that he/she fulfils or no longer fulfils the conditions required for stay, as provided for by law. Further, if a foreigner cannot prove that he/she is not a danger to the safety of others or if he/she is suspected of initializing actions that would endanger the Albanian public order, public security or public health, expulsion is possible. The right of residence as a family member is lost if the spouses are divorced, s or in cases where a removal order is issued.[230]

322. The actual decision ordering the removal from Albanian territory is never automatic. When a decision regarding the expulsion is taken, the person concerned must be heard in the process of decision-making. As a general rule, the same right to a hearing is also available to the spouse, if the spouse lives in Albania. The definition of 'spouse' follows the general definitions of family members in Section V of the Law 'On Foreigners'. The Law 'On Foreigners' requires all authorities involved in the decision-making regarding expulsion-matters to make a broad consideration of the effects of the decision. The general rule refers to the protection of family life and the best interest of the child, the protection of vulnerable persons, and health situation of the person who is the subject of the removal decision.[231]

323. It is imperative that the possibility to expel a person is not used in a way that would lead to a breach of Albania's obligations arising from international law. More precisely, the prohibition of refoulement, in the case of refugees and people benefiting from subsidiary protection, to areas where their life or freedom would be endangered or they would face a risk of persecution or serious harm, naturally, also have to be observed in expulsion cases. Special protection is granted, in any case, to children, victims of trafficking in human beings and other categories of persons in need.

324. If a decision on expulsion is taken in respect of USA citizens, or a citizen of the EU special rules apply. First of all, if an EU citizen has arrived in Albania in search of employment, is an employee or is self-employed, and can prove that this is the case, the right of residence can only be revoked on grounds of public order, public security or public health. EU citizens and USA citizens can only be extradited on grounds of public order, public security and public health or if that person has become a burden for the Albanian social security system. Family members of EU citizens and USA citizens, as a rule, enjoy the same level protection, but in instances where the family-tie is broken, their right to stay in Albania may not be lawful any more.

230. IOM, *E drejta migratore*, 183 (Tirane, 2009).

231. E. Canaj, *Analizë e disa problematikave mbi të drejtat e emigrantëve sipas Kartës së të drejtave themelore të Bashkimit Europian*, 87 (Jeta Juridike, No. 2, Tirane 2010).

§1. Loss in the Event of Non-renewal

325. The right of residence is lost if a residence permit is not renewed. Residence permits, as mentioned in paragraph 104, are initially always fixed-term permits, which may be renewed by a decision by the local police. The renewal of a residence permit is not automatic and the right of residence may be lost for a number of reasons. The basic rule is that a new residence permit is granted if the grounds for granting of the first residence permit are still present. It is for the applicant to show that the circumstances have not changed; that he/she, for instance, is still an employee, or a student, depending on the reason why the initial residence permit was granted.[232]

326. If the initial residence permit was granted for reasons of international protection, the holder of that permit is not per se required to show that the grounds for protection still exist when applying for renewal of the initial residence permit. In these situations, the assumption is that the need for international protection is continuous. An assessment of the application for renewal is only undertaken if there are very clear indications that the need for protection has ceased to exist. These indications can be connected to the grounds for cessation of refugee status, as provided for by international law (*see* paragraph 303).

327. A holder of a residence permit that has expired may be able to invoke on another ground than the one for which the residence permit was initially issued to stay in Albania. The general practice of the MoI is that all residence permits must be applied for from abroad and that inland applications in Albania are not possible. Thus, everyone who wishes to apply for a residence permit on a new ground, including those who are already lawfully present in Albania, must do so from abroad, in practice at the Albanian consular mission in their country of origin. However, there are exceptions to this general rule which is applied in an ad hoc manner, taking into account the circumstances of the individual case.

328. Nevertheless, if on the expiration of the validity of a residence permit, the holder wants to apply for a new residence permit on other grounds than the initial residence permit was issued for, he/she can do so and anew residence permit will be granted as a fixed-term residence permit, if the conditions set out in the law for the granting of the residence permit are met.

329. If the initial residence permit was granted for the purpose of temporary employment or self-employment, a continuous residence permit is granted after two years' stay in Albania. After a continuous residence permit has been issued, the holder of that permit is no longer required to continuously show that the conditions for issuing the residence permit are met.

---

232. E. Canaj, *Analizë e disa problematikave mbi të drejtat e emigrantëve sipas Kartës së të drejtave themelore të Bashkimit Europian*, 89 (Jeta Juridike, No. 2, Tirane 2010); IOM, *E drejta migratore*, 184 (Tiranë, 2009); L. Ikonomi, *E drejta migratore*, 57 (Tirana, 2014).

330. There are special rules for people who have stayed in Albania on the basis of a fixed-term residence permit for the purpose of study. If his residence permit expires when the foreign student still has to pass an exam at an Albanian institution for education, the right of residence is not, necessarily, lost. The Law 'On Foreigners', namely, provides former students with the right to be granted a fixed-term residence permit for the purpose of looking for a job in Albania after receiving their diploma. Although the residence permit is granted for another reason than the initial residence permit, a former student does not have to apply for this residence permit from abroad.

331. Similarly, if a residence permit has been granted on grounds of family ties in Albania, and the family ties cease to exist, that ground for renewal of the residence permit is no longer present. In these cases, a residence permit that is based on ties with Albania as a country can be applied for and is granted to the former family member notwithstanding the discontinuance of the family ties with no obligation to leave Albania.[233]

332. If the initial residence permit was granted on grounds of asylum or a special residence permit for victims of trafficking, a continuous residence permit is granted after six months of stay on a fixed-term residence permit in Albania.[234]

§2. Loss in the Event of Absence

333. Mostly, the assessment of the right to continue residence in Albania is undertaken in connection with an application for the renewal or continuation of a fixed-term residence permit. However, this assessment can also be made with regard to residence permits that are still valid, and have, thus, not yet expired. Residence permits can be annulled if their holder either has permanently left Albania or has stayed outside Albania for a continuous period of time of two years or more. Care must, therefore, be taken if the holder of a residence permit wishes to move abroad for a non-permanent period, that Albanian authorities are aware of the temporary nature of any arrangement. If there is a risk that a residence permit might be withdrawn on this ground and the holder of that permit wants to prevent this, an application not to have the residence permit withdrawn can be filed with the MoI. These applications are not automatically granted, but decisions are taken *in concreto.*

334. A residence permit can also be withdrawn if the authorities establish that the residence permit has issued on the basis of incorrect information concerning the applicant's identity or other circumstances that could have an effect on the decision to issue a residence permit if this information was provided to the authorities by the

233. *See Integrimi i refugjatëve në Shqipëri*, 28 (UNHCR, Tiranë, 2004); E. Canaj, *Analizë e disa problematikave mbi të drejtat e emigrantëve sipas Kartës së të drejtave themelore të Bashkimit European*, 89 (Jeta Juridike, No. 2, Tiranë 2010); E. Canaj & S. Bana, *E drejta e Bashkimit Europian* 39 (Tiranë, 2014).

234. *See Integrimi i refugjatëve në Shqipëri*, 13 (UNHCR, Tiranë, 2004).

applicant. The same applies to applicants who have held back information that, if known, would have had an effect on the decision to issue the residence permit.

335. Finally, if a residence permit has been granted on grounds of a reception agreement under the EU Researchers' Directive, that residence permit can be withdrawn when the reception agreement with the Albanian research institution ends. However, if the reception agreement is terminated as a result of the completion of the research project, the residence permit can be withdrawn, at the earliest, six months after the decision on termination is taken.

§3. Entry Ban

336. Temporary and permanent long-term resident permits can be withdrawn at any time if a Schengen-state requests the withdrawal because an entry ban has been imposed on the holder of a long-term resident permit and a decision on his or her removal from the Schengen territory has been taken based on the criminal conduct of that person or if that person is considered to be a danger to the society of the requesting State.[235]

337. Any residence permit loses its validity if the holder of that permit is expelled from Albania, or is granted Albanian nationality.

235. L. Ikonomi, *E drejta migratore*, 57 (Tirana, 2014); IOM, *E drejta migratore*, 182 (Tirane, 2009).

337–337 **Part IV, Ch. 1, Conditions under Which the Right of Residence**

Part V. Sanctions

Chapter 1. Sanctions

§1. Administrative Sanctions

338. Administrative sanctions have, as the term reveals, a sanctioning character. In the Republic of Albania certain types of administrative sanctions can be imposed, but their scope of application is limited to specific areas of law. Chapter VI of the Law 'On Foreigners' deals with the general conditions on removal and expulsion of aliens in the territory of the Republic of Albania. As far as irregular immigration is concerned, two forms of administrative sanctions can be applied. First, there are sanctions directed against employers using illegal labour force. These will be discussed in detail in Part VII, Chapter 3. The second form of administrative sanctions concerns carriers. They have an important role in preventing irregular entry to the territory.

339. Chapter VIII 'Surveillance and control of aliens' of the Law 'On Foreigners' deals with the control of non-nationals in the Republic of Albania and obligations imposed on carriers. The basis for this legislation is Council Directive 2001/51/EC of 28 June 2001 supplementing the provisions of Article 26 of the Convention Implementing the Schengen Agreement of 14 June 1985. According to Article 135 of the Law 'On Foreigners', a carrier, prior to departure, must verify that any passenger travelling to the Republic of Albania by air, land, rail or sea holds a valid travel document and visa, if required, and send, electronically, to the authority of the BCP of entry/departure, before departure, a list of the passengers and crew members on that flight. Upon arrival the carrier must present to the staff of the BCPs the full list of passengers and crew members. The driver of a vehicle, the master of a vessel or aircraft and the representative of the carrier on board are obliged to ensure that people not entitled to enter Albania do not enter that country without the permission of the border control authorities. In the case of detection of any stowaway on board, during the journey, the carrier must notify the border control authorities in advance or prior to their arrival at the BCP. Obviously, if the carrier violates the obligations described above, he/she is subject to financial penalty.

340. If a person is refused entry permission, the carrier is obliged to transport him/her to the country of embarkation or the country which issued that person the travel document on which he/she travelled; or any country to which that person is certainly going to be admitted. The obligation to return an incorrectly documented person apples to the carrier if a person in transit through the Republic of Albania is refused entry permission and if another carrier, which was supposed to transport that person to the country of destination, refuses to take him/ her on board; or if the authorities of the country of destination have refused that person entry permission and, as a consequence, that person has been returned to the Republic of Albania.

341. A carrier is obliged, if a person who has been refused permission to enter the territory of the Republic of Albania does not have sufficient funds for his or her return journey, to arrange his/her transport at its own cost. If immediate transport is not feasible, the carrier also bears any costs that arise from that person's stay in Albania. Upon enforcing the removal of a person not granted permission to enter Albania from the country, the border and migration police authorities may order the necessary number of escorts if the security of the vehicle or the enforcement of the decision on removal so requires. The carrier may submit a request to the border and migration authorities to order that the person to be returned is escorted.

342. A carrier is not obliged to return a person according to the terms of Article 135 of the Law 'On Foreigners' if the border control authorities have allowed that person to enter the country, unless an application for asylum is made at the border. If a person is refused entry permission at the border and this refusal is based on his/ her not holding the required travel document, visa or residence permit and the carrier requests an escort to return that person, then the carrier is obliged to pay for the costs of engaging an escort. If an escort is ordered by the Border and Migration Police authorities, the costs of engaging an escort are covered by the Border and Migration Police.

343. A carrier is not entitled to compensation by the State for any costs arising from the transport of irregular passengers. The carrier is obliged to return an asylum seeker, transported by him/her, to the Albanian border, if an application for asylum is made at the border and the decision on refusal to grant entry permission is issued within three months of entry into the country. When the local Border and Migration Police refuse entry permission they impose a fine on the carrier who transported the person who has been refused entry permission, unless entry permission is refused because of non-fulfilment of the additional conditions[236]by the foreigner or the invalidity of either the visa, or the residence permit, and if an error in the list of passengers is considered excusable. Additional documents are identified in Decision of the Council of Ministers No. 513 of 13 June 2013. This list of documents reflects those found in Annex I of Regulation 562/2006/EC. In fact, it is expressly stated that the foreigner must possess the necessary financial means for the period of stay and return to the country of origin: Article 13 is dedicated to financial guarantees, whilst Article 12 provides the possibility of an invitation by an

236. The additional conditions according to the type of visa requested are specified in Council of Ministers Decision No. 513, 13 Jun. 2013, https://www.ilo.org/dyn/natlex/docs/ELECTRONIC/97781/119213/F467343735/ALB-97781.pdf (accessed 15 May 2018).

Albanian national, who guarantees to reimburse any financial costs made by a foreign national. The carrier or his/her representative is heard before a fine is imposed on the carrier.[237]

344. An administrative sanction is imposed on a person or an organization if there has been an infringement of the law. It is also possible for the Albanian authorities to adopt an interim measure, such as a duty to report at regular intervals to the police or an obligation to hand over the travel documents to the authorities. These interim measures can contain elements that correspond with sanctions even if they do not constitute sanctions per se. The content of these interim measures is analysed in sub-chapter §3. The only administrative sanctions available as regards irregular stay or residence are those directed against employers who use illegal labour force. These will be discussed in Part VII, Chapter 3.

§2. Penal Sanctions

345. The legal basis for any criminal law measure, as is the case with the whole Albanian legislation, is the Constitution of the Republic of Albania. The other main source for criminal law obligations are international agreements, ratified by the Albanian government. The basic statute in Albanian criminal law is the Penal Code.[238] Besides the Penal Code, another source of criminal law is the Military Penal Code, approved by Law No. 8003 of 28 September 1995.[239] Sanctions in the Penal Code are defined and especially the alternative sanctions. The general principle regarding sentencing states that the sentence shall be determined so that it is in just proportion to the harmfulness and dangerousness of the offence committed, the motives to commit the act and the culpability of the offender as manifested in the offence committed. The general forms of punishment are imprisonment, fine, but there are also other, additional penalties: for instance community service.[240]

346. Persons who have committed crimes or criminal offence can be given one or more of the additional penalties, as provided for by Article 29 to Article 47, of the Penal Code of the Republic of Albania, along with the main sentence. The Law No. 10023, 27 November 2008, added other penalty alternatives to the Penal Code of the Republic of Albania. These alternative penalties are found in Chapter VII, of the Penal Code. The Penal Code was amended by Law No. 98, dated 31 July 2014;

237. *See* Art. 135, para. 12 of the Law 'On Foreigners'.
238. Law No. 7895, 27 Jan. 1995, *Official Journal*, No. 2, p. 23, http://www.hidaa.gov.al/ligje/kodi%20penal%20i%20rsh.pdf. *See* I. Elezi, S. Kacupi, M. Haxhia, *Komentari i Kodit Penal të Republikës së Shqipërisë*, 56 (Tiranë, 2012); I. Elezi, E *drejta penale, Pjesa e përgjithshme*, 79 (Tiranë 2008); I. Elezi, S. Kacupi, M. Haxhia *Komentari i Kodit Penal të Republikës së Shqipërisë*, 178 (Tiranë, 2012); Elezi, I., *E drejta penale, Pjesa e posaçme*, 93 (Botime Erik, 2007).
239. I. Elezi, S. Kacupi, M. Haxhia, *Komentari i Kodit Penal të Republikës së Shqipërisë*, 18 (Botimet Kumi, 2013).
240. Çela, K., Elezi, I. &Peza, G., *E drejta penale e Republikes së Shqipërisë, Pjesa e pergjithshme* III, 16 (Tirane, 1996); I.Salihu, *E drejta penale, Pjesa e Pergjithshme*, 78 (Tirane, 2010); I. Elezi, S. Kacupi, M. Haxhia, *Komentari i Kodit Penal të Republikës së Shqipërisë*, 23 (Tiranë, 2012).

Law No. 176/2014, dated 18 December 2014; Law No. 135/2015, dated 5 December 2015; Law No. 82/2016, dated 25 July 2016; Law No. 36/2017, dated 30 March 2017; and Law No. 89/2017, dated 22 May 2017.[241]

347. The penalty of imprisonment is imposed for a period of five days to twenty-five years.[242] For those who are minors at the time that they committed a crime, i.e., who have not reached the age of 18, the term of imprisonment may not be more than half the punishment provided by law for the offence committed.[243] The Penal Code provides the following additional penalties:[244]: a prohibition to exercise duties as civil servants or in the public service;[245] the seizure of the means used to commit the offence and its benefits;[246] a ban on driving;[247] the removal of decorations and honorary titles;[248] the withdrawal of the right to practice a profession or skill;[249] the withdrawal of the right to exercise executive duties of a legal person(the director, administrator, entrepreneur, liquidator, and any other duties pertaining to the quality of the legal person's representative);[250] a prohibition to stay in one or more administrative units;[251] expulsion from the territory;[252] the publication of court decisions[253] and the loss of parental responsibility.[254] Expulsion and removal from the territory of the Republic of Albania is imposed by Albanian courts on foreigners and stateless persons who commit a crime when it is considered that the presence of that person in the Republic of Albania is no longer desirable. An expulsion decision is revoked by a court, at the request of the subject of the expulsion order, if a person obtains Albanian citizenship.

348. According to Article 1 of Law No. 98/2014, which has amended Article 53/a of the Albanian Penal Code, a sentence of imprisonment for a fixed period not exceeding two years may be conditional (conditional imprisonment), unless the seriousness of the offence, the culpability of the offender or the criminal history of the offender requires the imposition of an unconditional sentence of imprisonment.

349. If an offender is sentenced to a fixed term of unconditional imprisonment of, at the most, one year this sentence will be changed to community service, unless

241. http://www.qbz.gov.al/botime/Kodi%20Penal-2017.pdf.
242. *See* Art. 32 of the Albanian Penal Code, as amended by Law No. 144/2013.
243. *See* Art. 51 of the Albanian Penal Code, as amended by Law No. 144/2013.
244. *See* Art. 30 of the Albanian Penal Code.
245. *See* Art. 35 of the Albanian Penal Code.
246. *See* Art. 36 of the Albanian Penal Code.
247. *See* Art. 37 of the Albanian Penal Code.
248. *See* Art. 38 of the Albanian Penal Code.
249. *See* Art. 39 of the Albanian Penal Code.
250. *See* Art. 40 of the Albanian Penal Code.
251. *See* Art. 41 of the Albanian Penal Code.
252. *See* Art. 42 of the Albanian Penal Code.
253. *See* Art. 43 of the Albanian Penal Code.
254. *See* Art. 43 para. *a* of the Albanian Penal Code.

the unconditional nature of the sentence of imprisonment, earlier community service orders or other weighty reasons bar the imposition of a community service order.[255]

350. Nowadays, the most common form of penalty in the Albanian Penal Code is a fine ... Today fining is the main sentence, for both criminal offences and some crimes. Fining is defined in terms of minimum and maximum fines, which are different for crimes and criminal offences. The Albanian Penal Code divides crimes and criminal offences in separate paragraphs in the same provision. This makes it possible to differentiate between the penalties that can be imposed. Criminal offences are punishable by fine or imprisonment, ranging from five days to two years. The minimum of fine is ALL (Albanian currency) 5,000 and the maximum is ALL 3000,000.

351. Article 297 of the Albanian Penal Code, as amended by Law No. 8279, of 15 January 1998, and by Law No. 9188, of 12 February 2004, states that the illegal crossing of the Albanian borders constitutes a criminal offence that is punishable by a fine or a term of imprisonment up to two years.

352. In addition, Article 298 of the Albanian Penal Code, as amended by Law No. 9188, 12 February 2004, Law No. 9686, dated 26 February 2007, and Law No. 23/2012, dated 1 March 2012, states that housing, accompaniment, making available or the use of vessels, flight or other means of transport or any other assistance to facilitate the illegal crossing of the border of the Republic of Albania or to the illegal entry of a person to another State is punishable with a term of imprisonment ranging from one to four years or a fine of ALL three million to ALL six million. If the assistance is given for profit, the sanctions applicable are: a term of imprisonment ranging from three to seven years or a fine of ALL four million to ALL eight million.

§3. Detention

353. For detention to be permitted under international human rights law, it must be in accordance with the law and not arbitrary. Detention conditions must be humane and the migrant must be entitled to take proceedings before a court so that it can decide on the lawfulness of the detention measure without delay. Where the migrants are victims of unlawful arrest or detention, they have a right to compensation.[256]

354. If the identity of a person or his or her travel route is unclear, it is possible that the authorities put him/her in detention upon arrival in the Republic of Albania.

255. *See* Art. 63 of the Albanian Penal Code.
256. International Covenant on Civil and Political Rights, Arts 9–10. *See also* International Convention on the Protection of All Migrants Workers and Members of their Families, n. 31, Art. 16, which provides additional protections for irregular migrants.

Detention should, however, as a general rule, be used as a measure of last resort. The application of the provisions in the Law 'On Foreigners' or the Law 'On Asylum' on detention may not restrict a detained person's rights any more than necessary. Accordingly, these acts provide other *interim measures* that should be applied prior to the rules on detention. Section IV of the Law 'On Foreigners' deals with these interim measures. Interim measures are taken by the local authority in order to prepare or ensure the enforcement of an expulsion order or to supervise the removal of a person from Albania. Interim measures are taken as alternative measures to detention in closed centre for irregular persons who are the subject of an expulsion measure. They require a case by case assessment of the individual situation and cannot impact on the enforcement of an expulsion order. Interim measures may be taken immediately following the issuing of an expulsion order, but, if appropriate, may be a substitute for a detention measure in a closed centre after the detention measure has been adopted and enforced.[257]

355. The first interim measure that the authorities may adopt is a measure obliging an alien to report at regular intervals to the police or border authorities. The obligation to report can be imposed if this is necessary to establish that a person meets the requirements for entry into the country or, in the alternative to prepare or ensure the enforcement of a decision to remove a person from the country, or to supervise the voluntary departure of a person from the country.

The obligation to report is in force until the person concerned departs from the territory.[258]

356. A second interim measure that can be adopted by the national authorities is to order a person to hand over his or her travel document and travel ticket to the police or border authorities or to give them a contact address where that person may be reached. Any interim measure that is adopted for the purpose of taking possession of these documents has to be approved by an order of the Minister of the Interior. The local authority may, as an interim measure, take possession of a non-national's financial means if and to the amount that is necessary to cover any return costs, if such costs might be incurred. The remainder of a financial guarantee has to be returned immediately to the person concerned the moment that he/she leaves Albanian territory. The Albanian authority responsible for border and migration, instead of other interim measures, or in combination with them, based on a case by case assessment, may request the alien to give a financial guarantee to cover the return costs.

357. A third interim measure that the local authorities may adopt is to restrict the personal freedom of a person. When such an interim measure is adopted the person concerned may not leave a specified territory. This interim measure can be imposed on a person whose return or expulsion cannot be ordered or enforced due to objective reasons, or an obligation entered into by the Republic of Albania under an international agreement; a person who has been issued a residence permit for

257. *See* in particular: Article 115 of the Law 'On Foreigners'.
258. *See* Art. 116 of the Law 'On Foreigners'.

humanitarian grounds; if the time limit for detention in a closed centre has expired and the removal of the person concerned is not possible; if the person concerned cannot be held in a closed centre due to humanitarian grounds or the Albanian public health authorities, recommend the isolation the person for the duration of the incubation period where there is a suspicion that that person is carrying a certain disease, as required by and in accordance with the International Health Regulations.[259]

358. Section V of the Law 'On Foreigners' deals specifically with the detention of a person in a closed centre. According to the law, a closed centre is an administrative institution with a defined security level and designed to restrict the freedom of a person who is the subject of forced removal or expulsion order. As a general rule, the closed centre must meet all of the requirements put in place to ensure human and decent treatment of the detained person as well as that person's fundamental rights. Any medical treatment that is necessary must be provided to those detained. If a person who is detained in a closed detention centre thus requests, the Albanian authorities must take immediate measures to ensure the care of any family member of the detained person who has been left without supervision and/or support.[260]

359. Detention in a closed centre is an administrative measure of last resort. Detention measures are adopted and enforced by the regional State authority responsible for non-nationals. A detention measure can only be imposed on a person who is the subject of an expulsion order and when all possible alternative measures have been exhausted; if an assessment reveals that such measures may not be enforced against the person concerned; or if the person concerned has to be readmitted according to a RA which has been concluded with the Republic of Albania if this is necessary to ensure his/ her return or readmission.[261]

360. If those exceptional case where the person who is the subject of a detention order is an unaccompanied minor, that person has to be accommodated in a State social centre which have been opened specifically for this purpose. In the alternative detention orders can be executed in another centre if this is done in cooperation with an international organization dealing with children, victims of trafficking in human beings or other persons in need. The unaccompanied minor may only be detained in a closed centre if this is in his/ her or his/her family's best interest or if they are housed in a different section than adults. In case of doubt of the age of a detained person, the Albanian authorities may request a specialized State institution to run a DNA-test in order to establish that person's age. If doubts remain concerning the age of a detained person after such a test, it is presumed that the person concerned is a minor. The opinion of a social worker or psychologist is taken into consideration before an unaccompanied minor is detained in a closed centre.[262]

259. *See* Art. 119 of the Law 'On Foreigners'.
260. *See* Art. 120 of the Law 'On Foreigners'.
261. *See* Art. 121 of the Law 'On Foreigners'.
262. *See* Art. 125 of the Law 'On Foreigners'.

361. The duration of detention in a closed centre must be as short as possible, in any case until the completion of legal procedures that will enable the detained person's removal from the territory of the Republic of Albania, within the time limits laid down in the Law 'On Foreigners'. The maximum period of detention in a closed centre is six months. This period can be extended with an additional six-month period, if the removal of the detained person is not yet possible and for one of the following reasons: the person detained refuses to provide data or personal information and the necessary travel documents to enable his/her return or has given false information; the person detained has, in different ways, hindered or prevented his/her return; the there is a delay in the issuing of a travel document or any other document that has been requested by the authorities of another country and is therefore necessary to return a person.[263]

362. Public security reasons may justify detention in a closed centre if the identity or purpose of stay of a person is unclear.[264] The person concerned must be informed in writing in a language of his/her understanding or at the very least in English that his/her detention in a closed centre has been ordered. This decision must specify the reasons justifying detention, the period of detention, the right to legal aid by a lawyer of his/her choice, or an ex officio lawyer as well as the right to communicate with his/her relatives.

363. A detention measure that is executed in a closed centre ends when the person detained is removed from the territory or when the detention period indicated in the detention order has expired. This is even the case if the person concerned has no right to remain. A detention measure also ends if the decision to detain a person in a closed centre is annulled, or when the measure ordering the detention of a person in a closed centre is replaced by another temporary measure as determined by the Law 'On Foreigners'. A person is also released from a closed centre if it is clear from the circumstances that the person concerned cannot be removed by force or if the Albanian courts have ordered the release of that person.[265]

364. In Albania there is only one centre where a person who is the subject of an expulsion order can be detained: Qendra e Mbylljes së Emigrantëve të Parregullt (Kareç, Vorë).

365. The official who is responsible for a decision to place a person in detention has to notify the Judicial District Court of the municipality where the alien is held in detention without delay and in any case no later than the day after that person was placed in detention. The Judicial District Court has to hear a detention case without delay and in any case no later than four days after the day on which the person was placed in detention. If the Judicial District Court rules that there are no grounds to hold a person in detention, that person has to be released immediately.

263. *See* Art. 123, para. 2 of the Law 'On Foreigners'.
264. *See* Art. 121, para. 3 of the Law 'On Foreigners'.
265. *See* Art. 124 of the Law 'On Foreigners'.

If the Judicial District Court orders that the detention measure has to be continued, it must rehear the case no later than two weeks after this decision.[266]

§4. Expulsion and Removal

366. Expulsion means that a person is required to leave the territory of the Republic of Albania and means that that person cannot lawfully re-enter the country while the order is in force. An expulsion decision invalidates any existing leave to enter or to return. According to the Albanian immigration rules, entry clearance and leave to enter is refused to any person whose expulsion has been ordered. Revocation of an expulsion order does not, however, entitle the person concerned to re-enter Albanian territory. It merely renders him/her eligible to apply for admission to Albania under the Immigration Rules. Albanian citizens cannot be expelled or removed from the territory of the Republic of Albania.

367. The Albanian Constitution includes a prohibition of collective expulsion of foreigners. This prohibition reflects the international obligations assumed by Albania and the obligations which follow from Albania's envisaged accession to the EU,[267] Albania has to respect the principle of *non refoulement* in absolute terms, which constitutes, among others, an attempt to codify the relevant case law of the ECtHR regarding Article 3 ECHR. Removal and expulsion of a non-national on personal grounds is allowed if in accordance with the conditions in the Albanian Law 'On Foreigners'. Chapter IV of this Law establishes the Albanian State's prerogative to regulate entry to and expulsion from its territory of non-nationals. When executing this responsibility, the Albanian authorities must take into consideration the evolving case law of the Strasbourg court regarding the protection of those, subject of an expulsion measure.

368. According to the Law 'On Foreigners', the detention regime and the same holds true for all alternative measures which can be adopted vis-à-vis irregular

---

266. *See* Art. 122 of the Law 'On Foreigners'.

267. *See* ultimately Art. 19 of the European Union Charter of Fundamental Rights (EUCFR). *See Explanations Relating to the Charter of Fundamental Rights* (2007/C 303/02), OJ C 303/17, 14 Dec. 2007. These explanations were originally prepared under the authority of the Praesidium of the Convention which drafted the Charter of Fundamental Rights of the European Union. *See* in doctrine O. De Schutter, V. Van Goethem (eds.), *Commentary of the Charter of Fundamental Rights of the European Union*, EU Network of Independent Experts on Fundamental Rights (June 2006); M.T. Gil Bazo, *The Charter of Fundamental Rights of the European Union and the Right to be Granted Asylum in the Union's Law*, 33 (Refugee Survey Quarterly, 27/2008). *See* ECtHR, *Tyrer v. United Kingdom*, Application No. 5856/72, 25 Apr. 1978, para. 31: 'The Court must also recall that the Convention is a living instrument which, as the Commission rightly stressed, must be interpreted in the light of present-day conditions'. *See* further O. Delas, *Le principe de non-refoulement dans la jurisprudence internationale des droits de l'homme*, 123 (Bruxelles, Bruylant, 2011) and M.T. Gil Bazo, *Refugee Status and Subsidiary Protection under EC Law. The EC Qualification Directive and the Right to be Granted Asylum*, 229 (A. Baldaccini, E. Guild & H. Toner, eds., Oxford, Hart, 2007).

migrants should ensure a humane and decent treatment of those detainees[268] and respect the fundamental rights of those individuals detained for the purpose of expulsion. A right to appeal decisions concerning detention in closed facilities is available.[269] Amongst the novelties of the Law 'On Foreigners' are the provisions concerning alternative measures to detain unaccompanied minors (UAMs), victims of human trafficking (VOT). These measures were included in the Law 'On Foreigners' following the recommendations of the UN Special Reporter in this respect.

369. The forced removal of a non-national from Albanian territory by the border and migration authorities is an administrative measure that can only be executed after an individual assessment. Forced removal is only permitted if the following conditions are satisfied. The person concerned: '*a)* has entered the territory of the Republic of Albania irregularly and there is information that he/she will transit irregularly to another country; *b)* has failed to leave the Republic of Albania within the time limit set in a removal order, if there is no objective reason to justify this failure or has re-entered the territory of the Republic of Albania after being removed from that territory before the period in which a prohibition of entry is in force; *c)* has not left the Republic of Albania for a period of up to 60 days after expiry of the period of stay, as indicated in a visa, residence permit or the period of stay foreseen by the Law "On Foreigners" that applies to those who do not need a visa to enter the Republic of Albania if there is a justified reason for the police authorities to assume that the person concerned intends to absconded; *d)* has been readmitted to another country under a Readmission Agreement concluded by the Republic of Albania with a third-country; *e)* has been declared an undesired person according to the terms of Article 9 of the Law "On Foreigners" and his/her presence in Albania is considered to be a threat to public order or security; according to the Albanian legislation; and *f)* has been convicted for a criminal offence which is sentenced to a minimum of three years of imprisonment.'

370. Article 121 of the Law 'On Foreigners' sets out the rules on detention in a closed centre for the purpose of expulsion by the authorities responsible for border and migration affairs. Detention is permitted until the enforcement of the expulsion order. If it is possible to use alternative *interim* measures, as defined in section IV of Chapter IV of the Law 'On Foreigners', such measure shall prevail over detention.

371. A migrant who is in an irregular situation who does not have a claim to international protection can be removed from the Albanian territory by the State. In these situations the State of origin is obliged, under international law, to readmit its own nationals. However, if the irregular migrant does not wish to return voluntarily,

268. Articles 120, 127, 128 Law No. 108/2013.
269. Articles 122, 123, 124 Law No. 108/2013.

forced removal is the alternative. Where there is an agreement regulating joint returns, the central Albanian authorities may cooperate with other countries when returning non-nationals.[270]

372. The person who is to be returned must be informed in writing, in a language that he/she understands, or in English, of the enforcement of an expulsion measure and provided with an explanation of the reasons why the order has been issued, the date and place of enforcement, the manner of transportation to the country of destination and the period of validity of the entry ban. How the expulsion order is actually executed has always got to be approved by the Minister of the Interior.[271]

373. A person who does not possess a travel document must appear in person or accompanied by the competent authorities before the diplomatic representations and consular posts accredited to the Republic of Albania, in order to be issued with such document. If there is no diplomatic representation or consular post of the country of which the person is a national in the Republic of Albania, the central authorities must lodge their request that a travel document is issued by the country of origin of the person concerned or by the diplomatic representation or and a consular post representation that country located in another country. If the diplomatic representation refuses to issue a travel document, the Albanian central authorities must issue a standard travel document as defined in a RA for the purpose of executing the forced removal of the person who is to be expelled. When enforcing these rules, the central authority responsible for border and migration affairs may issue a *laissez passer*, if the person who is to be expelled is not provided with a travel document by the authorities of the country of which he/she is a national.[272]

374. According to Article 113 of the Law 'On Foreigners' there is a category of persons who may not be expelled. This includes a person who has been issued a permanent residence permit, or was born in the Republic of Albania; who entered the Republic of Albania as an unaccompanied minor and has been issued a permanent residence permit; or who has been issued a temporary residence permit and is married to a person who has a permanent residence permit or holds the Albanian nationality. Expulsion is also not possible if there are justified reasons to suspect that the person concerned might be punished to death, subjected to torture, inhuman or degrading treatment or punishment for discriminatory reasons in the country of origin or another country; if the person concerned is an unaccompanied minor and the country of origin, another country or other institutions do not guarantee family

270. *See* Art. 109 para. 7 of the Law 'On Foreigners'. *See* L. Ikonomi, *E drejta migratore*, 132 (Tirana, 2014); IOM, *E drejta migratore,* 183 (Tirane, 2009); *Integrimi i refugjatëve në Shqipëri*, 89 (UNHCR, Tiranë, 2004); *Analiza e mangësive mbi legjislacionin dhe praktikën shqiptare të emigracionit krahasuar me standartet europiane dhe ato ndërkombëtare*, 59 (ONM, Tiranë, 2004); *Fjalorth i terminologjisë migratore*, 12 (ONM, Tirana, 2007).

271. *See* Art. 109 para. 7 of the Law 'On Foreigners'.

272. *See* Art. 109 pars 8 and 9 of the Law 'On Foreigners'.

reunification or proper health care; and if the person concerned is a family member of somebody who has been recognized as a refugee by the authorities of the Republic of Albania.

375. If a person poses a threat to public order and/or security or constitutes a threat to national security that person may, in exceptional cases, be expelled regardless of the fulfilment of the requirements mentioned above.[273]

376. A person cannot be expelled from Albania to a country where there are substantial reasons for believing that he/she faces a real risk of: (a) being unlawfully killed either by the State, or because that State is unable or unwilling to protect him as required by Article 2 ECHR or (b) suffering serious harm or other treatment contrary to Article 3 ECHR. The latter includes torture, as well as treatment or punishment that is degrading because it arouses in the victim a feeling of fear, anguish or inferiority capable of humiliating and debasing him, and possibly breaking his physical and moral resistance. Severe discrimination based on race, sex or other grounds may also constitute degrading treatment within the meaning of Article 3 ECHR.

377. According to the Albanian Immigration Rules and guidance, Article 3 ECHR also prevents the State from expelling a person who is suffering an illness that has reached such a critical stage (i.e., imminent death) that it would constitute inhuman treatment to deprive him of the care he/she is currently receiving in Albania. The logic is that sending a person to his/her home country under these circumstances would amount to an early death. However, if there is care available in the home country that ensures that the person will die in dignity, expulsion is permitted.[274]

378. To invoke Article 5 ECHR successfully the person who is the subject of an expulsion decision will have to establish that there are substantial grounds to believe that there is a real risk of a flagrant breach of the rights derived from this provision in the country to which he/she will be sent. Likewise, to successfully invoke Article 6 ECHR, the person subject of an expulsion decision must establish that there are substantial grounds for believing that there is a real risk: that there will be a fundamental breach of the principle of a fair trial as guaranteed by that provision.[275] This means that it will have to be established that there will be a miscarriage of justice that in itself constitutes a flagrant violation of the person's fundamental rights.

273. *See* Art. 113 para. 2 of the Law 'On Foreigners'. *See* L. Ikonomi, *E drejta migratore*, 145 (Tirana, 2014); IOM, *E drejta migratore*, 184 (Tiranë, 2009); *Integrimi i refugjatëve në Shqipëri*, 89 (UNHCR, Tiranë, 2004); *Analiza e mangësive mbi legjislacionin dhe praktikën shqiptare të emigracionit krahasuar me standartet europiane dhe ato ndërkombëtare*, 57 (ONM, Tiranë, 2004); *Fjalorth i terminologjisë migratore*, 70 (ONM, Tirana, 2007).

274. *See* ECtHR, *Bensaid v UK*, 2001, No. 44599/98, p. 82.

275. *See*, for example, UK House of Lords, *RB (Algeria) v. Secretary of State for the Home Department*, 2009, para. 10, 136.

Article 6 ECHR may also be invoked successfully by a person who has an outstanding civil claim in Albania for private law damages, e.g., a personal injury claim, or is a prospective party to such a civil claim which he/she is actively pursuing.

379. Article 8 ECHR may bar the execution of an expulsion decision if expulsion amounts to an interference with private or family life. In immigration cases a person's private life in Albania is assessed by considering the ties which that person has established with the Republic of Albania during the period that he/she was established in that country in terms of friends, education, work and leisure activities. Article 8 ECHR may also be engaged where the person claims that to expel him from Albania will separate him/her from his family resident in Albania. Expulsion would, under these circumstances, constitute a breach of his right to respect for family life in Albania. In deportation cases where the consequence of the decision may be the separation of a child from his/her parent(s), the decision maker should be prepared to consider hearing the views of the child directly, if this is requested or deemed necessary in the interest of the child.

380. The Albanian legislation provides an improved appeal mechanism against removal orders[276] and the expulsion[277] of foreigners. It promotes the voluntary enforcement of a removal order where irregular foreigners are concerned.[278] Article 110 of the Law 'On Foreigners' provides for a right to appeal an expulsion order issued by the authority responsible for border and migration affairs, as provided for by law. Until appeal proceedings are completed, the person appealing an expulsion decision has to be held in custody in accordance with the conditions that apply to alternative measures of supervision or detention in a closed centre, as provided for in an order that is issued specifically for this purpose.

276. Article 107 Law No. 108/2013.
277. Article 110 Law No. 108/2013.
278. Article 108 Law No. 108/2013.

Chapter 2. Sanctions Against Persons Helping Irregular Entry and Residence

381. This chapter deals with the legal framework on criminal measures that apply to trafficking and smuggling to and the facilitating of irregular entry into the territory of the Republic of Albania. This issue is at the nexus of migration and criminal law. The system of criminal law in Albania, as in other countries, especially the Member States of the EU is a central part of a complex and important part of the balance of the powers of the authorities, on the one side, and the rights of the citizen, on the other.

382. In developing policies to combat human trafficking and smuggling to Albania, both the international obligations and the obligations which follow from EU law have been considered. Article 29 of the Treaty on EU, that is concerned with the achievement of a high level of safety within the Area of Freedom, Security and Justice, requires the Member State to develop common action in the field of criminal law amongst themselves with a view to in prevent and combat crime, including the trafficking in persons. Council Directive 2004/81/EC of 29 April 2004 on the residence permit issued to third-country nationals who are victims of trafficking in human beings or who have been the subject of an action to facilitate illegal immigration, who cooperate with the competent authorities[279]was used by the Albanian authorities when they adopted the Law 'On Foreigners'.

383. The Council of Europe is the other organization that has adopted legislation that governs the fight against trafficking and smuggling of human beings. The main legal instrument adopted by the Council of Europe is the Convention Against Trafficking in Human Beings, that was ratified by Albania by Law No. 9642, dated 20 November 2006 and entitled: *'Për ratifikimin e Konventës së Këshillit të Evropës 'Për masat kundër Trafikimit të Qenieve Njerëzore'.*[280]

384. In recent years, irregular migration has increased considerably in recent years. This is reflected in the increased number of children and women who are trafficked. In the context of universal application of human rights, trafficking in human beings is an eminent modern phenomenon. To tackle this problem, Albania has signed RAs with a considerable number of third States. These agreements facilitate the readmission of persons who have been trafficked to those States or allow those people to transit the territory of those States.[281]

---

279. O.J. EC 2004, L 261/19.

280. *See* I. Zajmi, *A e kalon legjislacioni penal shqiptar për trafikimin e qenieve njerëzore pragun e standarteve ndërkombëtare?, Kuadri ligjor mbi trafikimin e qënieve njerëzore në Shqipëri dhe sfidat e hasura në praktikën gjyqësore,* 24 (Shkolla e Magjistratures, Tiranë, 2013) http://www.albania.iom.int/publications/research/School%20of%20Magistrate%20study%20on%20CT%20issues-ALB.pdf. (accessed 15 Jan. 2018).

281. Albania has signed a readmission agreement with the following countries: Republic of Italy, on 11 Sep. 1997; Switzerland, on 2 Feb. 2000; the Republic of Hungary, on 20 Mar. 2001, Belgium, on 17 Apr. 2002, the Republic of Bulgaria, on 07 Jun. 2002, the Republic of Romania, on 07 Jun. 2002, the United Kingdom of Great Britain and Northern Ireland, on 15 Oct. 2003 (entry into force: 16

§1. HUMAN SMUGGLING

385. The key international instrument dealing with the smuggling of migrants is the UN Convention against Transnational organized Crime ('Smuggling Protocol') and the Protocol against the Smuggling of Migrants by Land, Sea and Air, Supplementing the UN Convention.[282] Smuggling and trafficking differ from each other in the sense that the smuggling of a person includes the provision of a service, though illegal, to people who consciously buy the service in order to enter a country of which they are not a national. Irregular entry is defined as crossing borders without complying with the necessary requirements for legal entry into the receiving State.[283] Smuggling of migrants is characterized by a commercial transaction between the smuggler and the smuggled, involving a financial or other material gain for the former. Smuggling involves the crossing of an international border that is the irregular entry of non-nationals into or the transit to the destination State.

386. The smuggling of migrants often involves serious abuse and exploitation, both during the smuggling process and on arrival in the State of destination. Under international human rights law any State, in this case Albania, id obliged to take steps to prevent smuggling and to protect those who have been or may be smuggled. The power to manage migration must, however, be exercised with full respect for the human rights and freedoms of non-nationals, which are found in a wide range of human rights instruments and customary international law, regardless whether those persons are in a regular or an irregular situation. The specific purpose of international law is to prevent and combat the smuggling of migrants, as well as to promote cooperation amongst States Parties to the end, while protecting the rights of smuggled migrants.[284] Regardless of the irregular status of smuggled migrants, the Republic of Albania is obliged to ensure that their basic needs are met.

Aug. 2005), the Republic of Croatia, on 28 Jan. 2003 (entry into force on 15 Jun. 2005) and the Council of Europe, on 14 Apr. 2005. An agreement was signed on 27 Feb. 2006 by the Governments of the Republic of Albania and the Republic of Greece to provide protection and assistance to child victims of trafficking. An agreement between the Government of the Republic of Albania and the Swiss Federal Council on Police Cooperation and the Fight against Crime was signed on 21 Sep. 2005.

282. Protocol against the Smuggling of Migrants by Land, Sea and Air, Supplementing the United Nations Convention against Transnational Organized Crime, opened for signature: 15 Nov. 2000, 2241 UNTS 507, that entered into force on 28 Jan. 2004. In late 2011 there were 129 State Parties. The Republic of Albania ratified the Convention on 11 Jul. 2002 by Law No. 8920 and the Protocol on 20 Nov. 2006 by Law No. 9642 'Për ratifikimin e Konventës së Këshillit të Evropës 'Për masat kundër trafikimit të qenieve njerëzore'. *See also* I. Zajmi, *A e kalon legjislacioni penal shqiptar për trafikimin e qenieve njerëzore pragun e standarteve ndërkombëtare?, Kuadri ligjor mbi trafikimin e qënieve njerëzore në Shqipëri dhe sfidat e hasura në praktikën gjyqësore,* 24 (Shkolla e Magjistratures, Tiranë, 2013) http://www.albania.iom.int/publications/research/School%20of%20Magistrate%20study%20on%20CT%20issues-ALB.pdf. (accessed 15 Jan. 2018).

283. A. Koca, *Trafikimi i qënieve njerëzore. Këndvështrimi juridik', Kuadri ligjor mbi trafikimin e qënieve njerëzore në Shqipëri dhe sfidat e hasura në praktikën gjyqësore, 5* (Shkolla e Magjistratures, Tirane, 2013), http://www.albania.iom.int/publications/research/School%20of%20Magistrate%20study%20on%20CT%20issues-ALB.pdf. (accessed 15 Jan. 2018).

284. *See* A. Koca, *Një analizë krahasuese e ligjit dhe procedurës mbi Trafikimin e Njerëzve,* 55 (Konica 2006).

387. In 2011, Albania developed a new National Action Plan on the Fight against Trafficking in Human Beings in general and a National Action Plan on the Fight against Trafficking in Children and the Protection of Children, Victims of Trafficking 2014–2017. Actually Albania is developing a cross sectional Strategy on the Fight against Organized Crime, Trafficking and Terrorism for the period 2013–2020 which includes provisions on trafficking in human beings and trafficking in children.

388. The above-mentioned provisions complement the vision and specific provisions in the National Referral Mechanism for Identification, Referral and Assistance of VOTs (NRM). The latter, initially developed in 2005, was renewed in July 2012 [285] to enable the participation of more actors from the central government and civil society active in the assistance to VOTs. The NRM agreement and its Standard Operating Procedures (SOPs)[286] regulate the roles and responsibilities of all actors involved in the identification, referral, protection of and assistance to (potential) victims of trafficking in Albania.

§2. Human Trafficking

389. Trafficking is commonly and notoriously known as a criminal practice that takes place in the context of sex trade: woman and children are taken from one State to another, or moved within a State for the purpose of sexual exploitation. A general pattern of trafficking from poorer to wealthier countries is evident. Trafficking is a process that usually involves several actors. Once a victim is under the control of the traffickers, he/she is transported to the destination State, often through transit countries.[287] This requires the organization of passports and visa, including the forging of documents, or being smuggled across borders.

390. Albanian legislation on human trafficking was changed during the transition years. These changes are related to the mobility of organized crime and trafficking in the early 2000s. The main destination is Eastern and Central Europe. Albania has been, and unfortunately still is to be considered a source country for men, women and children subjected to trafficking in persons, specifically forced prostitution and forced labour. Albanians are not only victims of forced labour and sex trafficking in Albania, but also in Greece, Macedonia, Kosovo and Western

285. The revised text was signed on 15 Jun. 2012.
286. Adopted by Council of Ministers Decision No. 582 on 27 Jul. 2011.
287. S. Dollani, *Çështje të praktikës gjyqësore në lidhje me krimin e trafikimit të femrave, Kuadri ligjor mbi trafikimin e qënieve njerëzore në Shqipëri dhe sfidat e hasura në praktikën gjyqësore, 15* (Shkolla e Magjistratures, Tirane, 2013), http://www.albania.iom.int/publications/research/School%20of%20Magistrate%20study%20on%20CT%20issues-ALB.pdf. (accessed 15 Jan. 2018); A. Koca, *Trafikimi i qënieve njerëzore. Këndvështrimi juridik', Kuadri ligjor mbi trafikimin e qënieve njerëzore në Shqipëri dhe sfidat e hasura në praktikën gjyqësore, 5* (Shkolla e Magjistratures, Tir ane, 2013), http://www.albania.iom.int/publications/research/School%20of%20Magistrate%20study%20on%20CT%20issues-ALB.pdf. (accessed 15 Jan. 2018).

Europe. Approximately half of the victims referred for care in Albania were Albanian nationals, mainly women and girls subjected to conditions of forced prostitution, working in the most important Albanian cities Tirana, Durres, Vlore etc. Children are primarily exploited for begging and other forms of forced labour. There is evidence that Albanian men have been subjected to conditions of forced labour in the agricultural sector of Greece and other neighbouring countries.

391. The Albanian government has made significant efforts to combat human trafficking. The government has improved its capacity to identify, protect and reintegrate trafficking victims. It has also successfully prosecuted some sex trafficking offenders, imposing significant penalties. There are serious concerns, however, about the protection available for victims who have testified against their traffickers. The government has implemented a Nation Referral Mechanism and conducted meetings with relevant stakeholders to improve its functioning which has improved the protection of these victims. In addition, it has adopted several National Strategies during these two decades[288] and several laws,[289] amending the main articles in the Albanian Penal Code, such as Articles 110/a, 114, 128/b, 297 and 298.[290]

392. In terms of legislation in the area of trafficking in human beings and exploitation for labour purpose, it is important to highlight the following developments: The Law 'For the Protection of the Witnesses and Justice Collaborators' (2004) was amended by Law No. 10173, dated 22 October 2009. Article 28 of this law provides detailed rules on the protection of VOTs who are witnesses and justice collaborators. These rules are further specified in an Instruction of the Minister of Interior. In addition, a specific 'Law on the Prevention and the Fight against Organized Crime and Trafficking through Preventive Measures against Assets' (No. 10192) was approved on 3 December 2009. This law establishes the Agency for the Administration of Assets Confiscated and Sequestered by Organized Crime (including trafficking in human beings), which is part of the Ministry of Finance. Law No. 10192 is a novelty in the fight against trafficking as it foresees the establishment of a Special Fund for the compensation of victims of trafficking.

393. Albania has adopted a Strategy on the Fight Against Trafficking in Persons and Its Action Plan (2014–2017) which was are the roadmap for the anti-trafficking action. Regarding the current situation on human trafficking in Albania, it has made measurable progress in recent years in relation to the trafficking of human beings

288. *See* National Strategy on Preventing Human Trafficking, available at: http://www.crca.al/sites/default/files/publications/Strategjia%20kunder%20trafikimit%20te%20femijeve%20e%20miratuar%20me%20vkm.pdf. (accessed 21 Jan. 2018).
289. Law No. 9205 dated 15 Mar. 2004, 'Për mbrojtjen e dëshmitarëve dhe bashkëpunëtorëve të drejtësisë'; The Law No. 10023, dated 27 November 2008, that, amongst others added other penalty alternatives to the Albanian Penal Code.
290. L. Hasneziri, *Analiza juridiko-penale te veprës penale të 'trafikimit të personave', dhe problematika e hasur ne lidhje me kualifikimin e drejtë ligjor të kësaj vepre penale, Kuadri ligjor mbi trafikimin e qënieve njerëzore në Shqipëri dhe sfidat e hasura në praktikën gjyqësore* 34 (Tirane, 2013) http://www.albania.iom.int/publications/research/School%20of%20Magistrate%20study%20on%20CT%20issues-ALB.pdf (accessed 22 Mar. 2018).

due to the joint and comprehensive efforts of state and non-state agencies, and the continuous support of partner organizations – international and civil society ones.

394. The Penal Code of Albania was amended by Law No. 144/2013. The new provisions inserted into the Penal Code by this Law have made 'internal trafficking' in human beings a criminal offence. In addition, the benefits accrued from or the use of the services provided by trafficked persons, as well as exploitation following trafficking is now punishable by the law. The law recognizes that all forms of exploitation of children, including forced labour and begging, are a criminal offence punishable by the law. In particular, Article 124/b of the Penal Code, entitled 'Maltreatment of the Minor,[291] makes all situations in which a minor is forced to work to secure money for the family or to beg, punishable with imprisonment from two to five years (initially up to four years). If there has been serious harm to the minor's health or the minor has died, a sentence of imprisonment from ten to twenty years can be imposed. Article 128/b of the Penal Code, entitled 'Trafficking of Minors',[292] penalizes the trafficking of a minor with a term of imprisonment ranging from ten to twenty years (initially from seven to fifteen years and a fine). In addition, according to Article 114 of the Penal Code exploitation for the purpose of prostitution is punished with a term of imprisonment ranging from two to five years. When minors are exploited for the purpose of prostitution, the term of imprisonment ranges from seven to fifteen years.

395. According to Albanian law: 'The recruitment, transport, transfer, hiding or reception of persons through threat, the use of force or other forms of coercion, kidnapping, fraud, abuse of office or taking advantage of the social, physical or psychological condition of the victim, the giving or receipt of payments or benefits in order to get the consent of a person who controls another person, for one of the following purposes: exploitation, prostitution of others or other forms of sexual exploitation, forced services or work, slavery or treatment similar to slavery, the putting to use or transplanting of organs, as well as other forms of exploitation, are punishable with a term of imprisonment ranging from five to fifteen years and with a fine of two million to five million ALL '.[293] The organization, management and financing of the trafficking of persons are punishable with a term of imprisonment that ranges from seven to fifteen years and with a fine ranging from ALL four million to ALL six million.

396. In addition, when these offences are committed in collaboration or more than once the term of imprisonment is no less than fifteen years and can be subject of a fine ranging from ALL six to ALL eight million. This is also the case if the victim is maltreated or acts through the use of physical or psychological force, or suffers serious consequences to his/her health. If the offence has resulted in the

291. Article 2, added by Law No. 9859, dated 21 Jan. 2008, and changed by Law No. 23/2012, 1 March 2012.
292. Amended by Law No. 9188, dated 12 Feb. 2004, Art. 3; added by Law No. 9859, dated 21 Jan. 2008, Art. 3.
293. *See* Art. 110, para. 1 of the Albanian Penal Code.

death of the victim, the offence is punishable with a term of imprisonment of no less than twenty years or life sentence. In addition a fine ranging of from ALL seven million to ALL ten million can be imposed on the perpetrator. If the criminal offence is committed through the utilization of a State function or public service, the term of imprisonment and the fines are increased by one fourth of the punishment given.[294]

397. The recruitment, transport, transfer, hiding or reception of *women* through the use of threats, force or other forms of coercion, kidnapping, fraud, abuse of office or taking advantage of the social, physical or psychological condition or the giving or receipt of payments or benefits, in order to get the consent of a person who controls another person, with the purpose of exploitation of prostitution of others or other forms of sexual exploitation, forced services or work, slavery or forms similar to slavery, using or transplanting organs, as well as other forms of exploitation, are punished with imprisonment of from seven to fifteen years and with a fine of from ALL three million to ALL six million. The organization, management and financing of the trafficking of woman are punished with imprisonment from ten to fifteen years and with a fine of from ALL five million to ALL seven million.[295]

398. Inducing prostitution, mediating or gaining from these offences are punishable with a fine or up to five years of imprisonment.[296] When sexual exploitation involves: (1) minors; (2) a group of persons; (3) close relatives, i.e., such as in-laws, a person with whom the perpetrator has a custodial relation or if an official relation is taken advantage of; (4) by deception, coercion, violence or by taking advantage of the physical or mental incapability of a person; (5) against a person who has been forced or coerced to exercise prostitution outside the territory of the Republic of Albania; and (6) it is committed with accomplices, more than once or by persons who hold State or public functions/duties it is an offence punishable with a term of imprisonment ranging from seven up to fifteen years.[297]

399. The recruitment, transport, transfer, hiding or reception *of minors*[298]for the purpose of exploitation for prostitution or other forms of sexual exploitation, forced services or work, slavery or acts similar to slavery, putting to use or transplanting organs, as well as other forms of exploitation, are punished with a term of imprisonment ranging from seven to fifteen years or with a fine ranging from ALL four million to ALL six million.[299]

---

294. *See* Art. 110, para. 4 of the Albanian Penal Code.
295. *See* Art. 114/b, para. 1 of the Albanian Penal Code.
296. *See* Art. 114 of the Albanian Penal Code.
297. *See* Art. 114/a of the Albanian Penal Code.
298. Dh. Haveri, Trafikimi i të miturve. Problemet e hasura në praktikën gjyqësore, Kuadri ligjor mbi trafikimin e qënieve njerëzore në Shqipëri dhe sfidat e hasura në praktikën gjyqësore', Shkolla e Magjistratures, 62 (Tirane, 2013) http://www.albania.iom.int/publications/research/School%20of%20Magistrate%20study%20on%20CT%20issues-ALB.pdf. (accessed 21 Jan. 2018).
299. *See* Art. 128/b of the Albanian Penal Cade, entitled 'Trafficking of Minors' which, in addition, states that: 'The organization, management and financing of the trafficking of minors is punished with imprisonment of ten to twenty years or with a fine ranging from six million to eight million ALL.

400. Albania has taken some important steps to improve its efforts to identify and protect victims of trafficking.[300] The government funds and operates a reception centre that houses both victims of trafficking and irregular foreign migrants identified as such within the Albanian territory. When placed in this high-security reception centre, a victim's freedom of movement is often restricted. Regrettably, in some cases the State police officers do not provide real and maximum protection to trafficking victims when testifying against their traffickers, forcing victims to rely exclusively on Non-Governmental Organization (NGOs) for their protection. The National Coordinator for Victims Trafficking's office manages regional anti-trafficking working groups composed of the relevant stakeholders. These working groups reportedly do not always include civil society actors and do not always efficiently address trafficking cases brought to their attention. In November 2009, the government passed legislation to improve the registration process for new births and individuals in the Roma community, as the previous cumbersome procedures rendered unregistered Albanians and ethnic Roma highly vulnerable to trafficking.[301] The government of Albania provides free professional training to victims, and micro-credit loans to start private businesses, and integrates victims into schools.

401. Analysing official data on trafficked persons identified as being from Albania, and other information obtained from anti-trafficking stakeholders on the ground, we conclude that Albania remains predominantly a source country for the trafficking of men, women and children who are subjected to sex exploitation and forced labour. Many Albanian victims (adults and minors) are subjected to and exploited for the purpose of prostitution, internally, to neighbouring countries and beyond, especially to Belgium, France, Germany, Ireland, Italy, the Netherlands, Switzerland and the United Kingdom. Victims frequently accept fraudulent offers of employment in waitressing, bartending, dancing or singing especially in Kosovo, Greece and Macedonia.

As reported over the past five years, Albania is a source, transit, and destination country for men, women, and children subjected to sex trafficking and forced labour. Albanian women and children are subjected to sex trafficking and forced labour within the country, especially during the tourist season. Traffickers use false promises, such as marriage or employment offers, to force victims into sex trafficking. Traffickers increasingly use social media to recruit victims. Children are commonly

---

When this offence is committed in collaboration or more than once, or is accompanied by mistreatment and forcing the victim accusing physical or psychological force, or has serious consequences for the victim's health, it is punished with imprisonment of no less than fifteen years or with a fine ranging from six million to eight million ALL. When the offence has led to the death of the victim it is punished with imprisonment of no less than twenty years or with life imprisonment, or a fine of from 8 million to 10 million ALL'.

300. *See*, in particular, S. Simoni, *Trajtimi i viktimave të trafikimit si dëshmitarë gjatë procesit gjyqësor. Mundësitë ligjore për kompensimin e viktimave të trafikimit dhe nevoja për ndryshime ligjore. Probleme të hasura në praktikën gjyqësore, Kuadri ligjor mbi trafikimin e qënieve njerëzore në Shqipëri dhe sfidat e hasura në praktikën gjyqësore,* 75 (Shkolla e Magjistratures, Tiranë, 2013).

301. *See*, in particular, *Trafficking in Persons Report, 2010,* available on http://www.state.gov/j/tip/rls/tiprpt/2010/142759.htm.

forced to beg or perform other types of forced labour, such as selling small items. Albanian children, mainly from the Romani community, are exploited in Turkey for seasonal work.[302]

402. Other than the reported legislative developments in the area of child exploitation and child protection, the Penal Code still does not recognize forced child labour exploitation as a form of trafficking that amounts to a criminal offence, despite the fact that Albania has ratified the Palermo Protocol, which clearly defines this form of exploitation as trafficking in human beings. The Albanian authorities have frequently expressed their concern regarding the legal framework that regulates trafficking in human beings as the rules are found in various legal acts. Some of the recommendations made to the Albania government are: (a) to implement the law that exempts victims from penalties for unlawful acts committed as a direct result of being subjected to trafficking, particularly sex trafficking victims exploited in prostitution; (b) to train police, labour inspectors, and other frontline officials on proactive identification of victims; (c) to continue to vigorously investigate, prosecute, and convict traffickers under Articles 110(a) and 128(b) of the Penal Law; (d) to establish sustainable funding mechanisms for mobile units operated by law enforcement and civil society groups to identify victims; (e) to improve the protection of victims against threats and intimidation during court proceedings by facilitating participation in the witness protection programme and expanding training for prosecutors dealing with victim witnesses; (f) to increase funding of NGO-run shelters for trafficking victims and provide funding on a regular basis; (g) to improve the capacity of border and migration police to screen irregular migrants for trafficking indicators; and (h) to increase efforts to screen street children for signs of trafficking.

302. The government has maintained victim protection efforts. The government and NGOs identified ninty-five trafficking and potential trafficking victims, compared to 109 in 2015. Of these, 55 were adults and 44 were children (compared to 61 adults and 48 children in 2015), 11 were male and 84 were female (compared 22 male victims and 87 female victims in 2015), and eight were foreigners (compared to four foreign victims in 2015). Sixty-two were identified as potential victims and thirty-three were officially identified as victims, a status granted after a joint interview held by representatives from both law enforcement and State social services. The law guarantees equal services for both potential victims and officially recognized victims. *See* https://www.state.gov/documents/organization/271341.pdf (accessed 13 Feb. 2018).

Part VI. Legal Remedies and Procedural Safeguards

Chapter 1. Legal Remedies in Case of Refusal of Right to Enter, Stay or Reside

§1. Administrative Decisions on Entry

403. A refusal to grant permission to enter concerns, on the one hand, persons who are denied the right to enter Albania at the borders of the territory of the Republic of Albania and, on the other hand, persons either in or outside the territory of Albania whose application to be granted the right to enter Albania legally are refused. The latter instance includes decisions on visas, as well as decisions on international protection taken in the context of an asylum procedure. The Law 'On Foreigners' does not have a special section dedicated to legal remedies which are available to contest ae refusal to grant permission to enter, stay or reside. The available legal remedies are rather found in several articles found in that act.[303]

404. There are several reasons why a foreigner can be refused the right to enter Albania. Article 9 of the Law 'On Foreigners' mentions the situations where the alien cannot enter stay or reside in Albania. In particular, there are individuals who are declared non grata persons and by the Albanian law on immigration. A person can be declared persona non grata by the Minister of the Interior, if this is justified by major interests of the State, the Constitutional and legal order, national security and public order. Any decision to declare a person 'non grata' has to be motivated. A persona can be declared persona non grata is he/she has committed acts or has propagated against the sovereignty of the Republic of Albania, its national security, Constitutional or public order or security; is a member of a terrorist organization or supports and undertakes anarchist acts threatening the rule of law; is a threat to the

303. *See*, for example, Arts 9, 29, 36, 40, 46, 60, 63 and 68 of the Law 'On Foreigners'. *See* L. Ikonomi, *E drejta migratore*, 149 (Tirana, 2014); IOM, *E drejta migratore*, 184 (Tirane, 2009); *Integrimi i refugjatëve në Shqipëri*, 35 (UNHCR, Tiranë, 2004); *Analiza e mangësive mbi legjislacionin dhe praktikën shqiptare të emigracionit krahasuar me standartet europiane dhe ato ndërkombëtare*, 49 (ONM, Tiranë, 2004); *Fjalorth i terminologjisë migratore*, 89 (ONM, Tirana, 2007); *Kthimi i emigranteve te parregullt ne Shqiperi, nevojat dhe modalitetet*, ONM (Tirane, 2006): 52; *Përmbledhje aktesh juridike në fushën e migracionit*, 48 (ACIL/ONM, Tiranë, 2005); *Kthimi dhe ripranimi: Rasti i Shqiperise, sfidat dhe nevojat*, IOM (Tirane, 2006): 23.

country or poses a threat to the relations of the Republic of Albania with other countries; is suspected of entering and staying in the territory of the Republic of Albania to commit a crime or an act which poses a threat to the Republic of Albania; is involved in organized crime, trafficking in human beings, drugs, or any other form of illicit trafficking, based on the information received by the institutions responsible for national security.[304]

405. A person can be declared 'persona non grata' for a period of no less than five years from the date of declaration. During this period that person is not permitted to enter or stay in the Republic of Albania. The procedure of declaring an alien persona non grata by the Minister of the Interior and the sample of the Order of the Minister declaring an alien persona non grata shall be approved by Instruction of the Minister of the Interior. The Minister of the Interior, upon request of the person who has been declared persona non grata, can *only* reconsider an application for entry permission, a visa or residence permit, if that person has committed one of the above-mentioned acts when he/she was a minor.[305]

406. A refusal to grant entry permission is a negative decision that can be appealed.[306] The law does not specify the format for such a decision. In the case that a decision to e entry permission is adopted by the BMP at the border, the person refused entry permission receives an Order of Refusal to grant entry permission which states the reason(s) why entry permission was not granted. There is a right to appeal a decision to refuse entry permission which has to be addressed to the Directory of Border and Migration which is a unit in the Albanian Police force. Both the procedure to withhold entry permission and the template for the Order of Refusal has to be approved by Instruction of the Minister of Interior.

407. There is a list of circumstances that justify a decision to withhold entry permission in Article 10 of the Law 'On Foreigners'. This list includes the situations mentioned in paragraphs 43–44 in which there is no right to enter Albania. The Border and Migration Police have to withhold permission to enter, unless one of the general conditions for entry is not satisfied,[307] irrespective whether or not a visa has been issued, if the terms for issuing a visa have changed. The Border and Migration Police have also got to withhold entry permission if the terms for issuing a residence permit have changed or if the residence permit has been cancelled as required by the Law 'On Foreigners'.[308]

304. *See* Art. 9 paras 1 and 2 of the Law 'On Foreigners'.
305. *See* Art. 9 para. 3 of the Law 'On Foreigners'.
306. *See* Art. 10 para. 4 of the Law 'On Foreigners'.
307. Exemption from the requirements of letter (c), point 1 of Art. 6 of this law shall apply to those who: (a) reside legally in the Republic of Albania and are provided with residence permit; (b) are aliens who apply for asylum or temporary protection; (c) are provided with type 'D' visa; (ç) are provided with diplomatic passports.
308. The authority responsible for border and migration in the case of an entry refusal for the reasons mentioned in Art. 10 of the Law 'On Aliens'law shall place in the passport or the travel document of the alien, equivalent to the passport, the symbol determined by instruction of the Minister of the Interior and it shall notify the person, in a language of his or her understanding, through an act of

408. A refusals to grant entry permission is a negative administrative decisions on a visa application if the applicant: presents a false travel document; fails to prove the purpose of entry or does not satisfy entry conditions; fails to provide proof of secure means of support for the duration of stay in the Republic of Albania and return to the country of habitual residence; has exceeded the time limits of stay in the Republic of Albania; has stayed 90 days within 180 days in the territory of the Republic of Albania based on the issued visa; is the subject of an entry ban; is considered to be a threat to public security or public health; or fails to provide evidence of the authenticity of the submitted statements or fails to guarantee his/her departure from the territory of the Republic of Albania within the time limit indicated in the visa.[309]

409. Refusals to grant entry permission are adopted as a negative decision on a visa application. An appeal can be addressed to the competent authorities within the Ministry of Foreign Affairs. If the decision has been appealed, a new application for a visa can be made when this procedure has been completed. If a decision to refuse entry permission has not been appealed a new application for a visa can be made three months after the date of the decision to refuse the visa.

410. The administrative act to refuse an application for a visa is notified to the applicant, using the form approved by joint instruction of the Minister of Foreign Affairs and the Minister of the Interior and Director of State Intelligence Service.

411. An appeal against a decision to issue a visa can be made both on grounds of fact and law. Appeals must be made in writing and addressed to the competent court within thirty days of notice of the appealed decision.

412. Ordinary remedies are available in relation to all decisions in which the application is refused, – for instance decisions taken in the asylum procedure. The competent authority for the asylum procedure is the Office for Refugees. An asylum seeker has to lodge an appeal against a decision within fifteen days, starting with the day he/she receives the decision, with the National Commission for Refugees. The latter handles this appeal with priority in order to reach a final decision within the shortest possible period of time. The registration of an appeal suspends the decision of the Office for Refugees; the asylum seeker can remain in Albania for the

---

refusal, which template shall be approved by instruction of the Minister of the Interior. The alien, who has entered into the Republic of Albania and who, because of different reasons, may not be returned immediately, shall reside in the area determined for this category of persons until the arrival of the Travel Company or carrier that transported the alien.

309. *See* L. Ikonomi, *E drejta migratore*, 159 (Tirana, 2014); IOM, *E drejta migratore,* 184 (Tirane, 2009); *Analiza e mangësive mbi legjislacionin dhe praktikën shqiptare të emigracionit krahasuar me standartet europiane dhe ato ndërkombëtare*, 49 (ONM, Tiranë, 2004); *Fjalorth i terminologjise migratore*, ONM (Tirane, 2007): 89; *Kthimi i emigranteve te parregullt ne Shqiperi, nevojat dhe modalitetet,* ONM (Tirane, 2006): 52; *Përmbledhje aktesh juridike në fushën e migracionit*, 49 (ACIL/ONM, Tiranë, 2005); *Kthimi dhe ripranimi: Rasti i Shqiperise, sfidat dhe nevojat*, IOM (Tirane, 2006): 24.

duration of the appeal proceedings. Before adopting a decision, the National Commission for Refugees conducts a hearing with the asylum seeker, if it cannot reach a positive decision based on the information contained in the file. The National Commission for Refugees adheres to the same principles that guide the procedure of the Office for Refugees. The National Commission for Refugees has to adopt a decision no later than forty-five days from the day that the appeal was filed. The motivated decision of the National Commission for Refugees is delivered to the asylum seeker through the Office for Refugees. The decision of the National Commission for Refugees is final.

§2. Administrative Decisions on the Right to Reside

413. Administrative review is a non-statutory scheme. Thus police powers are solely regulated by in the rules in the migration guidance. Only one request can be made and this has to be done within fifteen days of the decision concerning the right to reside. Administrative review is usually completed as soon as possible. The applicant is notified of the decision in writing.

414. Administrative decisions on the right to reside concern, first, decisions on applications for a residence permit made within the territory of the Republic of Albania and, second, decisions on applications for a renewal of a residence permit that will allow the applicant to continue his/her stay in Albania.

415. According to the Albanian Immigration Rules there is a right to appeal any of the listed 'immigration decisions'. Where multiple decisions would result in multiple rights of appeal, these are subsumed into one appeal. All appealable grounds, as a general rule, can and should be raised in the appeal proceedings. Most, but not all, can be exercised by the appellant whilst in Albania.

416. A decision to refuse to issue or renew a residence permit or to annul a residence permit is communicated to the applicant in writing according to the format approved by Instruction of the Minister of the Interior. It contains *inter alia* the reasons for the refusal, the obligations imposed on the addressee following the refusal to issue a residence permit or to annul a residence permit as well as the right to appeal. There is a right to appeal the decision to refuse to issue, renew or annul the residence permit under administrative law. Appeals are to be lodged with the direct superior of the authority that has adopted the order to refuse to issue or annul a residence permit. The (administrative) appeal decision can be appealed in the court. The administrative and judicial appeal procedures may not exceed sixteen days from the day that the decision refusing to issue, renew or annul the residence permit was communicated to the applicant for or holder of a residence permit.

417. The competent court at the first appellate level is the Administrative Court in the area where the authority that adopted the decision is located. An appeal against a decision of the First Instance Administrative Courts can be lodged with the Supreme Administrative Court.

researchers or foreign specialists conducting scientific research, coming to the territory of the Republic of Albania in the framework of a bilateral governmental agreement or an agreement concluded between educational institutions; (v) trainers who come to the Republic of Albania within the framework of a cooperation agreement concluded between governmental institutions or educational institutions; (vi) staff employed by humanitarian organizations operating under international cooperation programmes.

424. An annual quota for the employment of non-nationals in the Republic of Albania is set until the first October of each year, as provided for in Article 82 of the Law 'On Immigration'. The Ministry of Labour, Social Affairs and Equal Opportunities, in collaboration with the Ministry of Economy, Trade and Energy, in consultation with the central State institutions responsible for employment, propose annual quotas for the employment of non-nationals which are then approved by decision of the Council of Ministers. The annual quota for the employment of non-nationals is determined in accordance with the migration and labour market situation in Albania. The decision setting the annual quota for the employment of non-nationals also defines the activities and occupations in which work is permitted, as well as the number of work permits that can be issued for the different activities and occupations. The annual quota for employment of non-nationals can include a quota for seasonal employment. The procedure for this institutional and inter-institutional cooperation to prepare the annual employment quota is approved by joint instruction of the Minister of Labour, Social Affairs and Equal Opportunities and the Minister of Economy, Trade and Energy.

425. Work permits may be issued in addition to the annual quota to non-nationals who are daily immigrant workers on the basis of bilateral agreements or to staff holding key positions in companies, branches and representative offices as well as staff that is transferred within enterprises, or companies, as part of an internal transfer where there is an agreement or collaboration is based on a cooperation programme; and to self-employed persons who manage their own company or who own more than 51% of the shares of the company. The same status is enjoyed by language teachers and lecturers in educational establishments who teach in language learning courses or to national minorities; foreign artists working in the Republic of Albania; employees conducting research in scientific research institutions, educational or legal entities in areas where there is no competence in the Republic of Albania or to professors, lecturers, instructors and other guest lecturers invited by an Albanian university or Foreign Language school.[316] An application for the worker's residence permit can be made either by the worker or by the employer.

426. When a foreigner has resided in Albania for an uninterrupted period of two years with a temporary residence permit granted on the basis of employment, he/she

316. *See*, in particular, Art. 83 of the Law 'On Foreigners'.

may apply for a continuous residence permit. Such a permit can be issued if the foreigner still meets the requirements for being granted a residence permit.[317]

317. *See Analiza e mangësive mbi legjislacionin dhe praktikën shqiptare të emigracionit krahasuar me standartet europiane dhe ato ndërkombëtare*, 49 (ONM, Tiranë, 2004); *Fjalorth i terminologjisë migratore*, 89 (ONM, Tirana, 2007); *Kthimi i emigranteve te parregullt ne Shqiperi, nevojat dhe modalitetet*, ONM (Tirane, 2006): 52; *Përmbledhje aktesh juridike në fushën e migracionit*, 49 (ACIL/ONM, Tiranë, 2005); *Kthimi dhe ripranimi: Rasti i Shqiperise, sfidat dhe nevojat*, IOM, 23 (Tirane, 2006); L. Ikonomi, *E drejta migratore*, 110 (Tirana, 2014).

Chapter 2. Conditions for Entitlement to Work in the Country as an Employed Person

427. Citizens from countries outside the EU and the USA need a worker's residence permit to work in Albania. The 'worker's residence permit' is the only specific permit category in the Law 'On Foreigners' in a separate Chapter. Other residence permits are not classified into separate permits, but as one residence permit which can be issued on different grounds (i.e., family ties, humanitarian grounds, employment etc.).[318]

428. A worker's residence permit doubles up as permit that gives its holder access to the Albanian labour market. There are several provisions in the Law 'On Foreigners' dedicated to this permit. Many of the provisions on the worker's residence permit also apply to other categories of residence permits that can be granted on the grounds of employment.

429. The legal definition of the worker's residence permit is that it is a permit that is required for a foreigner to reside in Albania or on board an Albanian vessel if the foreigner intends to take part in gainful employment to which he/she would not have the right under another residence permit or without a residence permit. Gainful employment is understood to mean work in return for payment in an employment relationship in the private or public sector, or some other employment relationship.

430. The type and duration of a residence permit for an employed person are determined by the employment contract.[319] If an employment contract is valid until further notice, even the first residence permit may be granted as a continuous permit, unless residence is intended to be temporary.

431. A non-national who wishes to take up employment in the Republic of Albania must, first of all, obtain a business registration certificate or a registration document for legal employment. A certificate of registration is issued for a period of stay up to sixty days within a period of one year.[320] Business registration certificates are

318. *See* L. Ikonomi, *E drejta migratore*, 112 (Tirana, 2014); IOM, *E drejta migratore*, 190 (Tirane, 2009); *Integrimi i refugjatëve në Shqipëri*, 3 (UNHCR, Tiranë, 2004); *Analiza e mangësive mbi legjislacionin dhe praktikën shqiptare të emigracionit krahasuar me standartet europiane dhe ato ndërkombëtare*, 22 (ONM, Tiranë, 2004); *Fjalorth i terminologjisë migratore*, 39 (ONM, Tirana, 2007).

319. F. Tashko, *Marrëdhëniet Individuale të punës, Komentar* 10 (Tiranë 2006); L. Ikonomi, *E drejta migratore*, 123 (Tirana, 2014); IOM, *E drejta migratore*, 185 (Tirane, 2009); *Përmbledhje aktesh juridike në fushën e migracionit*, 50 (ACIL/ONM, Tiranë, 2005).

320. *See* Art. 73 of the Law 'On Foreigners' which states: The certification for these categories of persons: (a) the audit and consultancy services providers; (b) lecturers who participate in joint seminars; (c) artists and technical staff participate in cultural activities such as opera, ballet, theatre, concerts, authors or actors of movies or TV shows; (d) aliens working in the circus or other entertainment activities to the public; (e) aliens working in fairs or exhibitions; (f) persons who instal machinery or constructions that are delivered by a foreign corporation and provide machinery repair service, as well as conduct employee training, be they Albanians or aliens, for their use.

issued for a period of stay up to ninety days within a period of one year to non-nationals who intend to work in the Republic of Albania as in the frontier transport of goods and people sector and are employed by a company whose headquarters are registered abroad; key personnel or board members who perform work for the company, but who are not employed by it; trainers coming to the Republic of Albania employed by foreign companies or their branches established in other countries providing vocational training activities based on cooperation programmes entered into between the institutions; experts in the field of the protection of cultural heritage, libraries and archives; pupils or students who come to Albania as cooperate relations, for training, or the exchange of experience etc.[321]

432. A certificate of registration of unlimited duration is issued to following non-nationals:

- persons involved in missions of technical assistance with the central institutions, independent institutions or institutions directly dependent of the aforementioned ones;
- consultants or advisors to central State institutions, independent institutions, or institutions directly dependent of the aforementioned ones who are employed under government agreement, or a project of international organizations;
- managers or staff of institutions, religious and charity foundations, non-profit organizations, which are recognized by and registered with the competent bodies of the Republic of Albania, who are not remunerated for their work;
- civil and military officials who come to work in the Republic of Albania within the framework of an agreement between the government of the Republic of Albania and the government of the country they come from;
- mass media representatives, reporters or foreign correspondents accredited in the Republic of Albania, working for a foreign employer; and
- lecturers, researchers or foreign specialists who come to the territory of the Republic of Albania within the framework of a bilateral governmental agreement or an agreement concluded between educational establishments.

433. The criteria and procedures for obtaining a certificate of registration are set by the Council of Ministers which also determines which documentation is required to establish that the conditions are satisfied. The Ministry of Youth and Social Welfare is the competent authority.[322] The format and content of the certificate of registration are approved by Decision of the Minister of the Ministry of Youth and Social Welfare. There are several actors that assist employers, for instance Business Albania, the Confederation of Employers Organization, the Albanian National Clothing Manufactures, Albanian Constructors Association and the Union of Industrialist. Examples of organizations that assist workers are: the Confederation of Trade Unions of Albania and the Union of Independent Trade Unions of Albania.

321. *Përmbledhje aktesh juridike në fushën e migracionit*, 51 (ACIL/ONM, Tiranë, 2005).
322. *See* for all the information the official website http://www.sociale.gov.al/ (accessed 12 May 2018).

Chapter 3. Sanctions for Illegal Participation in the Labour Market

§1. Sanctions Imposed on Employers

434. Like other countries, the Republic of Albania prohibits by law the employment of anybody who is illegally resident in its territory. Infringements of this prohibition are subject to the sanctions and measures laid down in Albanian legislation on migration and asylum, as well as under Criminal law.

435. The definition of employment encompasses its constituent elements, namely activities that are or ought to be remunerated, undertaken for or under the direction and/or supervision of the employer, irrespective of the legal relationship. The definition of employer can also include an association of persons, recognized as having the capacity to perform legal acts without legal personality.

436. According to Article 74 of the Law 'On Foreigners', the last employer, who has been issued a work permit is obliged to notify the competent authorities on any changes to the terms under which it was issued, requesting its approval if the amendment relates to the name and address of the employer, the valid employment contract covering the period for which the work permit is issued and all the activities that the person employed is authorized to undertake.

437. To prevent the employment of irregularly staying persons, employers are required, before they recruit anon-national, to verify whether that person has a valid residence permit or another authorization that is evidence of lawful stay in the Republic of Albania. This is also the case if the non-national is being recruited for the purpose of posting to another State in the context of the provision of services.[323]

438. According to Article 77 of the Law 'On Foreigners', a work permit may not be issued or renewed if, within the six months before submitting the request for a work permit, the employee for whom the working permit is intended has been released by the employer from duty for an indefinite period of time or has stipulated a contract that does not meet the requirements set out in Albanian legislation or international conventions on working and employment conditions. Likewise, if an employer does not provide the correct information and documents, if requested, a work permit will not be issued or renewed.[324] This means that employers need to receive all relevant information and documentation regarding the immigration status from their employees. Employers who have complied with the obligations set out in the afore mentioned provisions in the Law 'On Foreigners' are not held liable

323. *See*, in general, K. Çela & P. Haxhi, *E Drejtë e Krahasuar e Punës*, 15 (Iliar, Tiranë 2002); B. Bercusson, *European Labour Law,* 112 (King's College London Publication, London, 2009); Ph. Syrpis, *EU Intervention in Domestic Labour Law*, 69 (Oxford University Press, 2007); S. Hennion & M. Le Barbier, *E Drejta Sociale Evropiane dhe Ndërkombëtare*, 37 (Tirane Papirus, 2013).

324. *See* Art. 77 para. c of the Law 'On Foreigners'.

for employing a person who is residing irregularly in Albania if the competent Albanian authority later finds out that the document presented by an employee has, in fact, been forged or misused, unless the employer knew that the document was a forgery.

439. The most important provisions in the Law 'On Foreigners' concerning sanctions which can be imposed on employers are Articles 137–139 of the Law 'On Foreigners'. The employer recruiting non-national in the Republic of Albania is obliged, prior to employing that person, to request the latter to present a residence permit or another authorization of stay, valid for the period of employment and to copy or record the content of the residence permit, or other authorization of stay, prior to the start of employment either to store, at least for the duration of employment, copies or records which must be made available for inspection to the responsible state authorities controlling aliens in the territory and also to the inspectorate responsible for employment. Along the same lines, an employer is obliged to notify the responsible authorities of the start and end of employment by a non-national alien, within one week after employment is started and to cover all return costs if he/she has employed a foreigner unlawfully, if that person is returned by the Albanian authorities.

440. According to Article 137 of the Law 'On Foreigners', the employer should, in any case, be required to pay any outstanding remuneration for the work an employee has performed for him/her, even if employment was irregular as well any outstanding taxes and social security contributions and an administrative fine. If the level of remuneration cannot be determined, it is assumed to be at least the wage provided for by the applicable laws on minimum wages, collective agreements or practices in the relevant occupational branches. The employer can also be required to pay, where appropriate, any costs made to transmit outstanding remuneration to the country to which the irregularly employed person has (been) returned. If the employer does not take care of back payments then Albania is not obliged to fulfil this obligation on behalf of the employer.

441. When irregular employment has been established, the regional authority responsible for border and migration is entitled to propose measures to be adopted against the employer to the responsible State institutions (in this case the Directorate of the Ministry). Measures may include financial penalties and a contribution towards the costs of returning persons staying in Albania irregularly to a third country. The most important measures that can be taken against employers are the exclusion from the right to public benefits, assistance or funds for a period of up to five years and the exclusion from participation in public contracts for a period of up to five years. It is also possible to close down, either temporary or permanently, the legal or natural person where the violation was committed.[325]

442. To enforce the general prohibition and to deter infringements, Albanian law provides for appropriate sanctions. In some cases – such as repeated or knowingly

325. *See*, in particular, Art. 137 para. 4 of the Law 'On Foreigners'.

hiring undocumented migrants, or hiring children or victims of human trafficking – the employer is are punished for having committed a criminal offence for which Criminal law provides effective, proportionate and dissuasive penalties. Employers who subject migrant workers to particularly exploitive working conditions are also punishable under Criminal law. Subjecting a person to particularly exploitive working conditions is a criminal offence when committed intentionally, when it continues or is persistently repeated, or concerns the simultaneous employment of a significant number of irregularly employed persons. This is also the case if the offence is committed by an employer who hires workers from or uses the services of a person knowing that the persons performing the work or services are irregularly resident in Albania and a victim of human trafficking. There are special rules imposing sanctions for employers who employ minors irregularly.

§2. Sanctions for Workers

443. Chapter XI of the Law 'On Foreigners' deals with the sanctions in general which can be imposed on non-nationals who violate the law, in particular Articles 145 and 146 of the Law 'On Foreigners'.

444. The most important sanctions that can be imposed on workers, who are irregular participants in the labour market, are to cancel the work permit. This is stated by Article 80 of the Albanian Law 'On Foreigners', which allows the Albanian authorities to cancel a work permit before the deadline of its validity has expired if: it is established that the work permit was obtained by fraud or by submitting false information; after the issuing of the work permit, it is established that the documentation supporting the application is inaccurate; the alien acts or makes propaganda against the sovereignty of the Republic of Albania, its national security, Constitutional or public order.

445. In addition, the Inspectorate of labour of the Ministry of Youth and Social Welfare has the right to cancel a work permit before the deadline of its validity has expired if a temporary residence permit is cancelled, or if the person for whom the work permit was issued has left the Republic of Albania for a continuous period of more than six months, unless deployed by the employer in another country, or has left the Republic of Albania to attend education or to follow a vocational training, due to illness, baby-sitting or compulsory military service, and if the alien performs work other than what the work permit was issued for, unless the work is done by somebody who has been issued a permanent work permit.

446. Unemployment in itself is not a sufficient reason for the annulment of the 'residence permit for an employed person', unless the period of unemployment exceeds three months within a twelve-month period for the holder of the 'residence permit for an employed person', who has lawfully exercised activities as an employed person up to three years'; and six months within a twelve-month period for the holder of the 'residence permit for an employed person', who has lawfully exercised activities as employed person for more than three years.[326]

447. Within seven days after cancelling a work permit, the Inspectorate of labour notifies the responsible authority for border and migration.

448. Violation of the rules in the Law 'On Foreigners' is an administrative offence and the fine is imposed in accordance with the legislation on administrative offences. So, a person who is involved in remunerated employment or practices an occupation without having the right to gainful employment is punished with a fine ranging from ALL 20,000 to ALL 30,000.[327]

326. *See* Art. 40 of the Law 'On Foreigners' as amended.
327. *See* Art. 145 para. 1, point *c* of the Law 'On Foreigners'.

Chapter 4. Legal Remedies and Procedural Safeguards

449. The legal remedies and the procedural safeguards for the employment are the same as the procedures explained in Chapter I, Part V, Sanctions.

Part VIII. Access to Self-Employed Activities

Chapter 1. Overview of Applicable Legislation

450. The EU and the intention to join the EU have played a major role in the external dimension of labour migration policies in Albania. However, the Albanian government was also able to develop its own, very specific external dimension of migration policies based on the signing of bilateral agreements with other countries to regulate the recruitment of foreign workers.

451. Albania has a Civil law system similar to that in most other Continental European countries. It has enacted legislation in respect to property and contract rights. Considering the fact that Albania does not have a Commercial Code, relevant rules on these issues are found in, amongst others, the Foreign Investment Law;[328]the Commercial Companies Law;[329] the Bankruptcy Law;[330] the Employment Law;[331]the Taxation Procedures Law;[332] the Banking Law;[333] and the Concessions Law.[334] Companies interested in entering the Albanian market should contact the Albanian Investment and Development Agency[335] (former ALBINVEST) which provides direct assistance to investors.

452. Foreign investment enterprises registered in Albania as legal entities are allowed to own every type of land and companies investing in Albania have the right to employ foreign citizens. The most common type of organization for foreign investors is a limited liability company. The Law on Commercial Companies provides guidelines on the activities of companies and the legal structure under which they operate. Other forms of business entities include joint stock companies, joint

328. Law No 7764/1993, 2 Nov. 1993 'On Foreign Investments' amended by Law No. 10316, 16 Sep. 2010 and Law No. 46/2017, 13 Apr. 2017.
329. Law No. 9901 'On Entrepreneurs and Commercial Companies', entry into force: 14 Apr. 2008.
330. Law No. 8901, 23 May 2002, 'On Bankruptcy' (amended in May 2008). This Law is similar in organization to the German Bankruptcy Law.
331. Law No. 7961, 12 Jul. 1995.
332. Law No. 9769 / 2007 on Some Amendments to Law No. 8977, 12 Dec. 2002 'On the Taxation System in the Republic of Albania' (amended).
333. Law No. 8365/1998, 2 Jul. 1998 'On Banks in the Republic of Albania'.
334. Law No. 77/2015, 27 Jul. 2015' On Amendments and Additions to Law No. 125/2013 'On Concessions and Public Private Partnerships'.
335. *See* for more at: www.aida.gov.al.

ventures, unlimited partnerships, limited partnerships and sole entrepreneur enterprises. Employment relations between an employee and an employer are regulated by individual employment contracts pursuant to the Labour Code. The National Council of Labour, composed of government officials, trade unions and employers associations, aims to improve social dialogue between the government, management and employees.[336]

336. M. Blecher & J. Dine, *Komentar i Ligjit nr. 9901, 14 Apr. 2008, Për tregtarët dhe shoqëritë tregtare* 70 (Guttenberg, 2009).

Chapter 2. Conditions for Entitlement to Work in the Country as a Self-employed

§1. General Conditions

453. When applying for a residence permit to conduct business activities in Albania, the permit category is the residence permit for a self-employed person. The criteria for eligibility for this permit are: profitability of the business activity and guaranteed means of support for the person concerned. In addition the general professional and qualifications-related requirements relevant to the field of business have to be satisfied.[337]

454. The legislation regarding admission as a self-employed persons, i.e., the business registration and licensing procedures, is in line with the EU standards and aim at reducing administrative barriers for businesses operating in Albania.[338] Following the opening of the National Registration Centre for Businesses (NRC)[339] in September 2007, business entities are registered in a single place, in one day, for one Euro. Foreign and domestic investors have numerous options available to organize their business operations in Albania. [340]

455. Business entities that can be registered with the NRC are the following: Sole Entrepreneurs; Unlimited Partnerships; Limited Partnerships; Limited Liability Companies (Shpk); Joint Stock Companies etc.[341]

§2. Administrative Rules and Procedures

456. The NCR is a central public institution, with legal personality, resorting under the Minister responsible for economy. Its legal seat is in Tirana. Registration in the Commercial Register is obligatory for natural persons exercising a commercial economic activity; simple partnerships provided for by the Civil Code; commercial companies and any other entity subject to registration in accordance with Albanian law. To register a new company with the National Registration Centre the following documents are required:

(1) Application form: The applicant may fill out the form either at any NRC service desk with the help of the service desk clerk, if necessary, or via the Internet, using the NRC's 'Apply On-Line'-function.

---

337. F. Galgano, *E drejta tregtare,* 54 (Luarasi University Press Tiranë, 2009).
338. A. Malltezi, *E drejta shqiptare e shoqërive tregtare,* 49 (Tiranë, Mediaprint, 2011); M. Blecher & J. Dine, *Komentar i Ligjit nr. 9901, 14 April 2008, Për tregtarët dhe shoqëritë tregtare* 65 (Guttenberg, 2009).
339. Law No. 9723, 5 March 2007, 'National Registration Center' at www.qkr.gov.al.
340. *See* A. Malltezi, J. Rystemaj & L. Pelinku, *Aspekte të së drejtës së biznesit në Shqipëri,* 17 (Tiranë, 2014).
341. A. Malltezi, J. Rystemaj & L. Pelinku, *Aspekte të së drejtës së biznesit në Shqipëri,* 17 (Tiranë, 2014).

(2) The Charter: The statute or the organization chart of the registered person.
(3) Accompanying documents: Original personal identification document (ID card), other accompanying documents; the list of the accompanying documents for the initial registration is specific to different legal forms of companies.

§3. Conditions for Special Categories of Self-employed Persons

457. Foreigners who reside in Albania and have been issued a residence permit other than a residence permit for a self-employed person are also allowed to engage in business in Albania. The legal definition of the self-employed person is quite narrow, only including a person who is acting under his/her own unlimited business responsibility. A residence permit for a self-employed person is only issued if this definition is met and there is no other ground to reside in Albania.[342]

458. There are many cases where the law imposes special conditions for different categories of self-employed people, which also include foreigners. Compliance with these rules is entrusted to the National Licensing Centre (NLC)[343] that started life as a central public institution, resorting under the Minister responsible for economic issues in June 2009. The NLC assesses compliance with licensing or permitting criteria on the basis of the following information: *an* applicant's statements and documents issued by other public bodies or private institutions. In addition is makes its own assessments, performs preliminary inspections and tests, and conducts contests, interviews, hearings or any other adequate method.

459. The procedure to handle an applications for a license or a permits clear, simple, transparent and is governed by: (a) the 'silent consent' principle; (b) electronic communication and information means, including the possibility for *online* application; (c) the one-stop-shop model; and (d) the integrated exchange of information and documents between public bodies.

460. Licenses and permits, and/or respective sub-categories which fall under the competence of the NLC, are divided into three groups: *The first group* includes those categories or sub-categories that only require the applicant's statement, in order to evaluate whether the criteria are satisfied. *The second group* includes those categories or sub-categories that require both the applicant's statement and proof in the form of documents to be submitted by the applicant, for at least one of the criteria. *The third group* includes those categories or sub-categories for which assessment of (at least one of) the criteria also requires, an inspection, test, competition, interview, or any other assessment method.

342. *Ligj nr. 9901, datë 14.04.2008 'Për tregtarët dhe Shoqëritë Tregtare'. Ligj No. 9723 3 May 2007 'Për Qendrën Kombëtare të regjistrimit'*. Ligj No. 7850 29 Jul. 1994, *Kodi Civil i Republikës së Shqipërisë;* Th., Bachner, *Ligji i ri Shqiptar për Shoqëritë Tregtare – Interpretuar sipas burimeve të tij në të drejtën Evropiane*, 61 (Tiranë: Dudaj, 2009).
343. Law 'On National Licensing Center', No. 10081, 23 Feb. 2009.

Chapter 3. Sanctions Against the Irregular Exercise of Self-Employment

461. To detect migrants working in abusive conditions and irregular employment comprehensive legal framework has been established which is composed of, amongst others the new Law on Foreigners No. 108/2013, the National Action Plan on the Fight against Trafficking in Human Beings and the Strategy on the Fight against Organized Crime, Trafficking and Terrorism.

462. The National Strategy for Employment and Skills 2014–2020 approved by Decision of the Council of Ministers No. 818 dated 26 November 2014 has the overall objective to promote qualitative jobs and opportunities for developing skills for all Albanian males and females throughout their life cycle. The National Strategy for Employment and Skills focuses on four strategic priorities: (1) the promotion of decent employment opportunities through effective labour market policies; (2) the provision of qualitative education and vocational training for the youth and adults; (3) the promotion of social inclusion and territorial cohesion; and 4) the regulation of the labour market and the qualification system. The migration policy developed by and services offered by the Ministry of Foreign Affairs include *inter alia* the improvement of the treatment of non-nationals in Albania by guaranteeing non-nationals rights upon their arrival to Albania; the cooperation with other institutions dealing with non-nationals; and the facilitation of their right to enter Albania by removing the obligation to apply for a seasonal visa and the improvement of the procedure for the issuing of visa.

463. The administrative sanctions in Chapter XI of Law No. 108/2013 can be imposed on carriers, State bodies, public, legal or natural persons not complying with the obligations arising from the provisions of that Law, and on employers and employees who are unlawfully employed.

The Penal Code was amended by Law No. 144/2013 to make internal trafficking in human beings a criminal offence and to make the benefiting from or using the services provided by trafficked persons as well as the exploitation of people who have been trafficked punishable by law.[344]

464. Regarding the principle of equal treatment of migrants in an irregular situation in and the unlawful employment of a foreigner, Article 137(1)(dh) and (e) and (2) of Law No. 108/2013 obliges the employer to pay the outstanding remuneration for any work performed and any taxes and social contributions relevant to the employment of a foreigner who has been irregularly employed over a six month period, unless the employer can prove otherwise. Article 137(4) of the Law No. 108/2013 provides measures which can be imposed on an employer who has employed a foreigner unlawfully staying in the territory of the Republic of Albania.

344. ILO, *Migrant Workers and ILO Convention, 1975 (No. 143):* Albania–*Ratification (*CEACR*) (2006)* ILCs. (2014).

Chapter 4. Legal Remedies and Procedural Safeguards

465. The right to employment is founding the Albanian Constitution, more specifically in Article 49 that reads: 'Everyone has the right to earn the means of living by lawful work that he has chosen or accepted himself.' Everyone has the right to pursue a freely chosen or accepted occupation and to obtain a professional qualification.[345] This principle is phrased in gender neutral terms and thus applies to all citizens alike, both for men and for women.

466. The principle of equal treatment found in Article 18 of the Constitution is developed in the Labour Code where it stands as a fundamental right. According to section 9 of the Labour Code, any form of discrimination at work is prohibited. Discrimination means any distinction, exclusion or preference based on race, colour, sex, age, religion, political beliefs, religious origin, family relation, and any physical or mental defect that affects an individual's right to be treated as equal in employment and training. Distinctions, exclusions or preferences required for a particular job are not classed as discrimination. Measures taken by the Council of Ministers or in collective contracts designed to protect employees, as provided in the Labour Code are also not considered to amount to discrimination.[346]

467. Investors in Albania are entitled to legal protection of their rights related to their investment. Employers and employees have the right to form trade unions (Labour Code, Article 176). Trade unions are organized at the national level (according to the industrial sector) and at the company level. The right to strike is found in the Labour Code. Trade unions have the right to negotiate wages, working conditions etc., and collective agreements apply to both union and to non-union workers. Employment contracts can be for a limited or an unlimited period. As a general rule, employment contracts are signed for an unlimited period if the duration is not specified properly in the contract.

468. The parties to a dispute may agree to submit disputes for consideration by an arbitration institution. In the event that arbitration does not work, foreign investors have the right to submit a dispute to an Albanian court or to the Arbitration

345. *See*, in particular, Labour Code, Art. 115; Decision No. 220, 13 Feb. 2013 'On the Establishment and Functioning of Albanian School of Public Administration and Training of Public Administration Officers'. Albanian School of Public Administration (ASPA) has autonomy in administration and autonomy in determining curricula and training and training programs as well as training for the development of professional knowledge for public administration employees. *See* also Law No. 152/2013 'On Civil Servants, amended by Law No. 178/2014, dated 18.12.2014, published in Official Gazette No. 211. The Department of Public Administration establishes and administers the Central Personnel Registry, which is a unique database that includes professional data and other data on the employment relationships of each employee in state administration institutions, independent institutions and local government units (Art. 17). According to Art. 38 (The Right to Vocational Training) the Civil Servant has the right to improve professional skills through professional training and ongoing training funded by public funds, foreign donors or personal income. A civil servant is obliged to improve professional skills through professional training and ongoing training funded by public funds. (Art. 42 para. 3).

346. Law No. 10 221, 4 Feb. 2010 'On Protection from Discrimination'.

Court in Tirana. In the event of a dispute regarding discrimination, the transfer of assets, or the indirect expropriation of a foreign investment by the Government, the investor can submit the dispute to the International Centre for Settlement of Investment Disputes (ICSID). In Albania, ratified international agreements take legal preference over national legislation in matters relating to FDI.[347]

469. According to the law, the central authority for assessing the economic benefit of an activity engaged in by a self-employed person is the Ministry of Economy, Trade and Energy.[348] It is not regulated who the competent authority is to conduct the economic-benefit test if it has to be done for a self-employed person by the Ministry of Economy or upon request of the Ministry of Social Welfare and Youth. How these Ministries, both competent to issue work permits to self-employed persons and competent to perform the economic benefits test which is *sine qua non* for the granting of a work permit, have to cooperate as provided for by law.

470. There is no economic benefit test if a work permit is issued for self-employment in specific sectors of interest for Albania, in any region and for activities that will create employment opportunities in the country.[349]

347. *2012 Investment Climate Statement; Bureau of Economic and Business Affairs* (US Embassy), June 2012.
348. *See* Art. 4 of the Law 'On Foreigners'.
349. This article does not apply to foreigners who have worked in Albania and have stayed there lawful for more than two years within a period of five years.

Selected Bibliography

A. Aliu & H. Gashi, *E drejta familiare* (Prishtinë, 2007).

A. Anastasi, *E drejta kushtetuese e krahasuar: raste nga praktika kushtetuese dhe leksione për studentët e drejtësisë* (Tiranë, 2009).

A. Baldaccini, E. Guild & H. Toner (eds.), *Whose Freedom, Security and Justice?: EU Immigration and Asylum Law and Policy* (Oxford, Hart Pub., 2007).

A. Bërxholi, Veçoritë e vizualizimit të dinamikës së popullsisë, 156 (Atlasi gjeografik i popullsisë së Shqipërisë, Akademia e Shkencave, Qendra per Studime Gjeografike, No. 15, 2005).

A. Edwards, Human Rights, Refugees and the Right 'To Enjoy' Asylum, 299 (17 *Int'l J. Refugee L.* 293 2005).

A. Koca, *Një analizë krahasuese e ligjit dhe procedurës mbi Trafikimin e Njerëzve* (Konica 2006).

A. Koca, *Trafikimi i qënieve njerëzore. Këndvështrimi juridik', Kuadri ligjor mbi trafikimin e qënieve njerëzore në Shqipëri dhe sfidat e hasura në praktikën gjyqësore, 5 (*Shkolla e Magjistratures, Tirane, 2013).

A. Leka, *Albanian Migration during the post-Communist Transition and the European Integration in Global Era. An Intercultural Reflection*, 207 (*Academicus*, No. 8, 2009).

A. Malltezi, J. Rystemaj & L. Pelinku, *Aspekte të së drejtës së biznesit në Shqipëri* (Tiranë, 2014).

A. Malltezi, *E drejta shqiptare e shoqërive tregtare* (Tiranë, Mediaprint, 2011).

A. Malltezi, *Koncesionet në Shqipëri. Nga e drejta private në të drejtën publike*, 52–82 (Mediaprint, 2013).

A. Mandro *E drejta familjare* (Tiranë 2009).

A. Mandro, V. Mecaj T. Zaka & A. Fullani, *E drejta familjare* (Tiranë 2006).

A. Zezza, G. Carletto & B. Davis, *Moving Away from Poverty: A Spatial Analysis of Poverty and Migration in Albania*, 175–194 (Journal of Southern Europe and the Balkans Vol. 7, 2005).

Analiza e mangësive mbi legjislacionin dhe praktikën shqiptare të emigracionit krahasuar me standartet europiane dhe ato ndërkombëtare (ONM, Tiranë, 2004).

Analysis of Albanian Immigration and Practise as Compared to EU and International Standards. Gap Analysis on Migration Management in Albania (IOM, Tirana, 2004), available at https://www.albania.iom.int/publication/reports. (acce ssed 15 March 2018).

B. Bercusson, *European Labour Law* (King's College London Publication, London, 2009).

Selected Bibliography

Bank of Albania, *Bulletin 6M–1, 2011* (Tirana, 2012).

Banka Botërore, *Të bësh biznes, Të sjellësh ndryshimin për sipërmarrjet* (Palgrave MacMillan, IFC & Banka Botërore (Uashington D.C 2011).

Banka e Shqipërisë, *Analizë e zhvillimeve në sektorin e jalhtëm të ekonomisë*, 2012 (Departamenti i Politikës Monetare, Prill, 2013).

Bhuiylan, J.H., *Refugee status determination: analysis and application,* 123 (R. Islam, & J.H Bhuiyan, eds., Leiden-Boston, 2013).

Buletini Informativ nr. 41, Mbi aktivitetin e Strukturave te M.P.B. gjate muajit shkurt 2017, 37 (Ministria e Puneve te Brendshme, 2014) http://www.mb.gov.al/files/programs_files/17-03-23-11-51-41Buletin_mujor_shkurt_2017.pdf. (accessed 14 January 2018).

Buletini Informativ nr. 5, Mbi aktivitetin e Strukturave të M.P.B. gjatë muajit shkurt 2014, 27–30 (Ministria e Punëve të Brendshme, 2014).

C. Carletto & T. Kilic, *Moving up the Ladder? The Impact of Migration Experience on Occupational Mobility in Albania* (The World Bank, Policy Research Working Paper, n. 4908, 2009).

C. Carletto, B. Davis, M. Stampini, S. Trento & A. Zezza, *Internal Mobility and External Migration in Albania*, 4–13 (ESA Working Paper, Rome, 2004).

C. Mackenzie, *Return and Readmission. The Case of Albania*, 17–18 (IOM Tirana, 2006) available at https://www.albania.iom.int/publications/research/12%20Return%20and%20Readmission%20%20(last%20version).pdf (accessed 15 May 2018).

C. Nikas & R. King, *Economic Growth through Remittances: Lessons from the Greek Experience of the 1960s Applicable to the Albanian Case,* 235 (Journal of Southern Europe and the Balkans, Volume 7, No. 2, 2005).

Cahn, A., *Comparative Company Law*. Cambridge: University Press, 2010.

Council Directive 2001/55/EC of 20 July 2001 on Minimum Standards for Giving Temporary Protection in the Event of a Mass Influx of Displaced Persons and on Measures Promoting a Balance of Efforts between Member States in Receiving such Persons and Bearing the Consequences thereof, *OJ EU*, 2001, L 212/12.

D. Kule, A. Mancellari, Papapanagos & B. Nicholson, *The Tractor, the Shop and the Filling-station: Work Migration as Self-help Development in Albania,* 877–890 (*Europe-Asia Studies* 56(6), 2004).

D. Sokol, *The Working of EU Conditionality in the Area of Migration Policy: the Case of Readmission of Irregular Migrants to Albania,* 115 (East European Politics and Societies 26, 2012), DOI: 10.1177/0888325410386366.

Dh. Haveri, Trafikimi i të miturve. Problemet e hasura në praktikën gjyqësore, Kuadri ligjor mbi trafikimin e qënieve njerëzore në Shqipëri dhe sfidat e hasura në praktikën gjyqësore', Shkolla e Magjistratures, 86 (Tiranë, 2013).

E. Canaj & G. Bardeli, *Bashkimi familjar si një e drejtë themelore në ditët e sotme*, 141–152 (*Jus&Justicia*, UETPRESS, No. 13, 2016).

E. Canaj & G. Bardeli, *E drejta e bashkimit familjar. Në Bashkimin Europian dhe Shqipëri* (Tirane, 2018).

E. Canaj & A. Vasjari, *Family Reunification in Albania. A Comparative Study in the Context of Albanian Integration*, 681–690 (Mediterranean Journal of Social Science, Sapienza, Vol. 4. nr. 6, 2013) http://www.mcser.org/journal/index.php/mjss/article/view/350 (accessed 13 March 2018).

E. Canaj & A.Vasjari, *Family Reunification in Albania. A Comparative Study in the Context of Albanian Integration*, 681–690 (Mediterranean Journal of Social Science, Sapienza, Vol. 4. nr. 6, 2013) http://www.mcser.org/journal/index.php/mjss/article/view/350 (accessed 13 March 2018).

E. Canaj *The Right of Family Reunification. Albanian and Kosovo Cases*, in: '*Human Mobility.Migration from a European and African Viewpoint*' (ed. by) Giovanni Carlo Bruno, Immacolata Caruso, Bruno VendittoSoveria Mannelli (CZ), Rubbettino, 2013ISBN 978-88-498-4068-1http://www.issm.cnr.it/pubblicazioni/altre_pubbl/human_mobility/Human_Mobility.pdf.

E. Canaj & S. Bana, *E drejta e Bashkimit Europian* (Tirana, Onufri, 2014).

E. Canaj & S. Veliu, *Implementing European rules into Albanian legislation. The right of Family Reunification*, 35 (UETPRESS, Tirane, 2017).

E. Canaj, *The Right of Family Reunification. Albanian and Kosovo Cases*, 95 (G.C.Bruno & B.Venditto & S.Mannelli eds., Rubbettino, 2013) http://www.issm.cnr.it/pubblicazioni/altre_pubbl/human_mobility/Human_Mobility.pdf (accessed 12 May 2018).

E. Canaj, *Analizë e disa problematikave mbi të drejtat e emigrantëve sipas Kartës së të drejtave themelore të Bashkimit Europian* (Jeta Juridike, n. 2, Tiranë 2010).

E. Canaj, *Bashkimi familjar në dritën e zhvillimeve të reja europiane*, 75–91 (*Jus&Justicia*, UETPRESS, No. 7, Tiranë, 2012).

E. Canaj, *Lëvizja e lirë e personave në Bashkimin Europian* (UETPRESS, Tiranë, 2014).

E. Canaj S. Bana, *Il diritto al ricongiungimento familiare nel diritto internazionale e dell'Unione Europea e la sua tutela multilivello* (Edizioni Nuova Cultura, Italia, 2014).

E. Xhafera, *Investimi i huaj ne vendet e Europes Juglingore. Rasti i Shqiperise*, http//www.bankofalbania.org/Downloads/
Investimi_i_huaj_direkt_ne_vendet-
_ne_zhvillim_te_Evropes_Lindore_Rasti_i_Shqiperise.pdf.

European Commission *Albania Progress Report 2005*, https://ec.europa.eu/neighbourhood-enlargement/sites/near/files/pdf/key_documents/2016/20161109_report_albania.pdf. (accessed 20 October 2017).

European Commission *Albania Progress Report 2010*, https://ec.europa.eu/neighbourhood-enlargement/sites/near/files/pdf/key_documents/2016/20161109_report_albania.pdf (accessed 13 October 2017).

European Commission *Albania Progress Report 2013*, https://ec.europa.eu/neighbourhood-enlargement/sites/near/files/pdf/key_documents/2013/package/al_rapport_2013.pdf (accessed 15 October 2017).

European Commission *Albania Progress Report 2015*, https://ec.europa.eu/neighbourhood-enlargement/sites/near/files/pdf/key_documents/2015/20151110_report_albania.pdf. (accessed 20 October 2017).

European Commission *Albania Progress Report* 2016', https://ec.europa.eu/neighbourhood-enlargement/sites/near/files/pdf/key_documents/2016/20161109_report_albania.pdf (accessed 19 October 2017).

ExCom, *Conclusion No. 103 (LVI) Provision on International Protection Including Through Complementary Forms of Protection,* UNHCR, 56th Session, 2005.

Selected Bibliography

Explanations Relating to the Charter of Fundamental Rights (2007/C 303/02), OJ C 303/17, 14 (December 2007).

F. Galgano, *E drejta tregtare* (Luarasi University Press Tiranë, 2009).

F. Piperno, *Remittances Enhancement for Local Development in Albania: Constraints and Opportunities*, 57–64 (Working Papers 4/2003, CeSPI, Rome).

F. Tashko, *Marrëdhëniet Individuale të punës, Komentar* (Tiranë 2006).

Fjalorth i terminologjisë migratore (ONM, Tirana, 2007).

G. Appave, *Emerging Legal Issues in International Law on Migration*, 390 (B. Opeskin, R. Perruchoud & J. Redpath-Cross, eds. Cambridge U. Press, 2012).

G.S. Goodwin-Gill & J. McAdam, *The Refugee in International Law* (Oxford, Oxford University Press 2010).

Government of Albania, *National Strategy on Migration* (Government of Albania and IOM, Tirana, 2005) available at http://www.albania.iom.int/ (accessed 21 March 2018).

Guidelines for Integrated Border Management in the Western Balkans http://ec.europa.eu/enlargement/pdf/financial_assistance/cards/publications/ibm_guidelines_en.pdf.http://www.punetejashtme.gov.al/en (accessed 20 October 2017).

H. Lambert, *Safe Third Country in the European Union: An Evolving Concept in International Law and Implications for the UK*, 318–336 (Journal of Immigration, Asylum and Nationality Law Vol 26, 2012).

http://www.albania.iom.int/publications/research/School%20of%20Magistrate%20study%20on%20CT%20issues-ALB.pdf (accessed 22 March 2018).

http://www.albania.iom.int/publications/research/School%20of%20Magistrate%20study%20on%20CT%20issues-ALB.pdf. (accessed 21 January 2018).

http://www.albania.iom.int/publications/research/School%20of%20Magistrate%20study%20on%20CT%20issues-ALB.pdf. (accessed 15 January 2018).

https://www.state.gov/documents/organization/271341.pdf.

I. Elezi, *E drejta penale, Pjesa e përgjithshme*, (Tirane 2008).

I. Elezi, *E drejta penale, Pjesa e posaçme* (Botime Erik, 2007).

I. Elezi, S. Kacupi & M. Haxhia, *Komentari i Kodit Penal të Republikës së Shqipërisë* (Tiranë, 2012).

I. Elezi, S. Kacupi & M. Haxhia, *Komentari i Kodit Penal të Republikës së Shqipërisë* (Botimet Kumi, 2013).

I. Salihu, *E drejta penale, Pjesa e Pergjithshme* (2010).

I. Zajmi, *A e kalon legjislacioni penal shqiptar për trafikimin e qenieve njerëzore pragun e standarteve ndërkombëtare?, Kuadri ligjor mbi trafikimin e qënieve njerëzore në Shqipëri dhe sfidat e hasura në praktikën gjyqësore,* 24 (Shkolla e Magjistratures, Tiranë, 2013).

Integrimi i refugjatëve në Shqipëri (UNHCR, Tiranë, 2004).

IOM, *Analysis of Albanian Immigration and Practice as Compared to EU and International Standards. Gap Analysis on Migration Management in Albania,* 43 (IOM, Tirana, 2004) https://www.albania.iom.int/publication/researches-studies (accessed 20 October 2017).

IOM, *E drejta migratore* (Tirane, 2009).

IOM, *E drejta migratore* (Tirane, 2011).

J.H. Bhuiyan, *Protection of Refugees through the Principle of Non-refoulement* (Islam R. & Bhuiyan, J.H., eds., Leiden-Boston, 2013).

K. Barjaba, *Contemporary Patterns in Albanian Migration*, 57–64 (South-East Europe Review 3(2) 2000).

K. Barjaba, *Migration and Ethnicity in Albania: Synergies and Interdependencies* 231–239. (Easton Institute for International Studies), Summer Fall 2004, vol. xi, Issue 1.

K. Barjaba, Z. Dervishi & L. Perrone, *L'emigrazione albanese: spazi, tempi e cause* 513–537 (*Studi Emigrazione*, 29/1992).

K. Çela & P. Haxhi, *E Drejtë e Krahasuar e Punës* (Iliar, Tiranë 2002).

K. Çela, *E drejta e Punës*, 15 (Ilar, Tiranë, 2011).

K. Popp, *Regional Processes, Law and Institutional Developments on Migration*, 366 (B. Opeskin, R. Perruchoud & J. Redpath-Cross, eds. Cambridge U. Press, 2012).

K. Touzenis, *Irregular Migration, Migrant Smuggling and Human Rights: Towards Coherence* (International Council on Human Rights Policy, Geneva, 2010).

K. Touzenis, *Trafficking in Human Beings, Human rights and transnational criminal law, developments in law and practices,* 23 (UNESCO, Migration Studies 3, 2010).

Kodi Civil i Republikës së Shqipërisë (Tirane, 2014)

Kodi i Punës i Republikës se Shqipërisë, (Tiranë, 2014).

Komentari i Kodit Penal të Republikës së Shqipërisë, (Tirane 2014).

Kthimi dhe ripranimi: Rasti i Shqiperise, sfidat dhe nevojat, (IOM, Tirane, 2006).

Kthimi i emigranteve te parregullt ne Shqiperi, nevojat dhe modalitetet (ONM, Tirane, 2006).

Kuadri ligjor mbi trafikimin e qënieve njerëzore në Shqipëri dhe sfidat e hasura në praktikën gjyqësore, Shkolla e Magjistratures, 2013, http://www.albania.iom.int/publications/research/School%20of%20Magistrate%20study%20on%20CT%20issues-ALB.pdf. (accessed 15 January 2018).

L. Hasneziri, *Analiza juridiko-penale te veprës penale të 'trafikimit të personave', dhe problematika e hasur ne lidhje me kualifikimin e drejtë ligjor të kësaj vepre penale, Kuadri ligjor mbi trafikimin e qënieve njerëzore në Shqipëri dhe sfidat e hasura në praktikën gjyqësore* 34 (Tirane, 2013).

L. Ikonomi, *E drejta migratore*, (Tirana, 2014), also available at https://www.albania.iom.int/publications/manuals/4%20Migration%20Legislation.pdf, (accessed 14 May 2018).

L. Ikonomi, *E drejta migratore* (Tirana, 2014).

Ligj Nr. 9723 3 Maj2007 'Për Qendrën Kombëtare të regjistrimit'.

Ligj Nr. 9901, 14 Prill 2008 'Për tregtarët dhe Shoqëritë Tregtare'.

Ligj Nr. 9920 19 Maj 2008 'Për Procedurat tatimore në Republikën e Shqipërisë'.

Ligji N. 7703, 11 Maj 1993 'Për sigurimet shoqërore në Republikën e Shqipërisë', i ndryshuar.

Ligji Nr. 9121, 28 Korrik 2003 'Për mbrojtjen e Konkurrencës', i ndryshuar me ligjin 9499, 3 Prill 2006.

M. Blecher & J. Dine, *Komentar i Ligjit nr. 9901, 14 April 2008, Për tregtarët dhe shoqëritë tregtare* (Guttenberg, 2009).

M. Foster, *Responsibility Sharing or Shifting? 'Safe' Third Countries and International Law* 64–82 (Canada's Journal on Refugees, 25/2, 2008).

Selected Bibliography

M. Lerch, *Does Indirect Exposure to International Migration Influence Marriage and Fertility in Albania?* 95–114 (Springer Science + Business Media Dordrecht Research Paper, 2015).

M.D. Dubber, *The Comparative History and Theory of Corporate Criminal Liability* (10 July 2012). SSRN:https://ssrn.com/abstract=2114300 or http://dx.doi.org/10.2139/ssrn.2114300.

M.T. Gil Bazo, *Refugee Status and Subsidiary Protection under EC Law. The EC Qualification Directive and the Right to be Granted Asylum*, 229 (A. Baldaccini, E. Guild & H. Toner, eds., Oxford, Hart, 2007).

M.T. Gil Bazo, *The Charter of Fundamental Rights of the European Union and the Right to be Granted Asylum in the Union's Law,* 33 (Refugee Survey Quarterly, 2008/27).

Migracioni i kthimit dhe ri-integrimi në Shqipëri (INSTAT/IOM, 2014).

Ministry of Internal Affairs, Strategy on the Fight Against Trafficking in Persons and its Action Plan (2014–2017), ed. by Gjebrea L., available on file:///C:/Users/ecanaj/Downloads/ Albania_National_Strategy_Fight_Against_Trafficking_Human_Beings_2014_2017_en%20(2).p (accessed 21 January 2018).

N. Klein, *International Migration by Seaand Air,* 260 (B. Opeskin, R. Perruchoud & J. Redpath-Cross, eds. Cambridge U. Press, 2012).

N. Mai & S. Schwander-Sievers, *Albanian Migration and New Transnationalism,* 939–948 (*Journal of Ethnic and Migration Studies*, Vol. 29, 2003).

N. Mai, *Albanian Migration: Demographic and other Transformations*, 499–516 (Studi migrazione, Vol. Sept. 131/2007).

N. Tota, *Trafikimi i qenieve njerëzore. Aspekte penale juridike, krahasuese dhe kriminologjike* (UETPRESS, Tiranë 2018).

National Strategy on Preventing Human Trafficking, available at: http://www.crca.al/sites/default/files/publications/Strategjia%20kunder%20trafikimit%20te%20femijeve%20e%20miratuar%20me%20vkm.pdf.

O. De Schutter & O. Van Goethem, *Commentary of the Charter of Fundamental Rights of the European Union* (EU Network of Independent Experts on Fundamental Rights, June 2006), http://www.pedz.uni-mannheim.de/daten/edz-k/gdj/06/network_commentary_final%20_180706.pdf (accessed 13 May 2017).

O. Delas, *Le principe de non-refoulement dans la jurisprudence internationale des droits de l'homme* (Bruxelles, Bruylant, 2011).

Opeskin, B., Peerouchoud, R. & Redpath-Cross, *Conceptualising International Migration Law*, 1–16 (B. Opeskin, R. Perruchoud & J. Redpath-Cross, eds. Cambridge U. Press, 2012).

OSCE, Udhëzuesi i Praktikave më të Mira për Klimë Pozitive për Biznesin dhe Investimet Përkthyer nga Qendra për Kërkim dhe Zhvillim (OSBE, 2006).

Penal Code of Albania at http://www.hidaa.gov.al/ligje/kodi%20penal%20i%20rsh.pdf.

Përmbledhje aktesh juridike në fushën e migracionit (ACIL/ONM, Tiranë, 2005).

Përmbledhje e akteve ligjore në lidhje me përzgjedhjen e të huajve. Për policinë e Kufirit dhe Migracionit që merren me të huajt e parregullt (Ministria e Brendshme, Tirane, 2008).

Profili i Migracionit 2016 (Ministria e Brendshme Tirane, 2017).

Qeverisja e Korporatave, International Finance Corporation. Tiranë: World Bank Group, 2009.

R. Cholewinsky, *Family Reunification and Conditions Placed on Family Members: Dismantling a Fundamental Right,* 35–53 (European Journal of Migration and Law, 2002).

R. Islam, *Climate Refugees and International Refugee Law* (Islam R. & Bhuiyan, J.H., eds., Leiden-Boston, 2013).

R. Islam, *The Origin and Evolution of International Refugee Law*, 13 (Islam R. & Bhuiyan, J.H., eds., Leiden-Boston, 2013).

R. King & J. Vullnetari, *Migration and Development in Albania*, 7 (United Kingdom, 2003).

R. King & N. Mai & S. Schwandner-Sievers, *The New Albanian Migration* (Brighton, Sussex Academic Press, 2005).

R. King & N. Mai, *Out of Albania: From Crisis Migration to Social Inclusion in Italy* (New York and Oxford, Berghahn, 2008).

R. King, '*Albanians in Italy and Greece: A Study in Migration Dynamics and Social Exclusion*', 1–15 (Sussex Centre for Migration Research, University of Sussex, 2003).

R. King, *Across the Sea and Over the Mountains: Documenting Albanian Migration*, 283 (*Scottish Geographical Journal,* No. 119, 2003).

R. Mandal, *Protection Mechanisms Outside of the 1951 Convention* 8 (*UNHCR Legal and Protection Policy Research Series,* Department of International Protection, UNHCR, UN Doc. PPLA/2005/02, June 2005).

R. Panagiotou, *Albania and the EU: From Isolation to Integration,* 357–374 (Journal of Balkan and Near Eastern Studies, Volume 13/3, 2011).

R. Wallace & F. Janeczko, *The Concept of Asylum in International Law, 134* (Islam R. & Bhuiyan, J.H., eds., Leiden-Boston, 2013).

Return and readmission. The Case of Albania, 16 (IOM, Tirana, 2006).

Return Migration and Reintregation in Albania, 19 (IOM, Tirana, 2013).

S. Bariatti, *La famiglia nel diritto internazionale privato comunitario* (Milano 2007).

S. Dollani, *Cështje të praktikës gjyqësore në lidhje me krimin e trafikimit të femrave, Kuadri ligjor mbi trafikimin e qënieve njerëzore në Shqipëri dhe sfidat e hasura në praktikën gjyqësore,* 55–62 (Shkolla e Magjistratures, 2013).

S. Hennion & M. Le Barbier, *E Drejta Sociale Evropiane dhe Ndërkombëtare* (Tirane, Papirus, 2013).

S. Omari & A. Anastasi, *E drejta kushtetuese* (Tiranë, 2008).

S. Omari, *E drejta familjare* (Tiranë, 2008).

S. Phill, *EU Intervention in Domestic Labor Law* (Oxford U. Press, Oxford, 2007).

S. Simoni, *Trajtimi i viktimave të trafikimit si dëshmitarë gjatë procesit gjyqësor-.mundësitë ligjore për kompensimin e viktimave të trafikimit dhe nevoja për ndryshime ligjore. Probleme të hasura në praktikën gjyqësore. Kuadri ligjor mbi trafikimin e qënieve njerëzore në Shqipëri dhe sfidat e hasura në praktikën gjyqësore,* 75–85 (Shkolla e Magjistratures, 2013).

Sokol, D., (2012) The Working of EU Conditionality in the Area of Migration Policy: The Case of Readmission of Irregular Migrants to Albania, *East European Politics and Societies,* 2012 26: 115 DOI: 10.1177/0888325410386366.

Selected Bibliography

Strategjia e Zhvillimit të Biznesit dhe Investimeve (2013–2020) (Ministria e Ekonomisë, Tregtisë dhe Energjetikës Drejtoria e Pergjithshme e Politikave, April 2013).

Strategjia Kombëtare për Migracionin dhe Plani i Veprimit për Migracionin: rruga drejt menaxhimit të Migracionit, Tiranë, korrik 2005, available at: http://shtetiweb.org/wp-content/uploads/2014/05/strategjia_kombetare_e_migracionit_alb.pdf.

T. Dobi, *Investimet e huaja përballë pushtetit local si aktor kryesor në administrimin e tokës bujqësore, një betejë e humbur*, 73 (*Jus&Justicia*, No. 5).

Th. Bachner, *Ligji i ri Shqiptar për Shoqëritë Tregtare – Interpretuar sipas burimeve të tij në të drejtën Evropiane* (Tiranë, Dudaj, 2009).

Th. Kaime, *The Normative Framework for Children's Rights in Refugee Situations*, 401 (M.Rafiqul Islam-Md Jahid Hossain Bhyian eds., Martines Nijhoff Publishers, 2013).

The World Fact Book. Europe: Albania, 13 (Washington, DC, Central Intelligence Agency, 2009) available at https://www.cia.gov/library/publications/the-world-factbook/geos/al.html (accessed 18 January 2017).

Trafikimi njerëzor në europën juglindore dhe lindore.Probleme dhe perspektiva, Human Rights Defence Centre, 2007 available on http://www.ariadnet.net/pdfs/libri.pdf. (accessed 15 January 2018).

UNCHR, *Guidelines on Policies and Procedures in dealing with Unaccompanied Children Seeking Asylum* (February 1997).

UNCTAD-UNDP Albania, *Raporti i Investimeve te Huaja Direkte ne Shqiperi* (UNCTAD 2010).

UNDP Albania, Raporti i Investimeve te Huaja Direkte ne Shqiperi 2011 (OECD 2010).

UNHCR, *Complementary Forms of Protection: Their Nature and Relationship to the International Refugee Protection Regime,* Doc. EC/50/SC/CRP.18, 9 June 2000.

V. Chetail, *Sources of International Law*, 56 (B. Opeskin, R. Perruchoud & J. Redpath-Cross, eds. Cambridge U. Press, 2012).

V.K.M. Nr. 296, 06 Qershor 2005 e Këshillit te Ministrave të Republikës së Shqipërisë, availableat: https://www.parlament.al/wp-content/uploads/2015/11/legjislacioni_shqiptar_2001_2009.pdf. (accessed 18 January 2017).

V.K.M. Nr. 760, 19 Nentor 2004 e Këshillit të Ministrave të Republikës së Shqipërisë, available at: https://www.parlament.al/wp-content/uploads/2015/11/legjislacioni_shqiptar_2001_2009.pdf. (accessed 22 March 2017).

V.S. Khanna, *Corporate Criminal Liability: What Purpose Does it Serve*? 1477 (*Harvard Law Review*, Vol. 109, No. 7, 1996).

Vendimi nr.31, datë 14.6.2007, i Gjykatës së Shkallës së Parë për Krime të Rënda, Tiranë, 6.

Vendimi nr.310, datë 5.6.2009, të Gjykatës së Lartë; 9.

Vendimi nr.47, datë 23.10.2007, i Gjykatës Apelit për Krime të Rënda, Tiranë; 8.

Vendimi nr.47, të vitit 2012 të Gjykatës Kushtetuese të Republikës së Shqipërisë.

Vendimi nr.5, datë 17.1.2008, i Gjykatës së Shkallës së Parë për Krime të Rënda, Tiranë; 7.

Vendimi Unifikues i Gjykatës së Lartë, nr.4, datë 15.4.2011; 5.

www.aida.gov.al.

www.arsimi.gov.al.
www.minfin.gov.al.
Zh. Çuçi, *Sistemet e mbrojtjes shoqërore* (Ilar, Tiranë, 2007).

Selected Bibliography

Index

The numbers here refer to paragraph numbers.

Index

Made in the USA
Monee, IL
18 October 2026

66037588R10111